Past and Present Publications

Life, Marriage and Death in a Medieval Parish

Past and Present Publications

General Editor: T. H. ASTON, *Corpus Christi College, Oxford*

Past and Present Publications will comprise books similar in character to the articles in the journal *Past and Present*. Whether the volumes in the series are collections of essays – some previously published, others new studies – or monographs, they will encompass a wide variety of scholarly and original works primarily concerned with social, economic and cultural changes, and their causes and consequences. They will appeal to both specialists and non-specialists and will endeavour to communicate the results of historical and allied research in readable and lively form. This new series continues and expands in its aims the volumes previously published elsewhere.

Volumes published by the Cambridge University Press are:
Family and Inheritance: Rural Society in Western Europe 1200–1800, edited by Jack Goody, Joan Thirsk and E. P. Thompson*
French Society and the Revolution, edited by Douglas Johnson
Peasants, Knights and Heretics: Studies in Medieval English Social History, edited by R. H. Hilton
Towns in Societies: Essays in Economic History and Historical Sociology, edited by Philip Abrams and E. A. Wrigley*
Desolation of a City: Coventry and the Urban Crisis of the Late Middle Ages, Charles Phythian-Adams
Puritanism and Theatre: Thomas Middleton and Opposition Drama under the Early Stuarts, Margot Heinemann
Lords and Peasants in a Changing Society: The Estates of the Bishopric of Worcester, 680–1540, Christopher Dyer
Life, Marriage and Death in a Medieval Parish: Economy, Society and Demography in Halesowen 1270–1400, Zvi Razi
*Also issued as a paperback

Volumes previously published with Routledge and Kegan Paul are:
Crisis in Europe 1560–1660, edited by Trevor Aston
Studies in Ancient Society, edited by M. I. Finley
The Intellectual Revolution of the Seventeenth Century, edited by Charles Webster

Life, Marriage and Death in a Medieval Parish

Economy, Society and Demography in Halesowen 1270–1400

ZVI RAZI
Lecturer in Medieval History, Tel-Aviv University

CAMBRIDGE UNIVERSITY PRESS
Cambridge
London   New York   New Rochelle
Melbourne   Sydney

Published by the Press Syndicate of the University of Cambridge
The Pitt Building, Trumpington Street, Cambridge CB2 1RP
32 East 57th Street, New York, NY 10022, USA
296 Beaconsfield Parade, Middle Park, Melbourne 3206, Australia

© Past and Present Society 1980

First published 1980

Phototypeset in V.I.P. Times by
Western Printing Services Ltd., Bristol

Printed in Great Britain at the
University Press, Cambridge

British Library Cataloguing in Publication Data

Razi, Zvi
Life, marriage and death in a medieval parish.
– (Past and present publications).
1. Halesowen, Eng. – Population
I. Title II. Series
301.32′9′42493   HB3586.H/   79–41381

ISBN 0 521 23252 X

To the memory of my mother
Ada

Contents

List of Tables	*page* ix
List of Figures	x
Acknowledgements	xii
Abbreviations	xiii

Introduction		1
1	The Interpretation of Court-Roll Data for Demographic Analysis	11
	1 Methods and Techniques	11
	2 The Measurement of the Population Trend	24
2	The Population of Halesowen 1270–1348	27
	1 The Demographic Trend	27
	2 Male Replacement Rates	32
	3 Mortality	34
	4 The Marriage Trend	45
	5 Marriage Patterns and Age at Marriage	50
	6 Illegitimacy	64
	7 Size of Peasant Families	71
	8 Land Shortage and Population Growth	94
3	The Black Death	99
	1 Estimates of Black Death Mortality in England	99
	2 Mortality in the Parish of Halesowen during the Black Death	101
	3 Estimated Age-Specific Mortality in the Black Death	107
	4 The Aftermath of the Black Death	110
4	The Population of Halesowen 1350–1400	114
	1 The Demographic Trend	114
	2 Migrations	117
	3 Mortality	124
	4 The Marriage Trend	131
	5 The Age at Marriage	135
	6 Illegitimacy	138
	7 Size of Peasant Families and Social Stratification	139
	8 The Age Structure of an Adult Population in the Early 1390s	150

viii CONTENTS

Appendix: The Distribution of Marriage Fines over the Year 152

Bibliography 154

Index 161

Tables

		Page
1	The resident villagers identified in Halesowen court rolls 1271–1395	25
2	The growth of the population of Halesowen 1271–1349	31
3	Male replacement rates 1270–1348	33
4	Estimated actual male replacement rates 1270–1348	34
5	The number of male deaths, inter-peasant land transactions, pleas of debt and illegal gleaners obtained from the court rolls 1270–1348	37
6	The number of male and female deaths obtained from the court rolls 1270–1348	42
7	The intervals between the first appearance of villagers in the court rolls as tenants and their deaths 1300–48	44
8	Estimate of merchets 1293–1348	48
9	Brothers who were landholders in Halesowen at the same time 1270–1349	55
10	Sisters who married in Halesowen 1270–1349	56
11	Families whose sons obtained land and whose daughters married while the father was alive	59
12	Women paying leyrwyte in Halesowen 1270–1348	67
13	Families who had more than one female member who paid leyrwyte	68
14	Males noted in the court rolls 1270–1349 and their familial relationships	73
15	A comparison between the mean number of offspring of directly and indirectly reconstituted families 1270–1349	75
16	The number of offspring over the age of 12 in families reconstituted from Halesowen court rolls 1270–1349, by socio-economic status	84
17	The distribution of rich, middling and poor families reconstituted from the court rolls 1270–1349, by number of offspring	84
18	The socio-economic status of lessors, lessees, vendors and buyers of land in Halesowen 1270–1348	96

19 The status of villagers who took up or leased vacant holdings or parts of vacant holdings from the Abbot of Halesowen 1270–1348	page 96
20 The geographical distribution of mortality among the male tenants of Halesowen in the Black Death	106
21 The estimated age distribution of males who died in the plague of 1349	108
22 The estimated age-specific mortality of male tenants in the plague of 1349	109
23 The population movements 1351–95	117
24 Male immigrants identified in the court rolls 1351–95	118
25 Male replacement rate 1350–1400	119
26 Male deaths obtained from Halesowen court rolls 1350–1400	125
27 The estimated ages of males who died in the plagues of 1361–2, 1369 and 1375	128
28 Observed and estimated merchets obtained from the court rolls 1349–1400	133
29 Males noted in the court rolls 1350–1400 and their familial relationships	141
30 The number of offspring over the age of 12 in families reconstituted from Halesowen court rolls 1350–1400, by economic status	142
31 The distribution of rich, middling and poor families reconstituted from the court rolls 1350–1400, by number of offspring	142
32 The socio-economic status of lessors, lessees, vendors and buyers of land in Halesowen 1350–1400	148

Figures

Map of Halesowen	page xvi
1 The Melley family tree	18
2 The de Westeley family tree	20
3 The population trend in Halesowen 1271–1395	25
4 Number of male deaths recorded in the court rolls 1270–1349	36
5 Estimated marriage fines and male deaths 1293–1348	49
6a The Ordrich family tree	52
6b The Pyrie family tree	53
6c The Symon family tree	54

List of Figures

7	The distribution of rich, middling and poor families reconstituted from the court rolls in 1270–1349, by number of offspring	page 85
8	Number of male deaths and vacant holdings granted or leased by the Abbot of Halesowen 1270–1348	95
9	The course of the plague in the parish of Halesowen 1349	102
10	The geographical distribution of mortality among the male tenants of Halesowen in the Black Death	107
11	Male deaths obtained from the court rolls 1350–1400	126
12	The marriage trend in Halesowen 1300–99, based on estimated marriage fines presented as a percentage of the males identified in the court rolls	134
13	The distribution of rich, middling and poor families reconstituted from the court rolls 1350–1400, by number of offspring	143
14	The estimated age structure of the adult population of Halesowen in 1350 and 1393	151
15	The distribution of marriage fines over the year	152

Acknowledgements

In the course of my research and writing I have received the help of many people and institutions. Among the latter, I am especially indebted to the British Council and to Tel-Aviv University for financing my studies and research in Birmingham University; to Birmingham Reference Library for the use of the sources on which this work is based; to the University of Birmingham, and especially to the Department of History, for the research facilities and help they have given me; and to the Past and Present Society for promoting the publication of this work.

It is impossible to thank all the teachers, colleagues and friends who have helped over the years to bring this study to completion, but there are some whose contributions have been so valuable that they must be recorded. Foremost is Professor R. H. Hilton, who originally conceived the idea of this study and whose constant direction, fruitful suggestions, essential corrections and encouragement made it a reality; although, naturally, the responsibility for errors or short-comings is mine alone.

I am indebted also to Dr H. Stopes-Roe for invaluable assistance in preparing statistical material and for saving me from some pitfalls; to Dr R. M. Smith for his many useful suggestions and comments; to Mr T. H. Aston for the help and encouragement he has given me; to Jean Birrell and to Dr D. M. Palliser and Dr C. Dyer for their ready willingness to share with me findings from their own research into rural society; to Mary, Harry, Christopher and Helena Stopes-Roe who gave me love, a warm home and help when I had to stay in England on my own; to the librarians in the Local Studies Department, Birmingham Reference Library, and especially to Miss McCulla and Mr Andrews for their kindness and help; and to Mr W. J. Davies and Mrs Jane Van Tassel of the Cambridge University Press.

Finally, I must thank my wife Edna, and my daughters Tamar and Noa, for sustaining me through my long studies with love and patience.

Abbreviations used in the notes

BRL: Birmingham Reference Library
*Hales Court Rolls: Court Rolls of the Manor of Hales
1272—1307*, ed. J. Amphlett, S. G. Hamilton and R. A. Wilson.
2 vols. Worcestershire Historical Society, 1910–33

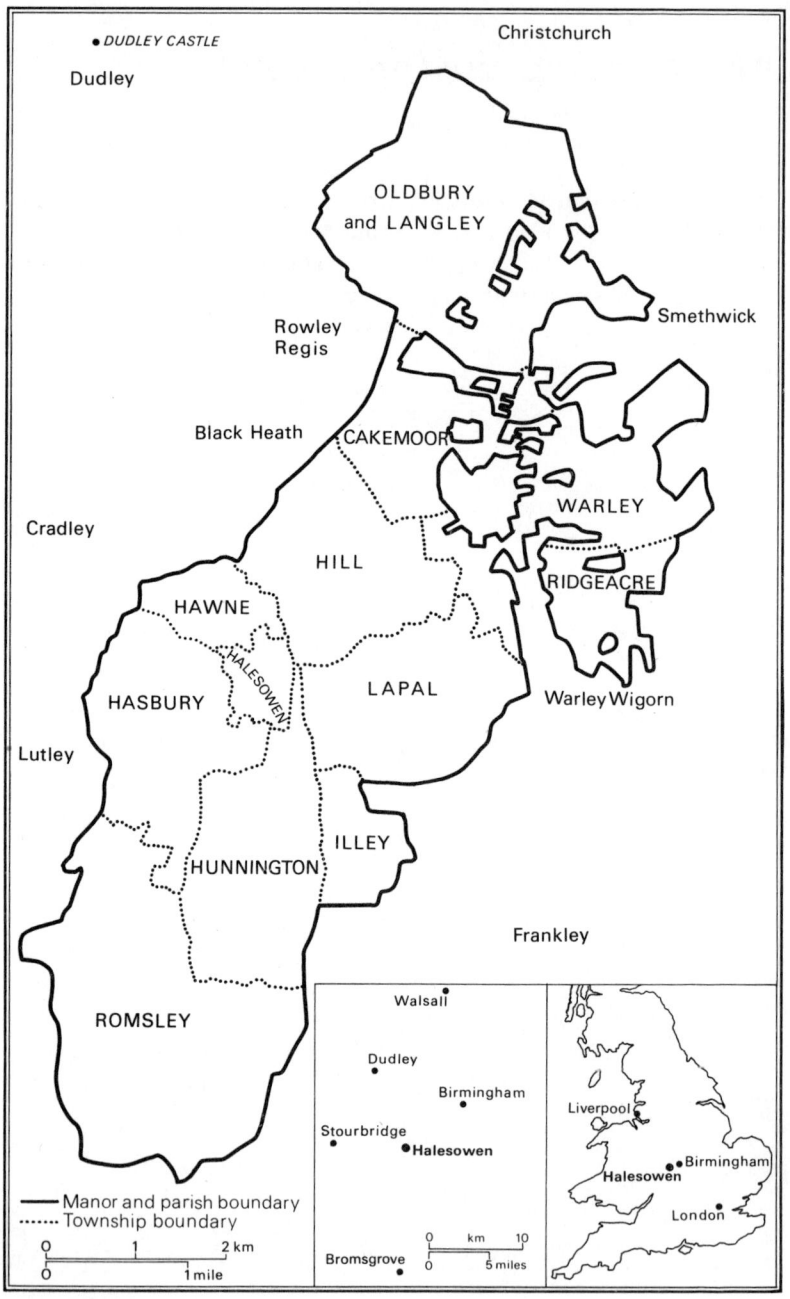

Map of Halesowen

Introduction

In the later Middle Ages English rural society underwent fundamental changes. The long-term trend of prices and wages was reversed as the prices of agricultural products fell and wages rose. The seigneurial economy declined and stagnated after a long period of prosperity. The landlords had to give up the direct cultivation of their demesnes and to relax control over their tenants. At the same time, the conditions of the peasants improved as the land became abundant and real wages rose and as serfdom and customary land tenure declined. Historians have pointed out that all these changes were to a large extent a result of a substantial recession of the population which occurred in the fourteenth century. However, there is a controversy about the cause and the date of this demographic change. Some historians claim that a severe subsistence crisis in the first quarter of the fourteenth century initiated the demographic recession.[1] Others argue that the turning point of the population trend occurred only in 1348–9 with the first visitation of the plague.[2] There is also a considerable disagreement about the rate of mortality in the Black Death, as estimates vary between 20 and 50 per cent of the total population.[3] Lastly, while some historians maintain that the demographic recession was primarily confined to the period between 1348 and 1375,[4] others argue that the population continued to decline in the last quarter of the fourteenth century.[5]

[1] M. M. Postan, 'Histoire économique: moyen âge', *Rapports du IXe Congrès International des Sciences Historiques* (Paris, 1950), 'Some agrarian evidence of a declining population in the later Middle Ages', *Essays on Medieval Agriculture and General Problems of the Medieval Economy* (Cambridge, 1973), pp. 186–213, and *The Medieval Economy and Society* (London, 1972), pp. 33–8; J. Z. Titow, *English Rural Society 1200–1350* (London, 1969), pp. 73–96.

[2] J. C. Russell, 'The pre-plague population of England', *Journal of British Studies*, V (1966), 1–21; B. F. Harvey, 'The population trend in England between 1300 and 1348', *Trans. Roy. Hist. Soc.*, 5th ser., XVI (1965), 23–42.

[3] See below, pp. 99–101.

[4] J. M. W. Bean, 'Plague, population and economic decline in England in the later Middle Ages', *Econ. Hist. Rev.*, 2nd ser., XV (1963), 435; A. R. Bridbury, *Economic Growth: England in the Later Middle Ages* (London, 1962), p. 23.

[5] J. C. Russell, *British Medieval Population* (Albuquerque, N. Mex., 1948), pp. 260–81; J. Saltmarsh, 'Plague and economic decline in England in the later Middle Ages', *Cambridge Hist. Journ.*, VII (1941).

All these debates arise because in the absence of sufficient demographic data the fourteenth-century population movements have been mainly studied by means of indirect evidence such as changes in settlement, land values, wages and prices. Undoubtedly these variables can reflect demographic changes, but they do not allow us to date or measure them accurately. J. C. Russell, however, in his pioneering study on the medieval population of England, has used direct demographic data to estimate the population trend in the fourteenth century.[6] But as these data are largely obtained from the records of the Inquisitiones Post Mortem, which dealt with the aristocracy, they do not necessarily provide an adequate measure of a population which was overwhelmingly rural. Admittedly, Russell has also derived some evidence about population movements in rural areas by comparing the population of a number of places estimated from the poll-tax returns of 1377 with the population of these places estimated from manorial extents before and after 1377.[7] But the results of this comparison cannot be accepted as valid: first, the sample is too small; secondly, it has not been shown that the areas included in these manors are identical to the areas taxed in 1377; and thirdly, it has been wrongly assumed that there is a direct relation between the actual population of a manor and the number of its recorded tenants. In order to observe and to understand more clearly the population movements in England in the later Middle Ages, new demographic data about the peasantry are needed. This study is an attempt to show that such data are available in manorial court rolls, which survive in great abundance.

Manorial courts dealt with land conveyances and transactions; disputes about inheritance, roads and boundaries; trespasses against the lord and neighbours; debts; breach of agreements; quarrels between neighbours; failures to render services, rents and other exactions; disturbances of the public order; infringement of village by-laws and the assize of ale and bread; and the election of jurymen, reeves and other village officials. In addition, the court recorded deaths, marriages and pregnancies out of wedlock of bondwomen; entries into tithing groups; and departures of villeins from the manor with and without permission. The range of these activities is so wide that it is hard to conceive how a villager could have avoided appearing before the court from time to time. Rich

[6] *British Medieval Population*, pp. 236–70. [7] Ibid. pp. 258, 266–7.

peasants, whether free tenants or villeins, turned up in the court more frequently than poor villagers, servants, sub-tenants and freeholders, but all of them attended it sooner or later during the course of their residence in the manor. Admittedly, women are not represented in court rolls to the same extent as men, and young villagers appear rarely in the records before the age of 12. Nevertheless, as adult males are almost totally represented, it is possible to measure the demographic trend fairly accurately. We can also obtain good data about mortality, life expectancy at 20, age at marriage, illegitimacy, male replacement rates and size of family. Moreover, the rich social and economic data available in court rolls enable us to study the reciprocal interaction between population, economic forces and social institutions.

However, the demographic data of court rolls have to be refined before they can yield reliable results. Until the middle of the fourteenth century surnames of peasants were neither fixed nor stable. Villagers appear in the court records under more than one name, and many appear under more than two. They were named indiscriminately by the scribes according to occupation or function, township, locality, place of origin and familial relationships. For example, Alexander, a villager from the township of Romsley, who appears in the records between 1274 and 1293, lived in the small hamlet of Kenelmestowe near the Church of St Kenelm and was a clerk by profession. He therefore had three surnames – 'de Kenelmestowe',[8] 'de St Kenelm'[9] and 'the Clerk'.[10] His son Clements was called 'Clements the son of Alexandre of St Kenelm'[11] and 'Clements Tandi'.[12] But in 1293 Clements married Emma de Folfen and entered with her the family holding. Henceforward he appears in the court rolls as 'Clements de Folfen'.[13] Moreover, many villagers had nicknames; for example, Roger Heath a rich villager from Lapal was called also 'Smart'.[14] In the post-plague era surnames stabilized and only a small number of villagers had aliases. But as the range of proper names and surnames used in the region was too narrow to give everybody a different name, one often finds two or more people with identical names, especially among those who had occupational surnames. Therefore it is essential to identify the villagers who appear in court rolls, to avoid the study and counting

[8] *Hales Court Rolls*, I, p. 50.
[9] Ibid. I, p. 260.
[10] Ibid. I, p. 57.
[11] Ibid. II, p. 173.
[12] Ibid. I, p. 348.
[13] Ibid. II, p. 170.
[14] Ibid. I, p. 130.

of names rather than of persons. Furthermore, in addition to the names of residents, manorial court records contain many names of outsiders: vagabonds, migrant labourers, non-resident tenants and plaintiffs attempting to recover debts or compensations for damages from local villagers. The frequent appearance of outsiders in court rolls tends as much as aliases to conceal the actual population of the manor. But when a good sequence of court rolls is available it is possible to overcome these problems and to obtain important demographic data. This I will show in the present study, which is based on Halesowen court rolls from 1270 to 1400.[15]

The manor of Hales, or Halesowen as it was later called, is located west of Birmingham, upon which it now borders. Very little is known about the history of the locality before the Norman Conquest. It is likely that Halesowen, like other northern and western districts in the West Midlands, was settled later than the Cotswolds, the river valleys and the dry plains of the south, probably during the Anglo-Saxon period.[16] In the Domesday Book the manor was assessed at 10 hides. On the demesne there were four ploughs, and the tenants – 36 villeins, 18 borders and 4 radmen – had between them forty-one and a half ploughs. There were also 8 male and 2 female slaves. A part of the manor, 1½ hides, was held by Roger the huntsman as a sub-manor. On the demesne there was one plough and five ploughs were in the hands of the tenants, 6 villeins and 5 borders. The local community had a church served by 2 priests. The manor was worth £24 in the time of King Edward but only £15 in 1086.[17]

[15] Halesowen and Romsley court rolls are deposited in BRL, nos. 34601 et seq., 350351 et seq. and 346790 et seq.
[16] See R. H. Hilton, *A Medieval Society* (London, 1967), p. 16.
[17] *Domesday Book,* vol. I (Record Commission, 1783), f. 308. The history of Roger Huntsman's part of the manor is obscure. However, one thing is certain: in the 1270s, when Halesowen court rolls began, the Abbey of Halesowen held directly the whole of the manor. The tenants of Romsley, Hasbury and Hamstead (Hunnington), the hamlets which probably constituted the sub-manor mentioned in 1086, appear in the court rolls of the manor of Halesowen as the tenants of the abbey. For example, in 1272 Henry de Folfen from Romsley gave the abbot 6 marks for the wardship of Thomas Squire, a villein from the same township *(Hales Court Rolls,* I, p. 43). In 1307 it was reported in the court that William Squire 'nativus domini' and his brother Richard were living in King's Norton. Thomas Squire their brother was ordered to bring them back to the manor (ibid. I, pp. 562–3). We do not know when the sub-manor was incorporated into the manor of Halesowen, but incorporation may have taken place after the foundation of the Abbey of Halesowen. Nash mentioned an ancient pleading of uncertain date, which necessarily must have been between 1214 and 1270, in which it is said that Stephen de Ashrug held Romsley, Hamstead

The manor, which was a part of Worcestershire, was granted by William the Conqueror to Roger Montgomery, Earl of Shrewsbury. It therefore came to be considered a part of Shropshire. However, the medieval parish of Halesowen, whose borders coincided with those of the manor, remained a part of the diocese of Worcester.[18] In 1102 Henry I confiscated the Earldom of Shrewsbury and the manor of Hales thus came into the hands of the Crown. It remained Crown property for seventy-five years until King Henry II granted it to David ap Owen, Prince of Wales in 1177, from which event Hales probably gained the additional name of Owen. After the death of David in 1204 the manor once more reverted to the king. In 1214 King John granted the manor to Peter de Roches, Bishop of Winchester, for the purpose of establishing a religious house. In 1215 the bishop gave the manor to the Premonstratensian Canons, who took possession of their new Abbey of Halesowen in 1217. The manor remained the abbey's property until the general dissolution of the religious houses in Henry VIII's reign.[19]

Halesowen was a large manor, eight miles long and about two and a half at its greatest width; its area amounted to some 10,000 acres.[20] The manor is situated in a broken hilly terrain of mixed heavy and light clays. The parish is watered by the river Stour, which flows from south-east to north-west through the townships of Romsley, Illey, Lapal and Hawne. In the south, a good part of the manor was covered by woods, and some of them, like Uffmoor Wood, still exist at the present day.

The hilly terrain of the parish shaped the structure of the local settlement, which was not concentrated in large nucleated villages, but scattered in small hamlets. In addition to the small market town

and Haselbury by serjeancy for which he had to find 3 foot soldiers for the king's army. Nash gives only a few details about the case and I was unable to trace the original record. But it seems that the abbot was required to render the services of 3 soldiers. To this he pleaded the foundation charter: 'ita quod a tempore concessionis carte predicte, et a fundatione domus sue dominus rex nunquam fuit in seisina de aliquo servitio Stephani de Ashrug' (T. R. Nash, *Collection for the History of Worcestershire*, 2nd edn, 2 vols. (London, 1799), I, p. 518).
[18] In February 1297 Agnes Gachard from Lapal came to Halesowen manorial court to clear herself of a false accusation made against her by her neighbour William Hay 'coram parochia de Hales' (*Hales Court Rolls*, I, p. 351).
[19] Ibid. I, introduction, pp. i–xxi. For the history of the abbey, see *Victoria County History of Worcestershire*, 4 vols. (London, 1901–24), II, pp. 163 et seq.
[20] The area of the old manor of Halesowen is given as 10,136 acres. See *Worcestershire County Council Handbook* (Worcester, 1910).

of Halesowen[21] there were twelve rural settlements or townships in the manor: Oldbury, Langley–Walloxhall, Warley, Cakemoor, Hill, Ridgeacre, Lapal, Hawne, Hasbury, Hunnington, Illey and Romsley.[22] Oldbury in the north and Romsley in the south were the largest settlements in the parish; each had about 30 to 35 families in *c*. 1300. The other hamlets had only between 10 and 20 families each, and Illey had no more than 6.

The rentals, customals and the great majority of the accounts of the manor of Halesowen have been lost.[23] Nevertheless, it is possible to glean from the court rolls some data about the local husbandry. On Wednesday in Easter Week 1281 the court ordered that 'all the fences round the common fields (rura communia) are to be closed by Sunday under a penalty of a plough share'.[24] This entry indicates clearly that the villagers of Halesowen practised open-field agriculture in common with other peasants in the West Midlands.[25] But unlike the old settled districts of the region, in Halesowen the field system was very irregular. Numerous references in the court records to failure on the part of the villagers to keep fences suggest that each township had its own system of open fields. In Oldbury there were five big open fields, and in Romsley three.[26] As a result of an extensive land reclamation carried out probably in the twelfth and thirteenth centuries a considerable part of the land under cultivation in the parish was held in severalty. Numerous crofts and enclosures were scattered all over the manor

---

[21] The Borough of Halesowen was erected by abbot and convent during the reign of Henry III. In the founding charter granted by the king, the townsmen were given the same liberties and franchises as the citizens of Hereford (BRL 351085). The court rolls of the Borough of Halesowen from 1272 to 1643 survive in good condition. The manuscripts are deposited in BRL 346512 et seq.

[22] It is likely that originally there were more than twelve hamlets in the manor. Kenelmestowe at the foot of the Clent hills was probably an independent hamlet which was incorporated with the township of Romsley in the thirteenth century. Langley and Walloxhall, which appear in the court records as one vill, were probably once two separated hamlets, and the same is true of Hunnington and Hamstead.

[23] Only three account rolls survive: for 1361–2, 1362–4 and 1368–9 (BRL 347130–2).

[24] *Hales Court Rolls,* II, p. 92.

[25] See Hilton, *Medieval Society*, pp. 7–22, 113–15.

[26] In 1359 the Abbot of Halesowen granted to Thomas son of William Sweyn and to Thomas Hill lands and meadows with their appurtenances in the five common fields in Oldbury, namely le Hyefield, Multworth, Radenhillfield, Rugeweyfield and le Netherfield (BRL 346342 24.7.1359). In 1396 the lord leased to Richard Squire and to his nephew Thomas Squire for twelve years his demesne lands 'lying in the three common fields in Romsley' (346823 28.4.1396).

in an irregular manner. The land in these small enclosed fields would often be ploughed, like the open fields, in ridges or selions and subdivided among different tenants.[27] Consequently, many villagers had land both in the open fields and in severalty.[28] There is further evidence that the peasant land in Halesowen was subject to three-course rotation,[29] and that the peasants sowed cereals and leguminous crops: wheat, rye, barley, oats, beans, peas and vetches.

On the pastoral side of the peasant economy in the parish, the rolls reveal that the villagers reared cattle, horses, pigs and sheep. In the pre-plague period, as a result of population pressures, the pastoral activities of the villagers were subordinated to arable farming.[30] However, in the second half of the fourteenth century, and especially in the fifteenth century, there is strong evidence which suggests that there was a greater specialization in pastoral farming in Halesowen.[31]

In Halesowen, as in other rural settlements, there were villagers engaging in non-agricultural activities: manufacture of textiles, metalworking, leatherworking, woodworking, building, food production and ale-brewing. However, there is no evidence which suggests that there was in Halesowen the thriving cloth industry

[27] In 1315 Agnes, Matilda and Alice the daughters of Thomas Colling sold to Henry Rutoner '3 selions of their father croft' (350359 11.6.1315). In the same year Thomas Don sold to Thomas Robert 2 selions in Pylecroft (ibid. 22.7.1315). In 1320 Margaret daughter of Rolf Grefory transferred to John de Wyteley 'medietatem campi qui vocatur Wildebestes Lord' (346238 23.4.1320). The names of some 146 small fields are mentioned in the court rolls between 1270 and 1400.

[28] In 1302 Thomas Symon transferred to his son Thomas II 'totam novam terram quam tenuit per particulas in superiori Oldebure que qui [dem] particule terre vocantur de la Waxlord' *(Hales Court Rolls,* I, p. 452). In 1293 Alexander de St Kenelm gave his daughter 'novam terram apud le Loneerd' (ibid. I, p. 260).

[29] The evidence is found in the fifteenth-century court rolls. But we can assume that the same rotation was practised during the period under study. See R. K. Field, 'The Worcestershire peasantry in the later Middle Ages', unpublished M.A. thesis, University of Birmingham, 1962, pp. 96–120.

[30] As a result of shortage of pasture many local peasants were understocked. On peasant livestock in the West Midlands in the second half of the thirteenth century, see Hilton, *Medieval Society,* pp. 106–10. See also M. M. Postan, 'Village livestock in the thirteenth century', *Essays on Medieval Agriculture and General Problems of the Medieval Economy* (Cambridge, 1973), pp. 214–48.

[31] In the court rolls between 1370 and 1400, 41 licences to sell foals and other fatstock and fines for unlicensed sales are recorded, whereas in the rolls from 1270 to 1349 there are only 11. In the fifteenth century, a large number of complaints of overstocking of the common pasture by tenants are recorded in Halesowen court rolls, which indicate that villagers were building up larger flocks and herds. See Field, 'Worcestershire peasantry', pp. 97–104.

which existed in the Cotswolds, or the industries that developed in the woodland districts of the region, such as woodworking of all kinds, iron-mining and working or pottery and tile-making.[32] In the court rolls from the first decade of the fourteenth century a coal-mine in the Coombs Wood in Hill is mentioned.[33] But as no other references to the mine can be found in later court rolls, we do not know if coal-mining in the area continued. Non-agricultural pursuits undoubtedly played an important role in the peasant economy. But so far as the court rolls indicate, agriculture was the major economic activity in the parish during the period under study.

The peasant holdings are often expressed in the court rolls in virgates and fractions of virgates. The exact size of a virgate in Halesowen is not given in the sources, but it is likely that it was equivalent to 25–30 acres. Only a small minority of the villagers, 18 per cent, were yardlanders in the period from 1270 to 1349, 39 per cent were half yardlanders and 43 per cent were quarter yardlanders and cottagers.[34] However, it should be stressed that as a result of population pressures and of an active land market, the yardland patterns of many peasant holdings were undermined.[35]

The rents and services rendered by tenants in Halesowen were

---

[32] See Hilton, *Medieval Society*, pp. 207–16; J. R. Birrell, 'Peasant craftsmen in the medieval forest', *Agric. Hist. Rev.*, XVII (1969), 91–107; E. M. Carus-Wilson, 'An industrial revolution of the thirteenth century', in *Essays in Economic History*, ed. Carus-Wilson, vol. I (London, 1954), pp. 41–60.

[33] In 1307 the abbot leased his mine in Coombs Wood to Henry le Knyth and Henry Hill for a year for a rent of £4. The grantees were to work the mine by making two pits in it with four spades ('duo fossata cum quattuor ligonibus in eadem minera') (*Hales Court Rolls*, I, p. 566). In 1309 Henry Hill 'recepit duos puteos minere carbonis maris apud la Combes' for a year. The rent this time was 7 marks (BRL 350353 16.4.1309). And in 1310 Henry Hill leased the mine again for a rent of 10 marks (350355 20.3.1310).

[34] See ch. 2, sect. 7. On the size of peasant holdings in the West Midlands, see Hilton, *Medieval Society*, pp. 113–15, and 'Social structure of rural Warwickshire in the Middle Ages', *The English Peasantry in the Later Middle Ages* (Oxford, 1975), pp. 126–7; E. A. Kosminsky, *Studies in the Agrarian History of England* (Oxford, 1956), p. 228.

[35] A large number of deceased tenants' holdings recorded in the court rolls were composed of messuages, curtilages, crofts, plots, small fields and a few selions in the open fields rather than of yardlands or fractions of yardlands. For example, in 1334 John son of Thomas of Hasbury died holding from the lord a tenement of 8 selions (BRL 346270 14.12.1334). In 1343 John Ordrich died holding 'messuage and various plots of land' (346303 7.5.1343). The smallholding of Nicholas Proudfoot who died in 1335 was composed of 'one messuage, one curtilage, one field called le Refeld, one field called le Loggesfeld and one field called Carpenteres'. His son Robert paid a 40*d*. entry fine (346270 3.1.1335).

much lighter than those on the long-established big Benedictine estates in Gloucestershire and Worcestershire, but comparable with those on the manors in the Forest of Dean, north Worcestershire, Warwickshire and Staffordshire.[36] In the reign of King John, before the foundation of the Abbey of Halesowen, yardland tenants paid an annual rent of 3s. 4d. and had to plough and to sow the demesne lands six and ten days respectively. All the tenants owed one day's 'boon work' for which they were given food at the lord's expense. They also had to mow the lord's grass and to fence his garden. They owed a suit of court every three weeks, but were exempted from suit of mill, as the king had no mill within the manor. On the death of a tenant his best beast was taken as heriot and the heir had to pay as a relief a sum of money equivalent to two years' rent, 6s. 8d. for a virgate, 3s. 4d. for a half virgate and 1s. 8d. for a quarter virgate. The villein tenants had to pay 2s. for permission to marry off their daughters outside the manor, and 12s. inside it.[37]

In the course of the thirteenth century, despite the vigorous resistance of the tenants, the abbey succeeded in forcing them to pay higher rents and entry fines.[38] The rate of entry fines was doubled to 13s. 4d. for a virgate, 6s. 8d. for a half virgate and 3s. 4d. for a quarter virgate. As the rate of entry fines was equivalent to two years' rent, it is likely that the annual rent was also doubled. The tenants were obliged to grind their corn in the mills built by the abbey and to pay tolls. In addition, the customary tenants had to pay tallages at the lord's will. However, it seems that labour services remained at their former level, and in 1327 they were commuted into money rents.[39]

---

[36] Hilton, *Medieval Society*, pp. 131–48, and 'Gloucester Abbey leases of the late thirteenth century' and 'Lord and peasant in Staffordshire in the Middle Ages', *English Peasantry*, pp. 141-7, 230.

[37] In 4 Edward I (1275), the Sheriff of Shropshire held an inquest to give evidence about the customs and services rendered by the tenants of Halesowen when the manor was in the hands of the Crown. A copy of the schedule of customs and services drawn up by the jury was published by Nash (*History of Worcestershire*, I, p. 512).

[38] The struggle between the Abbot and Convent of Halesowen and its villein tenants has been studied in detail by Hilton and by G. C. Homans. See Homans, *English Villagers of the Thirteenth Century* (New York, 1970), pp. 276–84; Hilton, 'Peasant movements before 1381', in *Essays in Economic History*, ed. E. M. Carus-Wilson, vol. II (London, 1962), p. 83, and *Medieval Society*, pp. 159–61.

[39] We have a record of the rents and services of the tenants of Romsley. The tenants were summoned to a court in July 1301 to do fealty and acknowledge their rents and services. Thomas le Squire a customary tenant of a yardland had to do three days' ploughing and three harrowing and three harvesting at his own table and to

In the absence of rentals or customals it is difficult to estimate the number of free and customary tenants in Halesowen in the period under study. However, at the court in July 1301, among the 26 tenants of Romsley listed 18 (69 per cent) were customary tenants and 8 (31 per cent) were freeholders.[40] Among the 788 families reconstituted from the court rolls between 1270 and 1349, 504 (64 per cent) were families of unfree status. Therefore we can assume that the percentage of customary tenants was between 64 and 69 and that of free tenants between 31 and 34.

The court rolls of the manor of Halesowen and of the township of Romsley between 1270 and 1400 survive in great abundance.[41] There are 215 rolls in which 1,667 court sessions are recorded. For the period of 131 years covered by the series, the rolls of only 16 years are missing.[42] Unfortunately, there are no tax returns for Halesowen and with the exception of three account rolls from the 1360s and a few deeds, no manorial extents, rentals and accounts survived.

The present study has been divided into four chapters. Chapter 1 is devoted to the methods used to interpret the court-roll data for demographic analysis. Chapter 2 deals with the population of the parish 1270–1348, chapter 3 with the Black Death and chapter 4 with the period 1350–1400.

---

mow the same as his neighbours, namely one day 'at the table of the lord'. The services of a few tenants included one day collecting nuts. Thomas Squire had to pay for his services a rent of 3s. 6d. It is possible that the 'assize rent' of Romsley tenants was not included in this list. See *Hales Court Rolls*, II, pp. 178–80. In another list of rents of a few freeholders from various townships recorded in 1299, the rents varied between 11s. 2d. and 10d. See ibid. II, p. 115. The labour services of the tenants of Halesowen were commuted into money rents for 100s., and those of the tenants of Romsley for 23s. See BRL 346251 4.3.1327 and 346800 21.3.1327.

[40] *Hales Court Rolls*, II, pp. 178–80, 183.

[41] Romsley, which was part of the sub-manor of 1½ hides mentioned in Domesday Book, was administered directly by the Abbey of Halesowen. Nevertheless, its manorial court was not abolished and the tenants of Romsley had to attend this court as well as the central court of the manor of Halesowen. It appears that the court of Romsley was not held as regularly as the court of Halesowen, and many of its records have been lost. The earlier records of the court of Romsley were sometimes copied on the back of the court rolls of the manor.

[42] The years for which records did not survive are 1273, 1283–92, 1296, 1303, 1360, 1365–6.

1. The Interpretation of Court-Roll Data for Demographic Analysis

1. Methods and Techniques

In order to identify the people whose names are mentioned in court rolls, a good sequence of detailed records is needed. Only if a name appears in the records repeatedly and frequently can the individual described by it be positively identified. But if the records of only a few of the court sessions held each year survive, or if there are too many gaps in the series, there is far less chance of identification and consequently of discovering the actual population of the manor. For example, J. A. Raftis has used the very fragmentary and scanty series of Warboys court rolls from 1290 to 1458 to measure population movements.[1] But if one looks closely at the list which according to the author represents the residents of Warboys it becomes immediately clear that this cannot possibly be the case. First, he overlooks the fact that surnames in the pre-plague period were unstable and assumes that each one represents a different person. But there are numerous cases in which two surnames could have described only one person. For example, in the court roll of 1294 the name 'Alexander Chamberlain' is mentioned and in 1316 'Alexander Chamberlain of Westow'.[2] It has been assumed that they are the names of two individuals, whereas it is clear that they could have been the names of one person. The same is true of the names 'Benedict son of Lawrence Parker' (who appears in the court rolls 1320–43) and 'Benedict son of Lawrence' (1316–45);[3] 'William Bonde' (1326–43) and 'William son of Robert Bonde' (1326); 'Thomas Sewyne' (1316) and 'Thomas Sewyne of Woodhurst' (1316); 'William Hyrst' (1322) and 'William son of John Raven of Hyrst' (1326); and many others.[4] Secondly, Professor Raftis assumes that a villager

---

[1] *Warboys* (Toronto, 1964), p. 213. From the original series of Warboys court rolls between the years 1290 and 1458, used in this study, the court records of only sixty-three years survived. Moreover, for these years, the records of only 75 court sessions are available.

[2] Ibid. pp. 19, 39.

[3] Here, and throughout, dates attached to names are dates of appearance in the court rolls, not dates of birth and death. A 'd.' appended to a date means that the person's death was recorded or indicated in the court rolls for the year or years named.

[4] Raftis, *Warboys*, pp. 14–40.

described by his occupation never appears under another surname. This surely cannot be true. For example, Hugo the Reeve (1292–9) also appears in the records under the name 'Hugo Beneyt' (1294–1347).[5] Thirdly, there are a large number of villagers who are mentioned in the records as servants of other villagers. They have no surnames and sometimes no proper names. Professor Raftis counts all these servants amongst the residents of the village, but as servants often change their employers this inevitably leads to double counting. If a servant has three employers in three years, the same person is counted three times. Fourthly, the list of residents of Warboys includes many outsiders. This inclusion has been justified by the dubious guess that the number of outsiders is almost balanced by those not listed in the court rolls.[6] As a result of these methodological errors Professor Raftis has thus made 'demographic' observations on names rather than on persons.

The methods used to discover the population of Halesowen through its manorial court records are straightforward but very slow. However, with the aid of a computer it is possible to save time in processing and analysing the data. The raw data available in Halesowen court rolls were refined in several stages: (1) registration, (2) spatial location, (3) family reconstitution, (4) identification.

(1) REGISTRATION

All the court appearances of each name were recorded on cards. On each occasion a name was mentioned, I transcribed onto the card the number of the roll, the date of the court session and the summary of the case. As the majority of the cases dealt with by the manorial court were fairly standard, it was possible to record them by using series of symbols and numbers. In addition, I included on the card all the rest of the names which were mentioned in the same entry, unless it was simply a list of villagers who did not attend the court or of those who brewed against the assize of ale. If, for example, 4 persons were involved in a case, its content was recorded four times on the personal cards of these villagers. As an example I will take the personal file of Richard le Bond. The information is given in an unabridged form.

---

[5] Ibid. pp. 16, 34, 244.   [6] Ibid. p. 213.

Richard le Bond
(1326–49d.)

BRL 346249 22.2.1326. Married Agnes Colines of Langley and both of them entered her family holding; entry fine 40*d*.
BRL 346250 1.10.1326. Elected to serve as an ale-taster.
BRL 346252 29.7.1327. Amerced 2*d*. for wrongly presenting that Matilda le Per brewed against the assize.
BRL 346252 30.9.1327. Elected as a forester.
BRL 346253 13.7.1328. Sued Roger Sweyn for not mowing his hay in Mormedewe as they had agreed. He claimed half a mark damage. Roger denied that any such agreement existed between them.
BRL 346254 5.10.1328. Amerced 2*d*. for trespass against Agnes le Per and ordered by the court to make amends to her.
BRL 346256 27.6.1330. Amerced 1*d*. for default of court.
BRL 346264 30.6.1333. Amerced 1*d*. for default of court.
BRL 346268 6.7.1334. Gave the lord 6*d*., his part of the rent due from the holding of Nicholas de Langley which he was holding with Thomas Barsfen and Thomas le Per.
BRL 346269 5.10.1334. Amerced 4*d*. for digging the lord's marl.
BRL 346271 19.4.1335. William King employed him to collect the rents from his tenants. Richard did not provide an account and the court ordered him to do so in the following session.
BRL 346271 10.5.1335. The account he provided showed that he owes William King 2*s*. 6½*d*. He promised to pay it.
BRL 346273 25.10.1335. Amerced 2*d*. for not pursuing a complaint of trespass he had lodged against William Belne.
BRL 346275 7.4.1336. Amerced 2*d*. for not grinding his corn in the lord's mill.
BRL 346279 12.3.1337. Amerced 2*d*. for not grinding his corn in the lord's mill.
BRL 346279 12.3.1337. Amerced 2*s*. for selling a horse without permission.
BRL 346279 23.4.1337. Sued William Belne for breach of agreement. William borrowed his horse for a day to carry dung but used the horse two days for carrying corn. As a result the horse suffered a damage. William Jurdan and Thomas Hykedys were called as witnesses. He won the case and William Belne was ordered to make amends.

BRL 346282 8.7.1338. Ordered to appear before the court for using abusive words against the cellarer and the abbot.

BRL 346283 19.8.1338. Amerced 1*d*. for wrongly impleading William Belne pledged by Thomas le Per and Thomas Jones.

BRL 346236 4.10.1340. Agnes his wife raised the hue and cry wrongly against Robert Disvaper; the amercement was excused.

BRL 346298 26.9.1341. He claimed that William de Langley took corn from his land causing 12*d*. damage. William denied, but both agreed to an inquiry by neighbours.

BRL 346300 17.7.1342. Sued by John Heath for a debt. He admitted that he owes him 2*s*. 6*d*. and promised to pay. Pledged by William Langley and Thomas Per.

BRL 346300 19.10.1342. Sued by Thomas Ironmonger for trespassing his hay.

BRL 346302 22.1.1343. Pledged Cristina the widow of Thomas Per.

BRL 346303 26.3.1343. Amerced 4*d*. for not taking part in an inquiry.

BRL 346304 20.8.1343. Sued John Langley for debt; pledged by Thomas Jones and John Gerald.

BRL 346305 30.3.1343. Sued John Brademedewe for trespassing his land.

BRL 346305 22.10.1343. Paid 2*d*. arrears of rent.

BRL 346307 21.7.1344. Sued John Heath for debt.

BRL 346308 6.10.1344. Raised the hue and cry against William de Langley.

BRL 346311 20.4.1345. Assaulted by Thomas Garyn and John de Langley who took malt from his house.

BRL 346311 11.5.1345. Owed Adam Radewall 10*d*. Amerced 2*d*. Pledged by Richard Burnet.

BRL 346313 24.5.1346. Owed Thomas Moor 15*s*.6*d*. for two cows he had bought from him. Promised to pay; 2*d*. amercement and 6*d*. damage were levied on him by the court.

BRL 346313 14.6.1346. Amerced 2*d*. because his horse trespassed on William King's land.

BRL 346333 5.7.1346. Owed money to Henry Parler. His beasts depastured John Percok's land. He had to pay 40*d*. damage and 4*d*. amercement.

BRL 346314 4.10.1346. Elected as a reeve and paid 20s. for the office.
BRL 346316 19.9.1347. Sub-let a part of his meadow for seven years to Robert Barsfen.
BRL 346316 3.10.1347. Amerced 4d. for not grinding his corn in the lord's mill. Elected as a forester; fine 40d.
BRL 346321 6.5.1349. Amerced 1d. for pledging Isabella Hamond who did not come to the court as she should have done.
BRL 346322 17.6.1349. Died holding a messuage and half a virgate. Heriot a mare valued at 3s. The holding was seized by the lord.
BRL 346323 13.1.1350. His holding was given by the lord to John the Miller for life. No entry fine is mentioned.

The name 'Richard le Bond' appears in the court rolls twenty-five times. There are names which appear only once or twice, but the great majority of them (80 per cent) appear more than ten times and some as many as two or three hundred times.[7] Each of the 5,002 names noted in Halesowen court rolls between 1270 and 1400 is mentioned on average fifteen times.

The name 'Richard le Bond' does not cause any problems because at that time nobody else on the manor bore this name. But there are many cases of common surnames like 'Miller', 'Smith', 'Green' and 'Heath' which were given to villagers who had the same Christian name. For example, in the 1320s there were three peasants in Halesowen called 'John Miller'.[8] Moreover, as it was customary to give the eldest son the Christian name of his father or his grandfather, it is difficult to distinguish between the members of the same family. The brothers William (1270–5d.) and Richard (1270–78/81d.) Tewenhall each had two sons also called William and Richard, and the six of them appear simultaneously in the court records.[9] The fact that many peasants had identical names and

[7] The name 'Richard Moulowe' (1348–1401d.) is mentioned 324 times.
[8] John Miller of Oldbury (1313–43d.) (BRL 346234–321); John Miller of Hunnington (1321–38) (346233–85); John Miller of Hill (1326) (346250).
[9] William Tewenhall (1270–5d.) (*Hales Court Rolls,* I, pp. 15–63); William II Tewenhall (1276–1306) (pp. 34–545); Richard son of William Tewenhall (1281–2) (pp. 184–90); Richard Tewenhall (1270–8/81d.) (pp. 11–102); Richard II Tewenhall (1280–2) (p. 204 and vol. II, p. 82); William son of Richard Tewenhall (1272–1314d.) (vol. I, pp. 38–577, and BRL 346233–5).

others had more than one surname creates such confusion that it is impossible to know who is who. The only way to solve the problem is to assume that each name mentioned in the court rolls describes a different person and then to test it in each case until positive identification is achieved. This can be done by finding the habitation of each villager and his place in a network of social and familial relationships.

(2) SPATIAL LOCATION

After I collected all the information available in the records about every name, they were classified according to the townships of the manor. The township of many villagers is noted in the records at least once during the term of their residence on the manor, since each township presented twice a year in the 'great court' the offences committed by its members. However, the habitation of a third of the peasants is not specified in the court rolls. To allocate these villagers we can use their neighbours and relatives whose habitation is known. The basis for this method is the fact that the litigation in the manorial court was frequently between neighbours and relatives, and that they pledged each other more often than villagers from other townships. Richard le Bond, whose file has been mentioned above, provides a good example. Richard lived in the township of Langley in the northern part of the manor. His name is associated with that of 25 villagers of whom 16 (64 per cent) belonged to the same township. As he appears in the records eight times with the brothers William and John Langley and five times with members of the Per–Sweyn family, it is likely that they were his close neighbours. There was, however, a group of rich peasants whose interests and activities were spread all over the manor and beyond. The litigation in which these notables were involved was not restricted to their immediate neighbours and relatives. Therefore they cannot be used to identify the geographical location of other villagers. But as far as the common peasant was concerned I found that the majority of the people with whom he was associated in the court were from his own township. Thus by using villagers whose location in the manor was known the location of the rest has been discovered. Eventually, most of the resident villagers were classified according to the twelve townships of the manor, and for many of them it has been possible to find even who were their closest neighbours.

The geographical classification of the villagers revealed many of those who had identical names. In these cases it was necessary to take all the information collected under these names and to relate every detail to the right person. This was done by the help of other villagers mentioned in the entries. For example, two peasants in the 1320s were called 'Thomas Hill' – one from Romsley, the other from Hill. In 1328 Thomas Hill complained that John Snode broke into his house and assaulted him and his guests. John Snode was from the township of Hill; therefore I assumed that the entry refers to Thomas Hill of Hill.[10] In 1320 Thomas Hill's blood was spilt by William de Westeley. As William was from Romsley, I assumed that the entry refers to Thomas Hill of Romsley.[11] When a court-roll entry mentions a name which was common to more than one villager and it was not clear whom it describes, the entry was disqualified. Fortunately, in most cases when there are important items of information about, for example, land transactions and conveyances, the records usually provide enough clues to identify the villagers mentioned, even though there were others with identical names.

When all the names which were temporarily assumed to represent unique persons were classified in twelve groups according to the townships of the manor, it was possible to reconstitute families.

(3) FAMILY RECONSTITUTION

Pedigrees of villagers are given very rarely in court rolls; the genealogical data found in them are largely incidental. Nevertheless, as many of the social and economic activities reflected in these records were conducted within a family framework, it is possible to discover the familial ties of villagers. In a good series of court rolls like that of Halesowen genealogical data are so abundant that most of the peasants can be linked to families. As an example of how this was done we will take the Melley family from the township of Illey (see fig. 1). Richard de Melley, a customary tenant, appears in the court rolls for the first time in 1270.[12] He had three brothers, Thomas, William and Gilbert. In 1274 he and his brothers Thomas and William were amerced for default of court, and in 1275 he was essoined by his brother Gilbert.[13] Richard had a son William who

---

[10] BRL 346385 3.1.1328.
[11] BRL 346239 8.10.1320.
[12] *Hales Court Rolls*, I, p. 2.
[13] Ibid. I, p. 66.

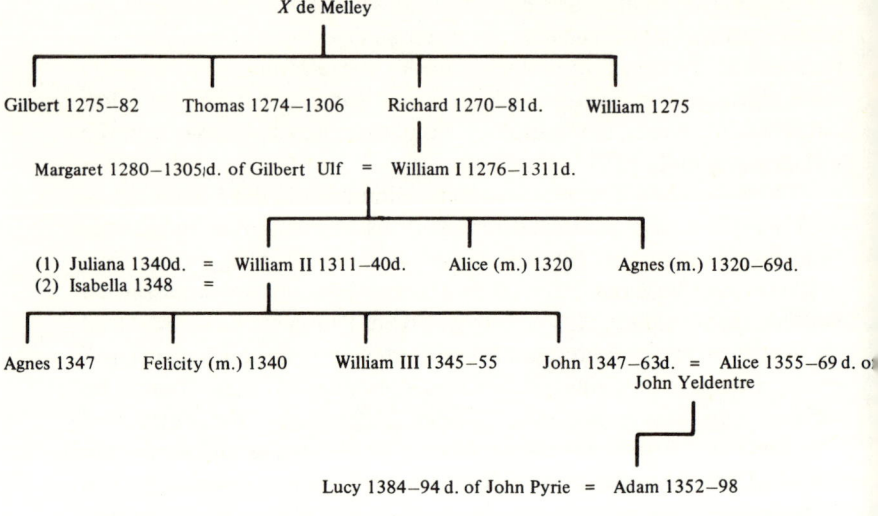

Fig. 1 The Melley family tree

was noted in the court records for the first time in 1276.[14] Richard died in 1281 and William entered the family holding for an entry fine of 16s.[15]

William I de Melley married Margaret the daughter of Gilbert Ulf of Illey and in 1306, when her father died, both of them entered a third of her father's holding.[16] Margaret bore him a son William and two daughters Agnes and Alice. In 1311 William I died and his son William II entered the land for 6s. 8d.[17] In 1320 William I's two daughters Alice and Agnes paid 4s. as a marriage fine.[18]

William II de Melley was married twice. His first wife Juliana died in 1340, and his second wife Isabella is noted for the first time in the records in 1348.[19] William II had two daughters: Felicity who paid merchet in 1340 and Agnes who was amerced in 1348 for trespass against a neighbour.[20] He also had two sons. The eldest, William III, is mentioned in the records for the first time in 1345, and his second son John is first mentioned in 1347.[21] William II died in the Black

[14] Ibid. II, p. 10.   [15] Ibid. I, p. 101.   [16] Ibid. I, p. 527.
[17] BRL 350357 10.3.1311.   [18] BRL 350238 27.2.1320.
[19] BRL 346292 25.10.1340; 346317 23.1.1348.
[20] BRL 346292 23.3.1340; 346317 23.1.1348.
[21] BRL 346310 16.3.1345; 346315 21.2.1347.

Death and, since his eldest son William III had left the manor, the family holding was given to John.²²

John de Melley married Alice the daughter of John Yeldentre a rich villager from Romsley.²³ John died in 1363 and his son Adam entered his father's half virgate in Illey and another half virgate in Romsley which he inherited from his mother.²⁴

Adam de Melley married Lucy the daughter and heiress of John Pyrie of Romsley, and in 1384 he entered her family holding, which amounted to half a virgate.²⁵ In 1398 Adam was still alive, and his descendants were resident in Halesowen in the fifteenth and sixteenth centuries.²⁶

It was possible to reconstitute 677 families like the Melleys who were resident in Halesowen between the years 1270 and 1400. The members of all these families are linked together on the basis of explicit genealogical data available in the court rolls. However, the links between the members of another 364 (35 per cent) reconstituted families are partly given in the records and partly hypothetical. For example, in the court rolls between 1270 and 1349 7 villagers from Romsley had the surname 'de Westeley'. Geoffrey de Westeley appears in the court rolls between 1270 and 1272.²⁷ In the records of 1279 the name 'William de Westeley'²⁸ is noted and in 1280 that of 'Tristran de Westeley'.²⁹ The link was made because the three of them, in addition to having a common surname, were engaged in ale-brewing, which in Halesowen was a trade practised by the same families for generations. In 1279 William was distrained for not paying heriot after the death of his mother, and in 1282 he was distrained because his sister married without permission, which suggests that he belonged to an old Romsley family and was not a newcomer.³⁰ William was married to Juliana daughter and co-heiress of Henry de Folfen, and in 1294 it was declared in the

---

²² After the death of William II de Melley in the plague (BRL 346321 6.5.1349) his holding was taken by the lord. But it seems that his son John took the holding, since he appears in the records from 1354 onwards as a landholder in the township of Illey. See 346333–49. William III his brother appears in the records in 1355 (346335). But in 1358 and again in 1362 it is reported that he was a fugitive serf.
²³ BRL 346329 3.10.1352.
²⁴ BRL 346349 3.10.1363 and 27.4.1370.
²⁵ BRL 346821 1.7.1384.
²⁶ R. K. Field, 'The Worcestershire peasantry in the later Middle Ages', unpublished M.A. thesis, University of Birmingham, 1962, pp. 207–8.
²⁷ *Hales Court Rolls*, I, pp. 4, 44.
²⁸ Ibid. II, p. 58.   ²⁹ Ibid. I, p. 153.   ³⁰ Ibid. I. pp. 117, 179.

court that his son William II would inherit the Folfen holding.[31] In 1316 William I died and his son William II entered the family holding.[32] In 1320 a villager called 'Thomas de Westeley' is noted in the court records.[33] I assumed that he was the brother of William II because he lived in Romsley and was involved often in quarrels with other members of the de Folfen family.[34] Moreover, in 1323 when Thomas bought a messuage and some land William II de Westeley was his surety; it was customary for close relatives to pledge each other in land transactions.[35] Thomas is mentioned for the last time in 1340, and in 1343 his son Thomas II appears in the records.[36] The last time William II de Westeley is mentioned in the court rolls is in 1334.[37] In 1335 Cristina de Westeley paid 2s. as a leyrwyte and from then onwards she was active as an ale-brewer in Romsley.[38] She could have been the widow of William II de Westeley or his daughter or the daughter of Thomas de Westeley. As it is now stated in the court records that she was a widow in 1335 when she payed a leyrwyte, the first possibility was ruled out. She was thus placed in the family tree as a daughter of either Thomas or William II de Westeley (see fig. 2).[39]

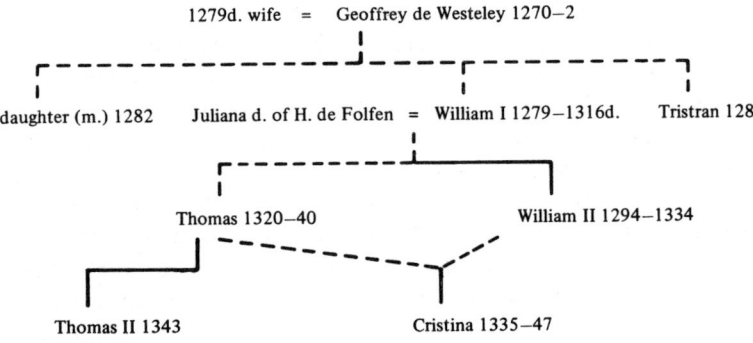

Fig. 2   The de Westeley family tree

[31] Ibid. I, pp. 273–4.
[32] BRL 346360 4.10.1316.
[33] BRL 346239 23.10.1320.
[34] BRL 346806 20.10.1335.
[35] BRL 346796 18.2.1323.
[36] BRL 346810 4.8.1340; 346305 30.2.1343.
[37] BRL 346804 4.4.1334.
[38] BRL 346805 31.3.1335.
[39] It is possible that Cristina Westeley died during the Black Death, since in 1351 the lord gave 'Westeley' holding which amounted to half a virgate to Thomas Taylor for a 6s. 8d. entry fine (BRL 346327 14.12.1351).

Hypothetical linkage was made only when villagers who had identical surnames lived in the same township; had the same neighbours and the same legal status; and pledged, co-operated and quarrelled often with each other. For example, Hugo de Melley (mentioned in the court rolls between 1293 and 1315)[40] was not linked to the Melley family from Illey because he was a free tenant and lived in Hawne, while the Melleys from Illey were bondmen. Obviously the margin of error in hypothetical nominal linkage is fairly wide, but it can be narrowed if used carefully and if the records are detailed enough to provide means to test the validity of such links. And the risk is worth taking because the method enables us to study many families in the lower echelons of village society which are usually underdocumented in court rolls.

(4) IDENTIFICATION

When the villagers were located geographically and families were reconstituted it was possible to find the names which describe more than one person. For example, the name 'John Heath' mentioned between 1280 and 1316 was the name of a villager from Lapal whose father was called Richard,[41] and of a villager from the township of Hill whose father was called Thomas.[42] The name 'Thomas Hill', which appears in the records from 1270 and 1349, was the name of 5 villagers from the township of Hill; the first one was the son of Edward,[43] the second the son of Geoffrey,[44] the third the son of Roger,[45] the fourth the son of Henry[46] and the fifth the son of Thomas.[47] However, it was still necessary to identify the villagers who had more than one surname. I took all the identical Christian names which were mentioned in the records every thirty years in each one of the townships and checked whether the different surnames attached to them describe different persons or not. This is a less complicated and time-consuming operation than it might appear to be, provided the information obtained from the court rolls on each villager is sufficiently detailed. Even in the township of Romsley, which was one of the biggest settlements in the parish, only

---

[40] *Hales Court Rolls*, I, pp. 256–565; BRL 350357–9.
[41] *Hales Court Rolls*, I, pp. 130–458.
[42] Ibid. I, pp. 70-544; BRL 346233–5 and 350351–60.
[43] *Hales Court Rolls*, I, p. 14.
[44] Ibid. I, pp. 13–438.
[45] BRL 346252–361 20.5.1332.
[46] BRL 346233–319.
[47] BRL 346319–23.

between 28 and 92 names of men and women required checking. It did not take long to check the identity of the Williams, Richards and Alices by using relatives, neighbours, data about legal and economic status and dates of marriages and deaths. For example, the names 'William ate Lyche'[48] and 'William Yeldentre'[49] mentioned in the records in the 1280s were the names of two different persons living in Romsley. The former was a bondman and had a half virgate of land; the latter was a freeman and had about a virgate of land. And the names 'Margaret Symon'[50] and 'Margaret Robin'[51] mentioned in the records in the first half of the fourteenth century were the names of two different women from Oldbury. The first was the daughter of William Symon and the second the daughter of Walter Robin.

Thus by checking every name the villagers who had more than one surname were identified. For example, Thomas le Archer and Thomas le Freeman appear in the court rolls between 1280 and 1300. Both lived in the township of Warley and both had a brother called Stephen. Therefore it was assumed that 'Thomas le Archer' and 'Thomas le Freeman' were one and the same person.[52] Both Richard Tewenhall and Richard le Feys from Ridgeacre mentioned in the records between 1293 and 1324 had a brother called William Tewenhall, an indication that the two Richards were one person with two surnames.[53] John Carpenter of Hill and John Fille of the same township appear in the court rolls between 1270 and 1300. But as both of them had a wife called Dionisia and a mother called Felicity, it is obvious that 'Carpenter' and 'Fille' were the aliases of John.[54]

[48] *Hales Court Rolls,* I, pp. 7–546.
[49] Ibid. I, pp. 57–562.   [50] BRL 346309.   [51] BRL 346271.
[52] On 15.2.1297 Thomas le Archer gave the lord 2s. to obtain permission to sell his holding to his brother Stephen. See *Hales Court Rolls,* I, p. 350. On 22.4.1237 Stephen le Freeman gave his daughter in marriage to Ralf Gregory with half of the holding he bought from his brother Thomas le Archer (ibid. I, 358).
[53] In 1234 Richard son of William Tewenhall entered the holding which belonged to William le Feys, for an entry fine of 20s. He was pledged by his brother William II Tewenhall, (*Hales Court Rolls,* I, p. 302). From 1237 to 1315 the name 'Richard le Feys' appears frequently in the records (ibid. I, pp. 363–524; BRL 346233–5 and 350355). But on 6.12.1312 (346234) Richard le Feys was granted some land by his brother William II Tewenhall. It is obvious that 'Feys' was the second surname of Richard son of William Tewenhall, attributed to him since he took the Feys holding.
[54] In 1271 William Mody was essoined by his stepson John (*Hales Court Rolls,* I, p. 29). In 1294 William Mody and Felicity his wife gave their house, half of a curtilage and half a virgate of land to John Carpenter; after their death he was to

Names of persons who could not be located in one of the townships or linked to families were disqualified because it was impossible to check their identity or to ascertain that they were residents on the manor. However, since the data obtained from Halesowen court rolls about individual villagers are in most cases abundant, it was possible to identify positively the great majority of them. In the court rolls from 1270 to 1400, 3,435 individual villagers – 2,057 males and 1,378 females – were identified as residents in the parish. Another 372 (11 per cent) persons noted in the records were disqualified as unidentified persons. This group includes villagers whose names were copied wrongly either by the scribes or by me, and those whose identity or residence in the manor was uncertain. In addition there were 178 people mentioned in the records who were also excluded from the sample because it was apparent that they were outsiders, like Richard atte Hey from Kidderminster,[55] who held land in Halesowen but never lived there, or William Bromyng from Harborne,[56] who came to Halesowen manorial court to recover a debt from Thomas Hickemons of Romsley.

In the absence of comparable studies it is difficult to assess the effectiveness of the methods described above and the quality of the sample population obtained from the court rolls. However, by chance there was an opportunity to test the methods and the sample. In a late stage of the study I discovered that I had overlooked several rolls which are not catalogued with the rest of the series. These rolls include the records of 98 court sessions held in the years 1307–11, 1314–17, 1321–2, 1326–7 and 1330. For these years only 90 court records had previously been available, and for the years 1308–10 and 1315–16 there were no records at all. In the newly discovered rolls the names of 642 resident villagers are mentioned, but only 32 (5 per cent) of them were not included in the prepared sample because they either emigrated or died imme-

---

inherit the whole holding. In return John promised to maintain them (ibid. I, p. 293). In 1234 Dionisia the wife of John son of Fille assaulted William Mody (ibid. I, p. 273). In the court held on 2.8.1234 (ibid. I, p. 230) John Carpenter undertook to bring pledges that his wife Dionisia would not again assault William and Felicity Mody. Therefore it is clear that John Fille and John Carpenter are the same person.

[55] In 1319 Richard atte Hey de Kiddeminster gave the lord 12d. for permission to hold land in Halesowen (BRL 346237 13.6.1319). His name is mentioned again only twice, in 1327 (346252 28.10.1327) and in 1337 (346279 14.5.1337), which suggests that he was not a resident of the manor.

[56] BRL 346348 1.11.1368.

diately after their first appearance in the records. Moreover, when I first counted the male residents of Halesowen appearing in the court rolls between 1311 and 1314, their number was 472. On re-counting the males mentioned in the records between 1311 and 1315, it was found that their number was 485, a difference of only 3 per cent. In the court records of 1315 the names of 264 males are noted, and if the methods used to identify the peasants were inadequate or if the court rolls are unrepresentative the difference between the two counts should have been much greater. Nevertheless, since the processing of the data obtained from Halesowen court rolls was done by hand, the margin of error is probably fairly wide. However, in future studies of court rolls this margin can be greatly reduced with the help of a computer.

2. *The Measurement of the Population Trend*

The court rolls' provision of a representative sample of the adult inhabitants of a manor enables us, if a consecutive series is available, to discover changes in population levels and to measure the rate of change. This can be done by frequent census-like enumerations of the villagers mentioned in the court records. However, since not all of them attended the manorial court every year, it is necessary to count them from the court rolls of more than one year to estimate their number. In order to obtain a large sample I counted the villagers identified in the court records of the first five years in each decade from 1270 to 1400, with the exception of the periods 1280–1300 and 1340–50, for which the count was done from the court rolls of the years 1280–2, 1293–5 and 1345–9. From the sample of 3,435 villagers identified in the court rolls between 1270 and 1400, 511 (14 per cent) were not enumerated at all, because they appear in the records only in between the periods under count. The results are presented in table 1 and fig. 3.

In table 1 one can see that the villagers have been counted each time from a different number of court records. Therefore it can be argued that the changes in the number of villagers reflect changes in the number of the court records rather than changes in the actual population of the parish. If this is true there should have been a direct relation between the number of individuals identified in them. But we can see clearly in table 1 that this is not the case. For example, for the period 1271–5 42 court records are available

Table 1. *The resident villagers identified in Halesowen court rolls 1271–1395*

Date	Number of court records	Number of males	Number of females	Total
1271–5	42	331	51	382
1280–2	39	392	71	463
1293–5	28	435	107	542
1301–5	44	457	147	604
1311–15	79	485	204	689
1321–5	88	412	170	582
1331–5	71	433	173	606
1345–9	66	470	205	675
1351–5	59	270	119	389
1361–5	42	255	103	358
1371–5	55	289	138	427
1381–5	69	275	127	402
1391–5	49	252	92	344

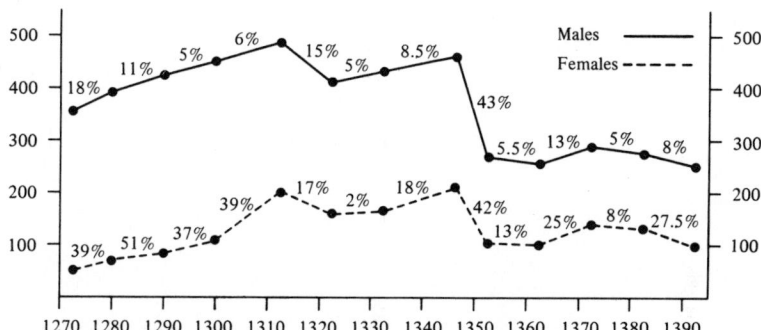

Fig. 3 The population trend in Halesowen 1271–1395

and for the period 1301–5 44; nevertheless, in the courts of 1301–5 38 per cent more males are identified. For the period 1321–5 88 court sessions are available and for the period 1293–5 only 28, yet in the courts of 1293–5 435 males were identified whereas in the courts of 1321–5 there are only 412.

The two curves in fig. 3 show the fluctuations in the number of men and women above the age of 12 identified in the court rolls between 1271 and 1395. Although the two curves follow the same course they fluctuate at different rates. But as men, unlike women, are almost fully represented in the court rolls, the changes in their number reflect more accurately the population trend in the parish. We can see that the population of Halesowen increased from 1270 to 1349, despite a temporary setback in the 1320s, and that after the Black Death it stagnated and declined. In the following chapters we will see evidence which will verify and explain this trend.

2. The Population of Halesowen 1270-1348

1. The Demographic Trend

In a series of articles M.M. Postan has put forward the view that the rural population of England declined some thirty years before the Black Death as a result of a 'Malthusian crisis'. He argued that since the productivity of medieval agriculture was low, the supply of food to support a growing population increased as long as the area under cultivation was expanding. But during the thirteenth century, as the reserves of reclaimable land were giving out, the growing demand for agricultural land resulted in divisions and subdivisions of holdings. Consequently, at the end of the thirteenth century almost half of the peasants did not have enough land to support their families. At the same time falling crop yields from exhausted soils reduced the supply of food. Under such unfavourable conditions the population ceased to expand and in the first quarter of the fourteenth century it even started to decline as a result of positive Malthusian checks which culminated in the 'great famine' of 1315-17.[1]

Plenty of indirect evidence has been brought forward to substantiate this view. It has been shown that at the end of the thirteenth century colonization in many parts of the country came to a halt, that land was in very short supply, that the proportion of smallholders among the peasants rose, that the 'great famine' took a heavy toll of life and that in the second quarter of the fourteenth century wages rose and holdings lay vacant in various parts of the country.[2]

---

[1] 'Histoire économique: moyen âge', *Rapports du IXe Congrès International des Sciences Historiques* (Paris, 1950), pp. 225 et seq., 'Some agrarian evidence of a declining population in the later Middle Ages', *Essays on Medieval Agriculture and General Problems of the Medieval Economy*, (Cambridge, 1973), pp. 186-213, and *The Medieval Economy and Society* (London, 1972), pp. 33-8.

[2] In addition to Postan's works mentioned above, see J. Z. Titow, 'Some differences between manors and their effects on the condition of the peasant in the thirteenth century', *Agric. Hist. Rev.*, X (1962), 1-13, 'Some evidence of the thirteenth century population increase', *Econ. Hist. Rev.*, 2nd ser., XIV (1961), 218-23, and *English Rural Society 1200-1350* (London, 1969), pp. 73 et seq.; I. Kershaw, 'The great famine and agrarian crisis in England 1315-22', *Past and Present*, no. 59 (1973), 3-50; A. R. H. Baker, 'Evidence in the "Nonarum Inquisitiones" of contracting arable lands in England during the early fourteenth

Yet, except for a study of mortality on some Winchester manors which has yielded questionable results, we have no direct demographic evidence that the rural population of England did decline before the Black Death.[3]

Postan's views on the demographic trend in the pre-plague period have been challenged. But no direct demographic evidence has been brought forward to show that the rural population *did* continue to increase until the first outbreak of bubonic plague in 1348–9.[4]

Halesowen court-roll evidence obviously cannot decide the issue. But it provides an opportunity to test empirically the validity of the assumption that a rural population could not have continued to increase and must have begun to decline once colonization on a large scale stopped and the supply of land decreased.

In 1086 there were 71 tenants in Halesowen, but in 1313–15 their number amounted to at least 215.[5] Although this comparison does not provide an exact measure of population growth, one might conclude that the population of the parish trebled between 1086 and 1313–15. Such an increase suggests that extensive land reclamation was carried out in the parish during the twelfth and thirteenth centuries. However, in the last quarter of the thirteenth and the first half of the fourteenth century, there are indications that the

century', *Econ. Hist. Rev.*, 2nd ser., XIX (1966), 518–32, 'Some evidence of a reduction in the acreage of cultivated lands in Sussex during the early fourteenth century', *Sussex Archaeol. Collections*, CIV (1966), 1–5, and 'Contracting arable lands in 1341', *Beds. Hist. Rec. Soc.*, X/IX (1970), 7–17; B. Waites, 'Medieval assessments and agricultural prosperity in northeast Yorkshire, 1292–1342', *Yorks. Archaeol. Journ.*, XLIV (1972), 134–45. For data about the rise in agricultural wages between the famine and the Black Death see J. E. Thorold Rogers, *A History of Agriculture and Prices in England 1259–1973*, vol. I (Oxford, 1866), pp. 264, 269, and *Six Centuries of Work and Wages*, 9th edn (London, 1908), pp. 217–18; W. H. Beveridge, 'Westminster wages in the manorial era', *Econ. Hist. Rev.*, 2nd ser., VII (1955–6), 20–2, 24.

[3] Postan and Titow, 'Heriots and prices on Winchester manors', in Postan, *Essays on Medieval Agriculture and General Problems of the Medieval Economy* (Cambridge, 1973), pp. 150–85. For criticism of the authors' observations see P. Goran Ohlin, 'No safety in numbers: some pitfalls of historical statistics', in *Industrialization in Two Systems*, ed. H. Rosovsky (New York, 1966), pp. 84–9.

[4] B. F. Harvey, 'The population trend in England between 1300 and 1348', *Trans. Roy. Hist. Soc.*, 5th ser., XVI (1965), 23–42; J. C. Russell, 'The pre-plague population of England', *Journ. British Studies*, V (1966), 1–21; W. C. Robinson, 'Money, population and economic change in late medieval Europe', *Econ. Hist. Rev.*, 2nd ser., XII (1959–60), 63–76; D. G. Watts, 'A model for the early fourteenth century', *Econ. Hist. Rev.*, 2nd ser., XX (1967), 543–5.

[5] See n. 30 below.

pace of land reclamation in Halesowen slowed down considerably. In the court rolls from 1270 to 1348, 83 assarts are recorded, but 63 (73 per cent) of them were of small or minute plots of land. In 1302, for example, the lord granted to John the son of Richard of Romsley a plot of wasteland to enclose and to build upon, for an annual rent of 1*d*. and a 6*d*. entry fine.[6] In 1301 Philip Sveynes was granted a plot taken out of the waste of Oldbury to increase the size of his courtyard, for an annual rent of one halfpenny and a 12*d*. entry fine.[7] And in 1282 Gilbert de Illey took a piece of land for an annual rent of one halfpenny and a 6*d*. entry fine, to enlarge his garden.[8] Although such reclamations were no more than a nibbling at the waste, the reserves of rough pasture in the manor were reduced already to such an extent that the villagers tried to curb further reclamations. In 1301 and 1302 the township of Oldbury paid the lord 14*s*. 6*d*. to ensure that two plots of wasteland 'should forever remain waste and be never enclosed for the common benefit of all the men of Oldbury'.[9] Similar concessions were obtained from the lord by the tenants of Warley (1309) and the tenants of Romsley (1327).[10] Moreover, there is evidence that sometimes the villagers tried to prevent assarts by force. In May 1306 the lord gave to Thomas Collyng for an entry fine of 4*s*. and rent of 2*d*. a plot in Lapal, 'sicut includitur sepibus et fossatis'. But some of Thomas Collyng's neighbours came and destroyed his enclosure.[11] In 1327 several villagers from Romsley destroyed and burnt the fence with which Nicholas Smith enclosed a plot of woodland.[12]

Land reclamation in Halesowen between 1270 and 1348 neither enlarged significantly the area under crops nor satisfied the growing demand for land. Although entry fines in Halesowen were customary and much lower than those paid by tenants on the Winchester or Glastonbury estates, there is evidence which supports J. Z. Titow's observation that customary low entry fines did not reflect the high

---

[6] 'Unam placeam terre de vasto domini ad includendum et super edificandum' (*Hales Court Rolls*, I, p. 472).
[7] Ibid. I, p. 413.   [8] Ibid. I, p. 210.
[9] 'Quod predicta placea vasti in perpetuum jaceat vasta, aperta, et nunquam inclusa sed ad commune asaimentum omnium hominum de Oldebury' (ibid. I, p. 457). For the grant of 1301 see ibid. II, p. 158.
[10] BRL 350353 29.1.1309; 346801 18.5.1327.
[11] *Hales Court Rolls*, I, p. 540. In the records of the court held in June 1306 it is noted that '... qui prostraverunt purpresturam quam dominus concessit Thomas Colling apud Lapole' (ibid. I, p. 546). The beginning of the entry is illegible.
[12] BRL 346810 14.7.1327.

market value of land.[13] When local tenants inherited land they usually paid the low customary entry fines. But whenever a villager acquired a vacant holding to which he had no right of inheritance, the rate of the entry fine was determined by the market value of land and consequently was quite high. For example, when in 1294 the lord gave to Henry Osbern a half virgate of land which previously belonged to Thomas Robin of Oldbury, the entry fine paid was not the customary one of 6s. 8d. but £6. 13s. 4d.[14] In 1301 William Lee acquired from the lord a vacant holding of a quarter virgate for an entry fine of £2. 7s. instead of 3s. 4d.[15] In 1345 the lord granted to Felicity Hypkyns a holding consisting of a cottage and a curtilage which had escheated from Thomas Symon for an entry fine of £1. 3s. 4d.[16]

As the demand for land in Halesowen far exceeded its supply, the number of villagers who did not have enough land to support their families was high; 43 per cent of the families who lived in the parish between 1270 and 1348 had only a quarter virgate of land or less. Yet, despite the fact that land in Halesowen was scarce and many families suffered from destitution, the population increased from 1271–5 to 1311–15 by 46 per cent (see table 2). This implies a compound annual rate of growth of 1.132 per cent. In the early 1320s the population was reduced by 15 per cent but recovered fairly quickly and on the eve of the Black Death had almost reached the peak of 1311–15. In the seventy-four years from 1273 to 1347 the population increased by a compound annual rate of 0.475 per cent. But before analysing this demographic trend we have to ask ourselves to what extent it was affected by migrations.

The inhabitants of Halesowen, like those of other medieval villages, did not constitute a closed population, as there were constant migrations to and from the parish.[17] Between 1270 and 1348 the departure from the manor of 67 men and women of unfree status, with and without licence, is recorded in the court rolls. Those whose new places of residence are given in the records did not go far away – they settled in Warley Wigorn, Kings Norton, Northfield, Birmingham, Aston, Smethwick, Dudley, Evesham, Warwick, Coventry,

---

[13] Titow, *English Rural Society*, pp. 74–8.
[14] *Hales Court Rolls*, I, p. 290.   [15] Ibid. II, p. 149.
[16] BRL 346312 13.7.1345. In 1276 William Tewenhall 'fecit finem pro quadam parva pecia terre 22s' (*Hales Court Rolls*, II, p. 9).
[17] For a study of peasant mobility in the thirteenth and fourteenth centuries see J. A. Raftis, *Tenure and Mobility* (Toronto, 1964), pp. 128–52.

Table 2. *The growth of the population of Halesowen 1271–1349*

Date	No. of males	Percentage (1271–5 = 100)
1271–5	331	100
1280–2	392	118
1293–5	435	131
1301–5	457	138
1311–15	485	146
1321–5	412	124
1331–5	433	131
1345–9	470	142

Wick in Worcestershire, Walsall, Newport in Shropshire and Hereford.[18] However, there is evidence that villeins left the manor without being registered in the court rolls, and it is likely that such cases were quite common.[19] And since the departure of freemen from the manor is not recorded at all, it is impossible to compile a full list of emigrants. As far as migrations to the manor are concerned, we cannot measure them either, because surnames in the pre-plague period were so unstable. Sometimes it is possible to identify immigrants like William Warde of Harborne who settled in Halesowen in the 1340s.[20] But often it is difficult to ascertain that a new surname noted in the records is the name of a newcomer rather than an alias of a local villager. Nevertheless, although the extent to which migrations affected the changes in the size of the population of the parish cannot be measured, it is possible to show that these changes were caused primarily by other demographic factors. Male replacement rates obtained from the court rolls suggest that the population growth between 1270 and the Black Death was sustained by a natural increase rather than by a constant inflow of immigrants. And data about mortality indicate clearly that the

---

[18] One villager was more adventurous. Philip le Feys alias Joye (1278–1310d.) from Langley left the village in 1282 and 'extitisset in partibus trans marinis' (*Hales Court Rolls*, I, p. 559). He returned to Halesowen in 1306 and only when he brought four pledges that he 'will not depart or remove himself from his land' was he allowed to take back his holding (ibid. I, p. 552).

[19] For example, the departure of Thomas Holy was not reported in the court. But in 1337 he came back and obtained the lord's permission to remain in the village (BRL 346278 19.2.1337).

[20] William Warde de Harborne (1342–75/7d.). He married Agnes the daughter of Thomas Heath of Lapal and settled in the village (BRL 346299–353).

number of villagers was reduced in the 1320s as a result of an upsurge in deaths and not of a sudden mass migration.

2. Male Replacement Rates

It is possible to calculate from court rolls male replacement rates, as Sylvia Thrupp has shown, by counting the number of sons who survived their fathers and who reached maturity, i.e. who are noted in the records as landholders.[21] For example, in 1321 the death of 6 tenants who had among them eleven sons is recorded in the court rolls. Ralf Ordrich (1274–1321d.) a quarter yardlander from Oldbury was succeeded by his son John (1295–1343d.); Thomas Richard (1272–1321d.) a yardlander from the same township left five sons, Richard (1293–1347/8d.) who inherited the family holding, Adam (1313–38), John (1316–35), Thomas (1318–48) and William who emigrated from the manor in 1326; John son of Roger de Walloxhall (1271–1321d.) a yardlander was succeeded by his son Roger (1320–38d.); Philip le King (1276–1321d.) a quarter yardlander from Langley was succeeded by his son William (1321–69d.); William II atte Pyrie a half yardlander from Romsley left two sons, William III (1313–48/50d.) who took the family holding and Symon (1315–55); and Thomas Godith (1280–1321d.) a half yardlander from Cakemoor was succeeded by his son Robert (1300–40).[22] The male replacement rates of 313 identified Halesowen tenants who died between 1270 and 1348 are presented in table 3.

The figures in table 3 show that the male replacement rates in Halesowen from 1270 to 1348, except in the crisis years between 1310 and 1319, were above unity. From this it appears that the reproductive capacity of the villagers in the pre-plague period was sufficient to maintain growth of the population. However, the replacement rates obtained do not provide a faithful measure of the actual rates of natural increase of the local population. On one hand they underestimate this increase, because the count of sons who survived their fathers is incomplete. Often sons of local villagers

---

[21] S. L. Thrupp, 'The problem of replacement-rates in late medieval English population', *Econ. Hist. Rev.*, 2nd ser., XVIII (1965), 101–19.

[22] John son of Roger Walloxhall died in February 1321 (BRL 350361 24.2.1321). Thomas Godith, Philip le King and Ralf Ordrich died in April (350361 8.4.1321; 346239 15.4.1321). Thomas Richard died in October (346242 21.10.1321) and William II atte Pyrie in November (346795 14.11.1321).

Table 3. *Male replacement rates 1270–1348*

Dates	No. of dead tenants	No. of sons over 20	Replacement rate
1270–82	38	55	1.447
1293–99	26	39	1.5
1300–09	33	48	1.454
1310–19	91	90	0.989
1320–29	46	54	1.173
1330–39	36	49	1.351
1340–48	43	47	1.093

appear in the records for some time and then disappear. Some of them undoubtedly died but others emigrated or simply acquired new surnames. On the other hand (as the deaths of cottagers and smallholders are underregistered in court rolls), if one counts only the sons of tenants whose deaths are registered, the replacement rates obtained are unrepresentative and consequently overestimated. Among the 313 tenants whose deaths are recorded in Halesowen court rolls between 1270 and 1348 only 93 (30 per cent) were poor tenants, whereas they constituted 43 per cent of the population.[23] The mean male replacement rate of the 313 tenants was at least 1.220, but that of the 93 poor tenants was at least only 0.713. In order to correct our figures, we can add to the sample of 313 tenants whose deaths are recorded 80 hypothetical cottagers and smallholders, which will provide a hypothetical but representative sample. Then, on the assumption that the mean male replacement rate of these poor tenants was at least 0.713, we can estimate the actual minimum male replacement rates of landholders in Halesowen (see table 4). The figures in table 4 suggest that Halesowen families in the pre-plague period were able not only to replace themselves from generation to generation but also to produce a surplus of offspring to maintain population growth.[24]

[23] The deaths of tenants were recorded either when their heirs entered the holding or when the heir was a minor who was taken into custody or when heriot and mortuary were taken by the lord. Many cottagers and peasants with minute holdings died without issue and as they had no beasts or other valuables their names do not appear in the list of villagers from whom death duties were collected. Often when such vacant cottages and small plots of land were given to new tenants, the lord's officials did not bother to mention the names of the former holders. Consequently the deaths of poor tenants are underrecorded in the court rolls.
[24] The data obtained by Russell from the record of the Inquisitiones Post Mortem have been use by T. H. Hollingsworth to calculate male replacement rates and then

Table 4. *Estimated actual male replacement rates 1270–1348*

Dates	No. of observed deaths	No. of hypothetical deaths	No. of observed sons over 20	No. of hypothetical sons over 20	Observed replacement rate	Estimated actual replacement rate
1270–82	38	49	55	62.8	1.447	1.281
1293–99	26	32	39	43.3	1.5	1.352
1300–09	33	44	48	55.8	1.454	1.269
1310–19	91	97	90	94.3	0.989	0.971
1320–29	46	59	54	63.4	1.173	1.072
1330–39	36	47	49	56.8	1.351	1.209
1340–48	43	55	47	55.6	1.093	1.010

Thrupp has calculated the male replacement rates of villagers in the pre-plague period from the court rolls of six eastern manors. In Redgrave and Hinderclay in Suffolk, although the rates declined in the first half of the fourteenth century, they did not fall below unit before the Black Death.[25] Unfortunately, the demographic trend on these manors was not measured by a count of the villagers appearing in the court rolls. If this were to be done so as to show that the population on these manors maintained growth until the first outbreak of the plague, it would confirm the observation made above about Halesowen.

3. *Mortality*

Usually the deaths of tenants only are recorded in court rolls. The exact date of death is not given; there was always an interval between the death and its registration when the heir of the deceased paid heriot and an entry fine or when he was taken into custody, or when the holding escheated for default of heirs or for failure to pay the customary fines.[26] The number of deaths obtained from the

to convert them into rates of natural increase. See Hollingsworth, *Historical Demography* (London, 1969), pp. 375–88. But as the male replacement rates obtained from the court rolls are very crude and minimal, I did not attempt to use his ingenious method to compute the rates of natural increase of the population of Halesowen.

[25] See Thrupp, 'Problem of replacement rates', p. 106.

[26] The death of Richard Tewenhall was recorded in 1314 when his son William came to the court and gave an ox, valued at 10s. 8d., as a heriot and paid 26s. 8d., as an entry fine (BRL 346234 13.3.1314). The death of Philip Lyrgan was recorded in 1314 when the lord seized his holding because his heirs failed to pay heriot and relief (ibid. 7.8.1314). The death of Richard Boyd is recorded in 1311 when his land was seized for default of heirs (350357 7.7.1311). The death of Richard Hill of Romsley

court rolls is far from being complete, because many of the records have been lost. However, a good number of unrecorded deaths were discovered indirectly through widows. For example, John Lappal is mentioned regularly from 1293 to July 1328.[27] In December 1331 his widow sued her brother-in-law for her dowry.[28] Therefore we can assume that John died between July 1328 and December 1331. As far as women are concerned, their deaths were recorded only when they were landholders. But from 1334 onwards lists of 'mortuaries' – a death duty of a beast which the rector was entitled to levy on his parishioners – were copied each year on to the court rolls. Consequently some data are available about the mortality of women and occasionally of men even though they were not tenants.[29] Nevertheless, despite these lists the overall number of dead females obtained from the court rolls is much lower than that of men.

As relatively good mortality data are available only for male tenants, we have to assume that their number did not change significantly between 1270 and 1348; otherwise we cannot use these data to trace the course of mortality during this period. In the absence of manorial extents or rentals for Halesowen it is difficult to estimate the size of its tenant population. However, a count of the male tenants appearing in the court rolls of the years 1293–5, 1313–15 and 1347–9 suggests that their number was fairly stable; in 1293–5 the names of 199 are noted; in 1315–17, 215; and 1347–9, 205.[30]

is recorded in 1345 when the custody of his minor son and heir John was given to Thomas de Stanlowe (346312 23.6.1345).

[27] John Lappal is mentioned for the first time in 1293 (*Hales Court Rolls*, I, p. 244) and for the last time in 1328 for brewing ale against the assize (BRL 346253 13.7.1328).

[28] BRL 346260 11.12.1331.

[29] Like many other medieval religious houses, the Abbey of Halesowen appropriated the local parish. The abbey presented to the vicarage, usually, a canon from 1270 to the dissolution of their house (see T. R. Nash, *Collection for the History of Worcestershire*, 2nd edn (2 vols., London, 1799, I, p. 532). Therefore the abbey was entitled to levy tithes and mortuaries which in Halesowen were called 'principalia'. In 1294 William of Warley died and, since the land which he held in the manor was a lease for life, the question arose whether the lord ought to have a heriot. The verdict of the twelve jurors was that 'herietum non debet nisi suum principale ad ecclesiam tantum' (*Hales Court Rolls*, I, pp. 284–5).

[30] I counted as a tenant any resident villager who inherited his holding or was given a holding by the lord or whose holding was surrendered to him in the court. I also counted as tenants resident villagers who were amerced for default of one of the regular courts. All the inhabitants of the manor had to attend, twice a year after

The number of dead villagers obtained from the court rolls has been calculated at three-yearly rather than yearly intervals, since the annual fluctuations in the number of deaths are often a result of deaths which occurred in one year but were registered or discovered in the records of the following year. The number of male deaths obtained from the court rolls between 1270 and 1349 is presented in fig. 4 and table 5.

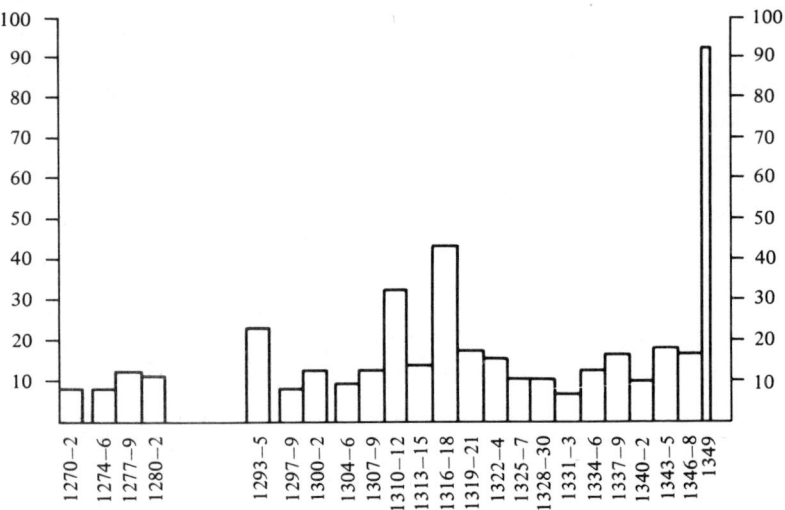

Fig. 4 Number of male deaths recorded in the court rolls 1270–1349 (per three years, except for 1349 when the parish was struck by the Black Death)

The annual average of recorded male deaths from 1270 to 1348, in the sixty-six years for which court rolls are available, is 4.84. We can see in fig. 4 that the number of deaths rose above the average in the years 1293–5, 1310–12, 1316–18, 1319–21, 1322–4, 1337–9, 1343–5 and 1346–8. As the manorial accounts of the Abbey of Halesowen did not survive, we do not know when the harvests in the parish were bad and when they were good. Nevertheless, it can be

Easter and Michaelmas, the so-called 'great courts' in which hundred jurisdiction was administered by the abbot. But attendance at the other regular courts was obligatory only to tenants. In Halesowen only tenants were chosen as jurymen, reeves, foresters and ale-tasters, and only resident tenants were accepted as pledges. Therefore an appearance in the court records of villagers in one of these functions is an indication that they were tenants. I have counted only male tenants because only the deaths of males are well recorded in the court rolls.

shown that in the years in which a high number of deaths was recorded the villagers experienced grave economic difficulties and dearth. Lean years are reflected in the court rolls by a rise in the number of pleas of debt, of inter-peasant land transactions and of illegal gleaners (see table 5). The reason for the rapid quickening of the inter-peasant land market during periods of economic crises is that smallholders and to a lesser extent half yardlanders had to sub-let and to sell land either to remit debts or to pay rents and fines and to buy food, seed corn and livestock.[31]

Table 5. *The number of male deaths, inter-peasant land transactions, pleas of debt and illegal gleaners obtained from the court rolls 1270–1348*

Years	No. of court sessions	No. of dead males	No. of inter-peasant land transactions (leases and sales) (extra-familial)	No. of pleas of debt	No. of illegal gleaners
1270–2	23	8	22	–	–
1274–6	36	8	3	3	–
1277–9	34	12	6	1	–
1280–2	39	11	21	6	–
1293–5	28	23	45	28	–
1297–9	21	8	5	8	9
1300–2	37	12	14	17	4
1304–6	27	9	16	12	1
1307–9	44	12	36	21	15
1310–12	43	32	38	32	25
1313–15	48	13	20	20	9
1316–18	36	43	47	34	33
1319–21	53	17	29	45	12
1322–4	49	15	52	23	24
1325–7	51	10	21	19	2
1328–30	46	10	19	20	2
1331–3	36	6	14	15	7
1334–6	54	12	16	30	18
1337–9	51	16	35	43	30
1340–2	38	9	22	70	2
1343–5	41	18	22	34	9
1346–8	39	16	31	54	20
Total	874	320	534	535	222

[31] Statistics of inter-peasant land transactions, compiled by Kershaw from the court rolls of three Hertfordshire manors of St Albans Abbey and the large Cambridgeshire manor of Chesterton, also show that the land market was brisker during periods of economic crisis in the village. See Kershaw, 'The great famine', p. 38.

The first mortality crisis in Halesowen in the period under study occurred in 1293–5 when the deaths of 23 male villagers were recorded in the court rolls. The index of prices of grains compiled by D. L. Farmer from a wide sample of manors shows that in 1294 and 1295 prices of corn reached famine level.[32] The sharp rise in the number of pleas of debt and of land transactions recorded in the court rolls of 1293–5 suggests that the high mortality in Halesowen in these years was caused by a subsistence crisis. There is a further indication which supports this observation. The deaths of cottagers and smallholders were not recorded in the court rolls as faithfully as those of better-off tenants. The total number of dead tenants obtained from the court rolls from 1270 to 1348 includes 30 per cent cottagers and smallholders although they constituted some 43 per cent of the population. But among the 23 tenants whose deaths were recorded in 1293–5, 9 (39 per cent) were either cottagers or smallholders. For example William Bercarius and John Symond of St Kenelm died in 1295. Both of them had two daughters and both of them were so poor that their daughters, instead of paying an entry fine, were allowed to take their holdings for an undertaking to perform four and eight days' work on the demesne in the autumn.[33] John Bedel died in 1293 without issue. His two nieces Agnes and Matilda entered the land for 2s., but as he had no beasts the lord took as a heriot a thrave and a half of oats.[34]

In the period 1307–9, the villagers of Halesowen again experienced hard times. The rise in the number of land transactions, pleas of debt and amercements for gleaning recorded in the court rolls suggests that the local harvest in 1307 and 1308 might have been as

The correlation between agrarian crises and the intensification of the land market in the village supports P. R. Hyams's criticism of Postan's sociological explanation of the existence of a peasant land market in England in the thirteenth and early fourteenth centuries. See Postan, 'The charters of the villeins', *Essays on Medieval Agriculture and General Problems of the Medieval Economy* (Cambridge, 1973), pp. 114–17, and Hyams, 'The origins of the peasant land market in England', *Econ. Hist. Rev.*, 2nd ser., XXIII (1970), 18–31.

[32] 'Some grain price movements in thirteenth-century England', *Econ. Hist. Rev.*, 2nd ser., X (1957–8), 212. See also Rogers, *History of Agriculture and Prices*, I, p. 192.
[33] *Hales Court Rolls*, I, p. 328.
[34] Ibid. I, p. 220 (2.3.1293). In the court held on 28.10.1293 we find the following entry: 'Una trava et dimidia avene considerantur per totam curiam de consuetudine domino pro herieto Johannis Bedelli quod unum averium non habuit' (ibid. I, p. 255).

The Population of Halesowen 1270–1348   39

bad as on other manors.³⁵ Yet the number of recorded deaths remains relatively low. It is possible that for some reason deaths were underregistered. But in view of the fact that the court rolls between 1307 and 1309 are very detailed and have survived almost intact, it seems to me that the figures are representative. Nevertheless, although mortality might not have risen in 1307–9, these lean years weakened the resistance of the population. Thus when the harvest of 1310 failed as a result of bad weather, mortality in Halesowen rose to a very high peak (see fig. 4).³⁶ It seems that the parish was hit again by a subsistence crisis, since it was found that among the 32 tenants whose deaths are recorded in the court rolls between 1310 and 1312, 14 (44 per cent) were cottagers and smallholders. Among them were Thomas Henry (1311d.) whose widow entered his curtilage for a 6d. entry fine;³⁷ Thomas atte Hall (1312d.) whose three daughters entered his cottage and curtilage for 6d.;³⁸ William Petynas (1310d.) cottager from Hasbury.³⁹ And John the son of Henry Garin a smallholder from Hasbury who died in 1312 paid a 2s. entry fine and a heriot of 12 chickens.⁴⁰

The great famine of 1315–17 which affected a wide area of northern Europe did not spare the villagers of Halesowen.⁴¹ Unfortunately, the records of the majority of the court sessions which were held in 1316 have been lost. Therefore, although the number of deaths, land transactions, pleas of debts and amercements for gleaning obtained from the court rolls in 1316–18 is high, it does not represent the true dimensions of the catastrophe. A number of

---

³⁵ Farmer, 'Some grain price movements', p. 212. See also Titow, *English Rural Society*, p. 98.
³⁶ Farmer, loc. cit. Titow, on the evidence of the account rolls of the Bishopric of Winchester, observed that the harvests of 1310 were outstandingly bad; see his article 'Evidence of weather in the account rolls of the Bishopric of Winchester 1209–1350', *Econ. Hist. Rev.*, 2nd ser., XII (1959–60), 403. The number of heriots collected on the Winchester manors rose to a high level in 1310–11. See Postan and Titow, 'Heriots and prices on Winchester manors', pp. 169, 177.
³⁷ BRL 346233 13.1.1312.
³⁸ His death is recorded in the court held on 6.12.1312 (BRL 346234). On 31.1.1313 his three daughters took his holding for a 6d. entry fine (ibid.).
³⁹ BRL 350357 28.10.1310.
⁴⁰ BRL 346233 19.4.1312.
⁴¹ See H. S. Lucas, 'The great European famine of 1315, 1316, and 1317', in *Essays in Economic History*, ed. E. M. Carus-Wilson, vol. II (London, 1962), pp. 49–72; Kershaw, 'The great famine', pp. 3–50, and his book *Bolton Priory: The Economy of a Northern Monastery* (Oxford, 1973), pp. 66–7; Postan and Titow, 'Heriots and prices on Winchester manors', pp. 169, 177.

deaths which occurred in 1316 were registered or discovered in the court rolls of 1317 and 1318, but it is nevertheless likely that more than 43 tenants died as a result of the famine. In any case the count of the male residents of Halesowen mentioned in the court rolls of 1311–15 and 1321–5 suggests that about 15 per cent of them lost their lives during the famine. Undoubtedly all the peasants suffered from the disastrous harvests of 1315 and 1316 and from the ensuing famine. Yet mortality was unevenly distributed among the various strata in the village. Among those 43 tenants whose deaths are recorded in the court rolls between 1316 and 1318, 22 (51 per cent) were poor villagers like William Walsh who had a 2-acre holding, Richard Smith a cottager from Warley, Thomas le Fisher a quarter yardlander from Cakemoor and the unnamed father of 14-year-old Henry Bonch whose custody and holding were taken by a neighbour for 20d.[42]

It is likely that the famine in Halesowen as in other parts of the country was accompanied by a pestilence.[43] The deaths of 6 rich peasants are recorded in the court rolls between 1316 and 1318. The fact that 5 of them died in their prime and 4 left minor sons suggests that they died from an infectious disease rather than from starvation. William Langley was about 25 years old when he died and his wife paid £2. 13s. 4d. for the custody of his 2-year-old son.[44] William atte Leye was about 40 years old and his wife took the custody of his 2-year-old son for £2. 10s.[45] Adam of Illey died at the age of 33 and his wife paid £1 for the custody of his 3-year-old son.[46] Richard Tewenhall was only 23 years old when he died and his

[42] The death of William son of Roger Wales is recorded in the court held on 21.9.1317 when his brother John entered his 2-acre holding (BRL 350360). The death of Richard Smith of Warley is recorded in the court held on 23.2.1317 when his widow Lucy entered his cottage for 12d. (350360). Thomas son of William le Fisher a smallholder from Cakemoor entered his father's land in 1311 for an entry fine of 3s. (346233 13.10.1311). He probably died during the famine with his family, since the lord seized his land in 1318 (346237 19.7.1318). The death of the father of Henry Bonch is recorded in the court held on 22.3.1318. The custody of Henry and his holding was taken by Wylimot of Oldbury (346236).

[43] See Kershaw, 'The great famine', p.11.

[44] BRL 350360 6.10.1316. William Langley appears in the records for the first time in 1312 for default of court (346233 26.7.1312).

[45] BRL 350360 6.10.1316. William atte Leye from Warley appears for the first time as landholder in 1297 for not paying his share in a sum of money levied on the tenants (13.5.1293: *Hales Court Rolls*, I, p. 363).

[46] BRL 350360 31.8.1317. Adam de Illey appears for the first time as landholder as a pledge on 28.7.1304 (*Hales Court Rolls*, I, p. 486). In 1307 he was elected as a juror (ibid. I, p. 577).

yardland holding with the custody of his 2-year-old son was given to a neighbour for £3. 6s. 8d.[47] and William atte Lowe another yardlander died at the age of 44, but in this case his son William was old enough to take the holding.[48]

In 1318 the terrible famine was over, but the agrarian crisis in Halesowen (as in other parts of the country) continued for four or five years more. The number of recorded land transactions, pleas of debt and illegal gleanings between 1319 and 1324 remains quite high. It is difficult to know if the crisis was caused by the murrain which affected cattle and oxen all over England in 1319 or by the bad harvests of 1320 and 1321 or by both.[49] However, since many of the weak villagers probably died during the famine of 1316-17, mortality did not rise much above average. In the court rolls of 1319 the deaths of 4 males are recorded; there were 6 in 1320, 7 in 1321, 6 in 1322, 6 in 1323 and 3 in 1324.

Mortality in Halesowen, which was below the average between 1325 and 1336, rose again in the twelve years which preceded the Black Death. The annual average of recorded deaths in the court rolls from 1325 to 1336 is 3.2, but from 1337 to 1348 it is 4.9. We can see in table 5 that the number of land transactions, pleas of debt and illegal gleanings recorded in the court rolls of 1337-48 also rises. This suggests that the peasants experienced economic difficulties during these years. In the absence of manorial accounts it is difficult to know if they were caused by bad harvests or by the heavy royal taxation.[50] However, it is important to note that mortality did not rise to such a high level as it did in the first quarter of the century; the annual average of observed deaths between 1300 and 1324 is 6.4 but is only 4.9 between 1337 and 1348.

The evidence about mortality in Halesowen in the years 1343-5

---

[47] BRL 350360 21.9.1317. Richard Tewenhall appears for the first time as landholder on 13.3.1314 paying heriot and entry fine for his deceased father William (346235).

[48] BRL 350360 31.8.1317. William I atte Lowe from Hunnington appears for the first time as landholder in the records on 14.10.1293, paying a fine for a field given to him by the lord (*Hales Court Rolls*, I, p. 253).

[49] See Kershaw, 'The great famine', pp. 13-15; see also Farmer, 'Some grain price movements', p. 212.

[50] See J. J. Maddicot, 'The peasantry and the demands of the Crown 1294-1341', *Past and Present Supplement*, I (1975), 41, 75. On Winchester manors the number of heriots rose in 1337-8, although prices did not rise. See Postan and Titow, 'Heriots and prices on Winchester manors', p. 170. For prices, see Titow, *English Rural Society*, p. 99.

is very interesting. Deaths of women are not registered in the court rolls to the same extent as those of men. Table 6 shows that although the numbers of observed male and female deaths rise and fall together, the number of male deaths always exceeds that of females, except in the years 1343–5. In 1343 the deaths of 6 men and 7 women are recorded; in 1344, 7 men and 3 women; but in 1345, 5 men and 17 women – a widow, 11 wives and 5 spinsters. This unusually high number of recorded female deaths cannot be explained away by a change in the registration of deaths, since the lists of mortuaries which provide these data are available from 1334. The price of corn was high in many parts of the country in 1344,[51] but if the rise in the number of deaths was caused by a food shortage, it is hard to see why more women than men died. Moreover, the number of recorded land transactions, pleas of debt

Table 6. *The number of male and female deaths obtained from the court rolls 1270–1348*

Years	Male deaths	Female deaths
1270–2	8	2
1274–6	8	2
1277–9	12	3
1280–2	11	3
1293–5	23	9
1297–9	8	0
1300–2	12	1
1304–6	9	3
1307–9	12	1
1310–12	32	6
1313–15	13	2
1316–18	43	10
1319–21	17	1
1322–4	15	4
1325–7	10	3
1328–30	10	3
1331–3	6	1
1334–6	12	3
1337–9	16	10
1340–2	9	5
1343–5	18	27
1346–8	16	9
Total	320	108

[51] See Titow, *English Rural Society,* loc. cit.

and illegal gleanings does not indicate that these were lean years (see table 5). Therefore it is possible that the parish was hit in 1343–5 by an infectious disease to which women were more susceptible than men.

In their study of mortality on the Winchester manors Postan and Titow have estimated that between 1292 and 1347 the annual crude death rate of male tenants above 20 was 52 per thousand and that their life expectancy at that age was twenty years.[52] The data about mortality obtained from the court rolls suggest that in the period 1300–48 Halesowen tenants lived longer and that their death rate was lower.

It was possible to obtain a sample of 196 well-documented tenants from the list of 250 tenants whose deaths are recorded in the court rolls between 1300 and 1348. The mean number of years between their first appearance in the records as tenants and their death is 30.2 (see table 7). As the minimum legal age for holding land in Halesowen was 20,[53] the expectation of life at that age for male tenants would have been at least about thirty years (30.2). This is a minimum figure, because the first appearance of a villager in the court rolls as landholder does not always coincide with his accession to property, and some villagers probably became tenants when they were over 20. At the same time this figure also overestimates the actual expectation of life at age 20 of Halesowen tenants. Our sample includes only 49 (25 per cent) cottagers and smallholders, whereas they constituted about 43 per cent of the tenant population. The estimated expectation of life at 20 of these poor tenants was only 20.8 years. In order to correct the overestimate of the life expectancy of the tenant population we can add 62

[52] See Postan and Titow, 'Heriots and prices on Winchester manors', pp. 159–60, 181–3.

[53] In 1293 Philip Hill died and his wife Juliana took the custody of his son John. 'Et custodia illius tenementi conceditur predicte Juliana usque ad terminum in quo dictus Johannes filius Philippi etatem viginti annorum poterit complere' (*Hales Court Rolls*, I, p. 226). In addition to this entry, there are many other cases which indicate that the minimum age for holding land in Halesowen was about 20. For example, in 1317 Roger Burnet died and his 12-year-old son John was taken into the custody of his mother Agatha (BRL 350360 8.6.1317). In 1325, 20-year-old John came to the court and formally took his father's holding (346248 6.2.1325). John le Clerk and his wife died in the Black Death of 1349 and their 2-year-old son Richard was taken into the custody of a relative (346322 19.8.1349). In 1367 when Richard was 20 he came to the court and entered the family holding (346347 6.10.1367). In all the other cases where the age of minors is given in the court rolls, I found that they did not enter land before they were about 20.

Table 7. *The intervals between the first appearance of villagers in the court rolls as tenants and their deaths 1300–48*

Years	No. of dead tenants	Interval between first appearance as landholder and death (in years)
1300–2	5	19, 51, 26, 31, 31
1304–6	6	44, 28, 30, 34, 18, 27
1307–9	6	8, 26, 37, 39, 38, 39
1310–12	20	30, 40, 15, 39, 36, 32, 34, 36, 34, 3, 21, 35, 20, 36, 9, 36, 16, 21, 41, 32
1313–15	12	20, 43, 33, 36, 32, 28, 16, 42, 40, 19, 22, 13
1316–18	38	5, 45, 21, 16, 41, 37, 36, 20, 22, 5, 34, 39, 4, 43, 47, 7, 9, 9, 36, 35, 18, 3, 24, 13, 13, 10, 47, 12, 22, 10, 24, 10, 37, 36, 25, 48, 4, 17
1319–21	13	39, 26, 12, 27, 13, 41, 47, 49, 50, 9, 35, 28, 41
1322–4	14	25, 27, 55, 35, 52, 10, 26, 40, 47, 30, 23, 20, 12, 19
1325–7	8	45, 48, 56, 50, 15, 37, 9, 38
1328–30	7	58, 24, 20, 23, 20, 32, 18
1331–3	6	36, 57, 56, 22, 10, 36
1334–6	10	17, 10, 16, 40, 42, 40, 40, 40, 35, 41
1337–9	18	66, 44, 29, 17, 25, 18, 22, 41, 17, 43, 25, 20, 60, 46, 46, 57, 30, 14
1340–2	7	47, 36, 39, 17, 24, 62, 45
1343–5	15	22, 16, 48, 27, 63, 36, 22, 34, 4, 6, 7, 35, 34, 19, 34
1346–8	11	65, 21, 45, 26, 41, 25, 26, 55, 46, 40, 41
Total	196	5,917

hypothetical poor tenants, to our sample of 196 tenants, which will provide us with a hypothetical but representative sample. If we assume that the expectation of life at 20 of these 62 hypothetical poor tenants was also 20.8 years, that of the whole group would have been at least 28 years. But it is reasonable to assume that among the poor tenants whose deaths are not recorded many were cottagers whose expectation of life at 20 was probably lower than tenants who had several acres of arable land and a cow or two. If we assume then that the expectation of life at 20 of the 62 hypothetical poor tenants was only ten years, that of all the tenants in our sample would have been 25.3 years. Therefore the estimated actual expectation of life of male tenants in Halesowen in the first half of the fourteenth century could have been between at least 25 and 28 years.⁵⁴ In a stationary population such life expectancy corresponds to a death rate of between 36 and 40 per thousand. Therefore the annual crude death rate of landholders in Halesowen above the age of 20 would have been about 36-40 per thousand. These figures are crude and should be regarded as tentative estimates until further demographic studies based on court rolls have provided comparable results.

We have seen that between 1293 and 1318 Halesowen was hit by three subsistence crises which took a heavy toll of life especially among the cottagers and smallholders, the harvest-sensitive element in rural society. The most devastating of these crises, the great famine of 1316–17, reduced the population of the parish by about 15 per cent. Nevertheless, the count of the villagers appearing in the court rolls between 1270 and 1349 reveals that the population of Halesowen increased during this period and that the 'great famine' did not reverse this trend but only slowed it down. This is by no means a unique demographic phenomenon. Pre-industrial populations suffered from periodic outbreaks of famine and pestilence which caused heavy mortality. But such crises often relieved pressures on limited resources and were followed by a fall in death rates, a sharp rise in marriages and births and a subsequent fast recovery within twenty to twenty-five years.⁵⁵ The marriage trend obtained from Halesowen court rolls suggests that the recovery of the population in the parish after the demographic crisis of the 1310s followed a similar pattern.

4. *The Marriage Trend*

In Halesowen, as on other contemporary manors, customary tenants who married off their daughters were required to pay a licence

⁵⁴ J. C. Russell has estimated the expectation of life at 20 of the tenants-in-chief at 28.74 for those born before 1276, 25.19 for those born in the period 1276–1300 and 23.80 for those born in the period 1301–25. See his *British Medieval Population* (Albuquerque, N. Mex., 1948, p. 186). D. Herlihy has estimated the expectation of life at 20 in Pistoia in 1427 at 25.4. See his *Medieval and Renaissance Pistoia* (London, 1967), p. 283.

⁵⁵ See P. Goubert, 'En Beauvaisis: problèmes démographiques du XVIIIe siècle', *Annales: ESC*, VII (1952), 453–68. For a general discussion of the problem see E. A. Wrigley, *Population and History* (London, 1969), pp. 62–70. During the period 1526–30 there were severe harvest failures and outbreaks of the plague in Languedoc which caused heavy mortality. Yet the rapid population growth in the region which started about 1500 continued at the same pace until 1570. See E. Le Roy Ladurie, *The Peasants of Languedoc* (Chicago, 1974), pp. 51, 135–41.

fee to the lord. The fee varied between 12*d*. and 6*s*. 8*d*., but in most cases the rate was 2*s*. The tenants attempted often to evade paying merchets, as about 30 per cent of the fines recorded in Halesowen court rolls were paid for marriages without permission. The use of marriage fines to trace the marriage trend is problematic. In the absence of statistical analysis of marriage fines recorded in other contemporary series of court rolls, it is difficult to know if the fluctuations in the number of merchets obtained from Halesowen court rolls reflected the fluctuations in the number of marriages or the changes in the collection or registration of the fines by the manorial administration. Nevertheless, until comparable data are available, we will assume as a hypothesis that the trend of merchets represents the marriage trend in Halesowen. As merchets were underregistered in the court rolls of the early 1270s and the court records of the years 1283–92 are missing, we will study the marriage trend only in the period 1293–1348.

The number of merchets obtained from court rolls depends to a large extent on the number of court records available for each year. Marriage fines which were registered in court records which have been lost cannot be discovered, as can many deaths, in the following records which survived.[56] Therefore it is necessary to correct the underenumeration of merchets in the years for which the complete court records did not survive. For all the years under study except two (1296 and 1303) a sufficient number of court records survived so that it was possible by checking the rolls and by measuring the

[56] The difference between the number of observed merchets and the estimated ones is 24 per cent. Therefore, if I had applied the same method to correct the underenumeration of deaths, the difference between the number of observed and estimated deaths would have been the same. But since from the total number of 320 deaths obtained from the court rolls between 1270 and 1348, 38 (12 per cent) were discovered through widows, I preferred not to compensate for the missing records. Moreover, the death of a tenant was often mentioned more than once. For example, in the records of the court which was held on 24.11.1311 it is noted that Thomas Henry died and that his holding was seized by the lord (BRL 346233). On 12.1.1312 his widow came to the court and after she paid 6*d*. as heriot and relief, the holding of her deceased husband, which consisted of a curtilage, was given to her with the custody of John, Thomas's son (ibid.). In 1384 John atte Pyrie from Romsley died and his daughter Lucy and her husband Adam de Melley entered his holding for 6*s*. 8*d*. (346821 1.7.1384). But in the list of mortuaries which was copied on to the court rolls of the year 1385 the name of John atte Pyrie is mentioned again (346364C). If deaths are noted in the court rolls more than once, a correction of the number of observed deaths in relation to the missing records would result in an overestimate of the actual deaths.

The Population of Halesowen 1270–1348   47

intervals between contiguous pairs of court sessions to estimate the number of court sessions held each year. Then, on the assumption that each year the same number of merchets was registered in the missing court records as in those which survived, the number of estimated merchets was obtained.[57] The results are presented in table 8 and in fig. 5.

The average annual number of estimated marriages of bondwomen is 4.6. We can see in fig. 5 that the number of marriages was well above the average in the years 1293–5, 1310–12 and 1325–48. In the periods 1293–5 and 1310–12, as mortality was high and many young villagers inherited land or husbands lost their wives, the number of marriages rose sharply. The subsistence crisis of 1316–17, however, was so much worse than the previous ones that, although land was available and many husbands probably lost their wives, marriages had to be postponed. A similar sharp drop in marriages during a severe famine has been observed in rural parishes in Beauvais in 1693–4 and in other pre-industrial societies.[58] Although the 'great famine' was over in 1318–19, the number of marriages in Halesowen not only failed to rise but even declined during the years 1319–24. This was a result of the severity of the agrarian crisis in the parish during these years, and probably also of the high mortality of young adults from the disease which accompanied the famine. Only in the mid 1320s when the economic conditions in the village improved did the marriage rate rise to its pre-famine level; between 1293 and 1315 the annual average of estimated merchets is 4.4, and from 1325 to 1335, 4.3.

In the last thirteen years which preceded the Black Death there was a substantial rise in the number of marriages; the annual average of estimated merchets between 1336 and 1348 is 6.4, a rise of 49 per cent. The sudden jump in the number of young adults who married during these years suggests that the famine of 1316–17 was followed by a baby boom and that fertility rates in the 1320s were generally high. If this hypothesis is true it explains the rapid recovery of the population of Halesowen observed in the court rolls from the 1330s and 1340s. In his study of the villages in the Paris area Fourquin has observed that despite the heavy mortality caused by the famine of 1315–17, the population recovered fairly quickly as a

[57] See appendix.
[58] See Goubert, 'En Beauvaisis', pp. 459–61, and Wrigley, *Population and History*, pp. 82–3.

Table 8. *Estimate of merchets 1293–1348*

Year	No. of available court sessions	No. of estimated court sessions	No. of observed merchets	No. of estimated merchets
1293	11	15	4	5.5
1294	11	15	4	5.5
1295	6	15	2	5.0
1297	10	14	3	4.8
1298	2		1	4.8
1299	9	14	2	3.5
1300	9	17	1	1.9
1301	17	17	8	8.0
1302	11	17	1	1.5
1304	8	17	0	0.0
1305	8	17	5	10.6
1306	11	17	2	3.1
1307	15	17	0	0.0
1308	14	16	4	4.5
1309	15	17	5	5.6
1310	12	16	1	1.3
1311	13	17	5	6.5
1312	18	18	8	8.0
1313	18	18	8	8.0
1314	16	17	3	3.1
1315	14	18	1	1.3
1316	4		2	3.4
1317	15	17	3	3.4
1318	17	17	3	3.0
1319	17	17	3	3.0
1320	18	18	3	3.0
1321	18	18	3	3.0
1322	15	19	1	1.3
1323	16	19	4	4.7
1324	18	18	2	2.0
1325	18	18	2	2.0
1326	18	18	4	4.0
1327	15	18	9	10.8
1328	18	18	5	5.0
1329	13	18	3	4.1
1330	15	18	5	6.0
1331	9	18	3	6.0
1332	10	17	2	3.4
1333	17	17	2	2.0
1334	16	18	1	1.1
1335	19	19	4	4.0
1336	19	19	11	11.0
1337	17	17	5	5.0
1338	17	17	8	8.0
1339	17	19	3	3.3
1340	16	19	7	8.3
1341	7	17	2	4.9
1342	15	18	3	3.6
1343	14	17	6	7.3
1344	15	19	4	4.9
1345	12	18	8	12.0
1346	12	19	2	3.0
1347	10	19	1	1.9
1348	17	17	10	10.0
Total	742	904	202	250.9

The Population of Halesowen 1270–1348

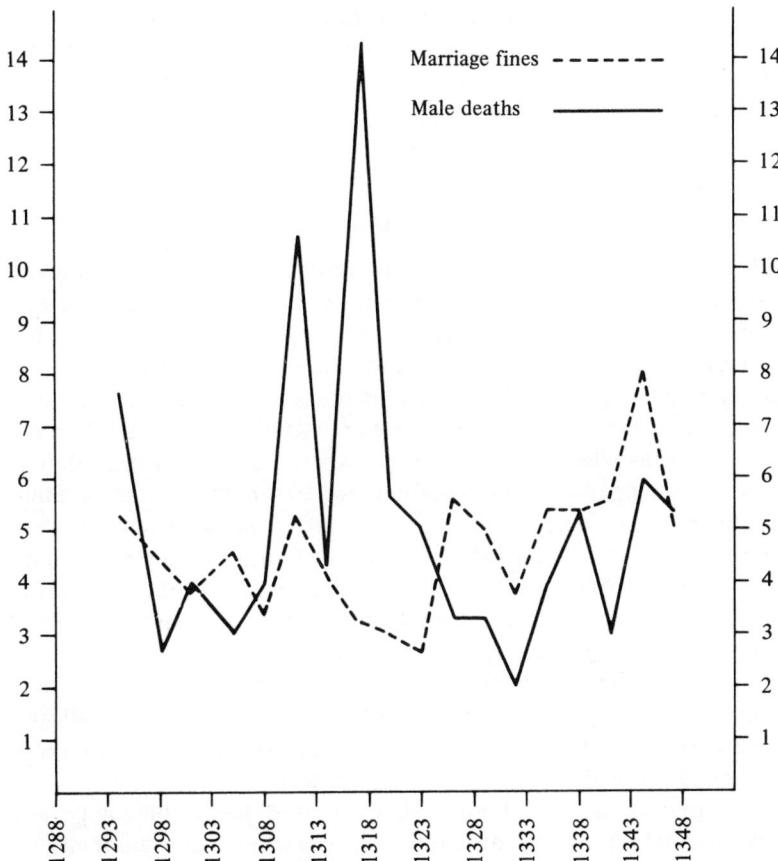

Fig. 5 Estimated marriage fines and male deaths 1293–1348 (three-year averages)

result of a sharp rise in births after the famine. He has also claimed that there is no indication in the sources that the famine initiated a lasting fall in the population in the area.[59]

From the evidence brought forward so far it appears that the census-like enumerations of the villagers appearing in Halesowen

[59] G. Fourquin, *Les campagnes de la région parisienne à la fin du Moyen Age* (Paris, 1964), pp. 191–2. On p. 192 n. 6 the author quotes from the contemporary chronicle of Jean de Venette, who observed that 'Mullieres quam solito abundancius concipiebant'.

court rolls faithfully represent the population movements in the parish. In the following sections I will try to show how the population increased despite the fact that land was in short supply, that almost half of the families lived below or on the edge of subsistence and that mortality was quite heavy.

5. Marriage Patterns and Age at Marriage

The most detailed treatment of the marriage patterns of medieval peasants can be found in G. C. Homans's book on English villagers in the thirteenth century.[60] He has argued that, as peasants could not marry until they acquired land, the majority of them had to defer marriage until the retirement or death of their fathers and consequently had to marry rather late in life.[61] He has also claimed that in areas where primogeniture was the dominant inheritance custom, younger sons and daughters were compelled either to emigrate or to remain single all their lives in their native villages. He has observed that sons who did not inherit the family holding sometimes succeeded in obtaining land and founding families of their own. But as the supply of land was limited, and younger sons and daughters who stayed on the family holding were not allowed to marry, the majority of them had to remain single.[62] The evidence obtained from Halesowen court rolls does not support these generalizations, and it strengthens J. Hajnal's hypothesis that medieval villagers followed a non-European marriage pattern.[63]

Despite the fact that land in Halesowen in the pre-plague period was in short supply and that primogeniture was the dominant inheritance custom, in a great number of families more than one son and one daughter settled in the village and married. Parents tried to pass on to their heir a holding large enough to support his future family and to maintain its status in the village. At the same time, any additional land which was acquired through marriage or by pur-

[60] *English Villagers of the Thirteenth Century* (New York, 1970), pp. 133–76.

[61] Ibid. pp. 154–8. Russell has accepted Homans's view on the age of marriage; see *British Medieval Population*, p. 164.

[62] Homans, *English Villagers*, pp. 133–43. For a criticism of Homans's rigid distinction between the settlement patterns of sons in areas in which partible inheritance was practised and areas where impartible inheritance was dominant see R. J. Faith, 'Peasant families and inheritance customs in medieval England,' *Agric. Hist. Rev.*, XIV (1966), 85–6.

[63] See Hajnal, 'European marriage patterns in perspective', in *Population in History*, eds. D. V. Glass and D. E. C. Eversley (London, 1965), 116–120, 133–5.

chase in the market, as well as accumulated capital, was used to provide younger sons and daughters with the means to start their own families in the village.[64] When parents did not do well in life, they were often prepared to cut down the size of the holding which was to be the inheritance for their heir, in order to provide for other children. In such cases, although younger sons and daughters were usually given only a small part of the family tenement, they started families of their own. For example, Ralf Ordrich (1274–1321d.) a smallholder from Oldbury had two sons who survived to maturity.[65] John the eldest appears in the court rolls for the first time as a landholder in 1297.[66] Eleven years later in 1308 he paid a marriage fine for his daughter Matilda.[67] He had another daughter Agnes who married in 1322 and a son Richard who inherited the family holding in 1343 when John died.[68] Richard neither emigrated nor remained single all his life. In September 1301 his father gave him a plot of land opposite his door on which to build a dwelling.[69] This can hardly be called a 'living', yet Richard married, probably shortly after building his cottage, since when he died in 1317/18 he left a 15-year-old son.[70] The genealogy of the Ordrich family (see fig. 6a) shows that Ralf a smallholder had in his early fifties a married

[64] In 1294 Thomas Pit bought land from William Lech. In the purchase agreement registered in the court records it is stated that 'si plus de tenemento illius Willelmi vendi debet, predictus Thomas illud emat si velit ad opus alicuius pueri sue herde suo excepto' (*Hales Court Rolls*, I, p. 299). In his study of the land market on the manors of Peterborough Abbey in the years 1086–1310, E. King has observed that land was purchased by the peasant in order 'that their younger sons should have some small independent position; that their daughters should have a dowry, even were it only half an acre of land' (*Peterborough Abbey 1086–1310: A Study of the Land Market* (Cambridge, 1973), p. 124). Peasants' wills published by A. E. Levett show that members of the family who were not to inherit were provided for; see 'Wills of villeins and copyholders', *Studies in Manorial History* (Oxford, 1938), pp. 208–34.

[65] Ralf Ordrich is noted in the court rolls for the first time on 22.5.1274 (*Hales Court Rolls*, I, p. 49) and for the last time on 15.4.1321 (BRL 346239).

[66] *Hales Court Rolls*, I, p. 368.

[67] In the court held on 31.7.1308 John son of Ralf Ordrich paid 2s. 2d. to marry his daughter Matilda outside the manor (BRL 350352).

[68] BRL 346242 3.2.1322; 346304 18.6.1343. Richard entered his father's land for 3s. 4d.

[69] 'Memorandum quod Radulfus Ordrich per licentiam domini dedit Ricardo filio suo unam placeam terre de capite unius selionis terre in Oldebure ex opposite porte sue ad super edificandum et tenendum ad totam vitam ipsius Ricardi. Ita scilicet quod si dictus Ricardus alibi in feodo domini terram vel tenamentum adquirire possit ... liceat illud edificium ab inde movere et pro sua voluntate in suo proprio tenemento iterum levare sine impedimento alicujus et pro ista licentia idem Ricardus dat domino duodecim denarios' (*Hales Court Rolls*, I, p. 425).

[70] 346236 1.3.1318.

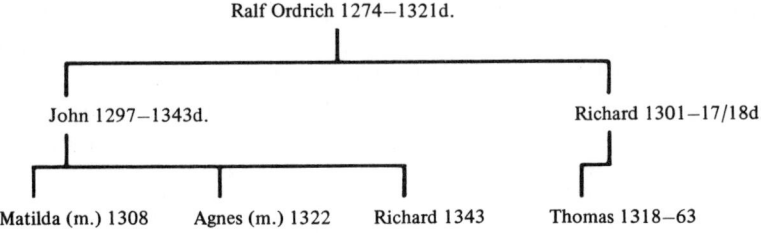

Fig. 6a   The Ordrich family tree

granddaughter, and in his early sixties another granddaughter and two grandsons. William II atte Pyrie from Romsley (1293–1321d.), a half yardlander, had two sons and two daughters. All of them settled and married in Romsley, and three of them did so while he was still alive. The number of William's descendants who lived in Romsley in the first half of the century numbered eleven (see fig. 6b). In the period 1270–1349, the descendants of Thomas Symon a rich villager from Oldbury (1271–6) numbered twenty-six – eleven females and fifteen males (see fig. 6c).

When the head of the family died the eldest son usually took the responsibility for helping his brothers and sisters to acquire land and to marry, which he often did by giving them a part of his holdings.[71] For example, Richard Aleyn of Romsley (1293–1314/18d.) died between 1314 and 1318.[72] In 1330 his son John (1313–49d.) endowed his sister Margaret with a dowry: a cottage, a garden and a curtilage which were part of the family holding.[73] In 1280 Thomas Schirlet of Hunnington granted half of his holding to his brother Richard.[74] In 1302 Richard Malle of Romsley granted to his brother John and his bride Margaret a butt of land to build on and hold for the life of each of them at a rent of $1\frac{1}{2}d$.[75] In 1304, Adam Green and

[71] On some of Crowland Abbey's Cambridgeshire manors the local custom decreed that the eldest son, who inherited the family holding, had to provide his brothers with some land. See F. M. Page, 'The customary poor law of three Cambridgeshire manors', *Cambridge Hist. Journ.*, III (1930).

[72] Richard Aleyn of Romsley appears in the records for the last time on 10.15.1314 (BRL 346235). On 12.1.1318 Agnes widow transferred to her son her lands in Romsley and also her dower (346794). Therefore we know that Richard Aleyn died between 1314 and 1318. Richard II Aleyn died in 1328 and his brother John entered the land (346801 23.3.1328).

[73] BRL 346802 19.5.1330. Two months earlier Margaret had paid 2s. as a marriage fine (BRL 346802 14.3.1330).

[74] *Hales Court Rolls*, I, p. 152.   [75] Ibid. II, p. 186.

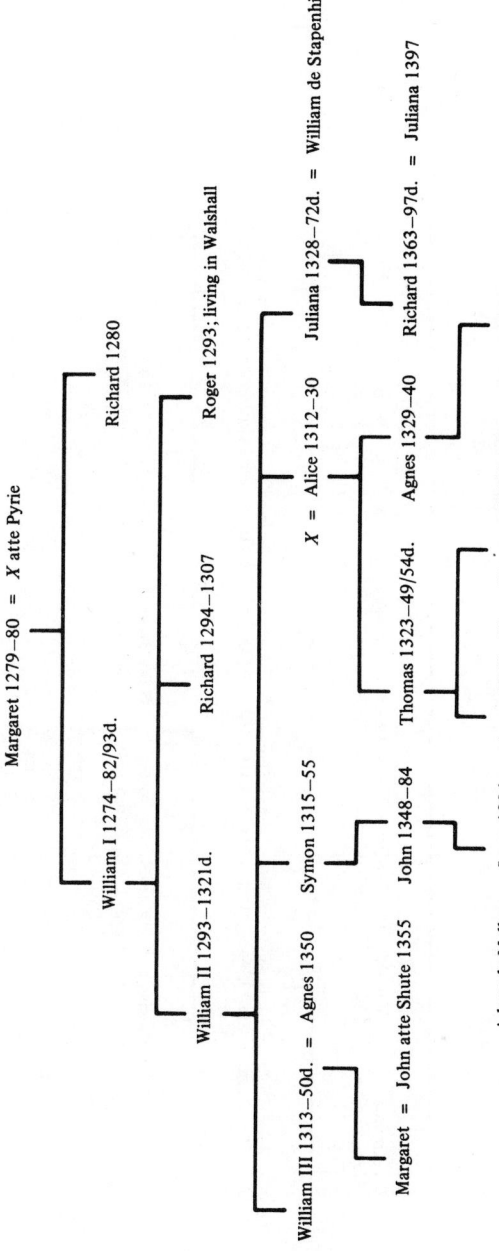

Fig. 6b The Pyrie family tree

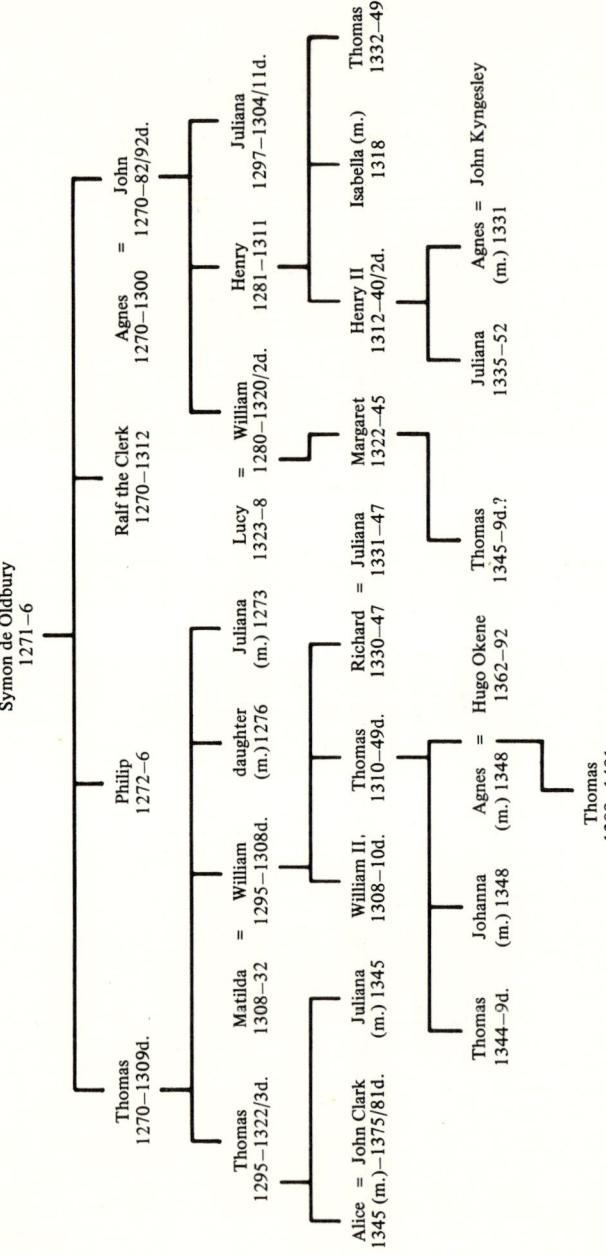

Fig. 6c The Symon family tree

his wife Agnes 'surrendered in the lord's hand' 2 selions. The lord granted the land to Adam's brother Richard and to his heirs 'ad tenendam et super edificandam'. Richard subsequently married and had two daughters.[76] Thomas Symon of Oldbury transferred in 1330 for the use of his younger brother Richard two plots of land taken from his holding.[77] In 1331 Richard married the daughter of Ralf Candina and in order to support his family he leased between 1331 and 1339, 43 selions for various terms of years. Only in 1344 did his father-in-law give him and his wife Juliana his half-yardland holding.[78]

Undoubtedly there was emigration of younger sons and daughters, and those who remained in Halesowen did not always succeed in obtaining land and marrying. However, the evidence obtained from Halesowen court rolls indicates that a much higher proportion of younger sons and daughters than has been assumed by Homans married and settled in the village. It was possible to reconstitute 590 families from Halesowen court rolls between 1270 and 1349 who had sons above the age of 12. Among these families only 290 (49 per cent) had more than one son. In table 9 we can see that in 140

Table 9. *Brothers who were landholders in Halesowen at the same time 1270–1349*

No. of brothers who were landholders	No. of families	Total no. of brothers who were landholders
Two	86	172
Three	34	102
Four	19	76
Five	1	5
Total	140	355

[76] Ibid. I, pp. 48–314. His two daughters were Felicity, mentioned on 13.5.1321 (BRL 346240), and Alice, noted on 17.12.1325 (346798). His widow Alice is mentioned for the first time on 17.5.1318 (346236). Richard probably died during the 'great famine'.

[77] BRL 346256 6.6.1330.

[78] In 1331 he leased from his parents-in-law 12 selions for a term of fifteen years on a crop-sharing basis (BRL 346259 5.6.1331). In 1332 he leased from them another 12 selions for twenty-three years on the same agreement of crop-sharing (346261 13.5.1332). In 1337 he leased 2 selions from Richard Thomas for six years and 3 selions from Geoffrey Robines for nine years (346279 25.6.1337). In 1334 Ralf Candina and his wife transferred to him and to their daughter Juliana his wife their half-virgate holding (360307 9.6.1344).

(48 per cent) of these families at least two brothers were landholders at the same time.[79] Moreover, there is evidence that among the 355 brothers who were landholders at least 269 (76 per cent) were married. Unfortunately, because of the underrepresentation of women in court rolls, we can obtain information only about the marriage of bondwomen. Nevertheless, evidence is found that in a large number of families more than one daughter married. At least 318 families who were resident in Halesowen between 1270 and 1349 had daughters above the age of 12. Among these families 106 (33 per cent) had more than one daughter. In table 10 we can see that in 44 (41.5 per cent) of these families at least two sisters were married. This is only a minimum figure, not only because some of these 106 families were probably families of freeholders but also because the list of marriage fines obtained from the court rolls is incomplete.

It is true that in Halesowen, as in other contemporary villages, peasants married only when they had land. But the amount of land with which many of them were prepared to start a family was in many cases only a cottage or a smallholding of a few acres. Therefore, despite the fact that land was in short supply in Halesowen and that primogeniture was the inheritance custom, many younger sons and daughters founded families of their own rather than remain unmarried in the parental household. As the supply of land was limited, the settlement of more than a son and a daughter per family obviously increased the number of villagers whose holdings were

Table 10. *Sisters who married in Halesowen 1270–1349*

No. of married sisters	No. of families	Total no. of married sisters
Two	34	68
Three	7	21
Four	3	12
Total	44	101

[79] In Broughton in Huntingdonshire, as in Halesowen, the villagers practised impartible inheritance. Nevertheless, in 23 per cent of the families resident in Broughton between 1288 and 1340, more than one son acquired land in the village. See E. Britton, *The Community of the Vill* (Toronto, 1977), pp. 60–4.

too small to support their families. But it seems that Halesowen villagers were prepared to face economic hardships and destitution rather than to remain bachelors and spinsters. Consequently, impartible inheritance did not secure, as Homans has argued, a stable adaption of the village society to its economic conditions.[80]

The study of the history of Halesowen families in the pre-plague period has revealed that in many families sons and daughters acquired land and married before the death of the father. For example, Alexander of Kenelmestowe alias Clerk (1274–95) had two sons and a daughter. In 1282 he probably helped his eldest son Henry (1280–1312d.) to buy two plots of land.[81] Henry subsequently married, since nineteen years later in 1301 his son Walter appears in the court rolls as a landholder.[82] In 1293 Alexander married his second son Clement (1293–1318d.) to Emma the heiress of Matilda de Folfen, and endowed his daughter Margaret (1293–1312) with a dowry, a plot of land reclaimed from the waste.[83] John Hurne a quarter yardlander from Hasbury (1293–1339d.) had a son and four daughters. He managed to provide his son with a cottage and a curtilage and to marry off three of his daughters before his death.[84]

Fathers settled their sons in the village while they were still alive, either by giving them a part of the family holding, or by buying them land, or by helping them to acquire land, or by marrying them to brides with dowries in land. In 1279, for example, William Abovebroc gave to his son William II half of the family holding.[85] In 1302 Thomas Symon transferred to his son Thomas II a part of his holding which consisted of 'new-land' held in severalty, 'ad super edificandum'.[86] Henry II settled in the village on a small plot of land given to him by his father Henry de Halen (1312–48) in 1335, for which he paid a 12d. entry fine.[87] In 1318 Robert Curteys of Romsley (1304–41) bought for his eldest son Thomas the holding of

[80] Homans, *English Villagers*, p. 159.   [81] *Hales Court Rolls*, I, p. 195.
[82] In 1301 Henry's son Walter recognized in the court that he was holding land from the lord for 12d. rent (*Hales Court Rolls*, II, p. 179).
[83] Ibid. II, p. 170; I, p. 260.
[84] In 1338 he gave Adam his son a cottage and curtilage (BRL 346285 7.10.1338). Adam left the village in 1333 but came back in 1338. In 1314 he gave to Felicity 2 selions as a dowry and paid 3s. as merchet (350359 27.11.1314). In 1320 he paid 2s. merchet for his daughter Margaret (346239 8.10.1320). His third daughter Alice paid merchet in 1335 (346273 11.10.1335).
[85] *Hales Court Rolls*, II, pp. 55–6.
[86] Ibid. I, p. 452.   [87] BRL 346271 10.5.1335.

Adam Green, but as Thomas was under age at that time, he entered the land only in 1325.[88] In 1317 Henry (1317–49d.) son of Thomas Robert obtained from the lord the vacant holding of William Don for an entry fine of £2, which he probably got from his father Thomas (1282–1326) a yardlander from Hasbury.[89] In 1295 John Depslough took the holding and the custody of Johanna the daughter of Thomas Sibile a rich villager from Ridgeacre, and with the lord's permission, which cost him £2, he married her to his eldest son Thomas.[90]

Sometimes the acquisition of land by the eldest son coincided with his father's retirement. However, in the majority of families for which evidence is available sons established families of their own before the retirement of their fathers.[91] For example, in 1333 Roger le Per of Langley (1311–49d.) granted his half-yardland holding to his son Thomas, who undertook to provide his keep.[92] Thomas had been an independent landholder since 1328, when he obtained from the lord Thomas Deye's holding.[93]

Table 11 sums the number of families reconstituted from Halesowen court rolls between 1270 and 1349, whose offspring obtained land and married while the father was alive.[94] We can see that the offspring settled in the village and married in 76 per cent of the rich families, in 42 per cent of the middling and in 14 per cent of the poor families, and that on average in rich families more offspring per family did so than in less-well-off families. Rich peasants settled their children while they were alive more often than their poorer neighbours, not only because they had more means to do so, but also because they lived longer and more of their children survived to maturity. In section 7 below evidence will be brought forward to show that the rate of survival of children in the village was determined to a large extent by the wealth of their parents. As far as life expectancy of adults is concerned, although our data are crude, they strongly suggest that rich villagers lived longer than poorer peasants, who often suffered from malnutrition. The oldest

[88] BRL 346794 17.2.1318 and 31.10.1325.
[89] BRL 350360 26.1.1317.   [90] *Hales Court Rolls,* I, p. 330.
[91] From 178 fathers whose sons entered land before the fathers' deaths, the sons of only 21 (12 per cent) acquired land when the fathers retired.
[92] BRL 346263 20.1.1333.   [93] BRL 346252 10.2.1328.
[94] The total number of families reconstituted from Halesowen court rolls between 1270 and 1349 is 788. Nevertheless, I included in table 11 only 720 families, because the socio-economic status of 40 families is not clear and 28 families had no offspring.

Table 11. *Families whose sons obtained land and whose daughters married while the father was alive*

Status	No. of families	No. of families whose sons obtained land while the father was alive	No. of sons	No. of families whose daughters married while the father was alive	No. of daughters	Total no. of families whose sons obtained land and daughters married while the father was alive	Total no. of offspring
Rich	131	73	140	40	60	99 (76%)	200
Middling	285	81	115	40	50	119 (42%)	165
Poor	304	24	28	21	26	42 (14%)	54
Total	720	178	283	101	136	260 (36%)	419

peasants who died in Halesowen in the pre-plague period were yardlanders: John Schirlet from Hunnington, for example, who died in 1337, was at least 86 years old, and Thomas Squire from Romsley, who died in 1342, was about 82. Among the 43 peasants who lived more than sixty years, 22 (51 per cent) were rich, although the rich constituted only 18 per cent of the population.

The fact that the percentage of rich families whose offspring settled in the village and married while the father was alive was much higher than that of poor and middling families suggests that age at marriage for the sons and daughters of well-to-do families was probably lower than that of children of poorer families. Undoubtedly there were cases of sons and daughters of middling and poor families who reached maturity but had to wait until the father's death in order to obtain land or a dowry. But it is very likely that a great many offspring of such families, who suffered often from destitution, settled in the village and married only after the death of the father simply because they were previously too young to hold land and to marry. For example, Thomas Adam a half yardlander from Hasbury married Edith in 1318, but when he died sixteen years later his eldest son Thomas was only 3 years old.[95] It is difficult to estimate the number of families whose children were too young to hold land and to marry before the death of their father. But it is reasonable to assume that such families constituted at least 50 per cent of the 720 families reconstituted from the court rolls between 1270 and 1349, because the expectation of life at 20 for smallholders, who constituted 43 per cent of the population, was only about twenty-one years and because many parents must have lost their small children in one of the subsistence crises between 1293 and 1321. In this case, 72 per cent of the families who could have grown-up offspring settled and married them while the father was alive.

Manorial court rolls do not provide data to compute the mean age at first marriage of males and females. But it is possible to take three-generation families and to estimate crudely the age at marriage of a number of men and women. If sons in Halesowen did not have to wait until their father's death to obtain land, and if they were prepared to start their independent life with a part of the family lands and sometimes even with quite a small holding, it is likely that

[95] BRL 346237 19.7.1318; 346270 14.12.1334. Thomas died holding from the lord a half virgate.

many of them did so as soon as they reached the age of 20, the minimum legal age for holding land. Many other sons must have obtained land at about 20, either because they were at that age or because they were minors when their fathers died. If this hypothesis is true, and as on average tenants appear in the records at least once in three years, we can assume that when a son of a resident villager appears in the court rolls for the first time as landholder, he was between the ages of 20 and 23. If between seventeen and twenty-three years later his son appears in the records as landholder, we can assume that he was married at about the age of 20. And if he had a daughter who is noted in the records for paying merchet, say, sixteen years after his first appearance as landholder, we can assume that she was married between the ages of 16 and 19. The method described above is effective only in those cases when the first-born son or daughter survived to maturity. If only the second- or third-born son or daughter of a villager survived to maturity, they appear in the records – the son as landholder and the daughter for paying merchet – more than twenty-three years after his first appearance in the records as landholder. As infant and child mortality was heavy in the period under study, such cases must have been numerous.

Roger Burnet a half yardlander from Langley appears in the court rolls for the first time as landholder in 1300.[96] In 1317 he died and his 12-year-old son John was taken into the custody of his mother Agatha.[97] In 1325, 20-year-old John came to the court and formally took his father's holding on condition that he would render all the customary services.[98] John married in that year, since twenty years later, in 1345, his son Richard entered two plots of land and bought the holding of Thomas Jones of Langley.[99] Richard probably married in 1345 when he acquired a holding, because when he died in 1349 he left a minor daughter Felicity. Felicity was taken into the custody of her grandfather John, who was then only 44 years old.[100]

Adam son of Thomas Adam a half yardlander from Hasbury is noted in the court rolls in 1302, three years before the death of his father.[101] Adam died in his prime in 1311 and his son Thomas was

---

[96] *Hales Court Rolls*, II, p. 132.
[97] BRL 350360 8.6.1317.
[98] BRL 346248 6.2.1325.
[99] BRL 346311 20.4.1345.
[100] BRL 346322 17.6.1349.
[101] *Hales Court Rolls*, I, p. 456 (4.6.1302). He entered his father's half virgate in 1305 (ibid. I, p. 500).

taken into the custody of his mother Margaret.[102] In 1318 Thomas appeared in the court and paid a fine of 6s. 8d. to marry Edith a bondwoman and to enter her land.[103] We can therefore assume that Thomas was between the ages of 16 and 19 when he married.

Thomas son of Nicholas atte Mersh (1312–49d.) a smallholder from Hawne appears in the court rolls for the first time as landholder in 1312 when he entered his deceased father's holding for 3s.[104] In 1333, twenty-one years later, his son William obtained the lord's permission to marry Cristina the daughter of Thomas Halen and to enter her land.[105] Therefore we can assume that William was about 21 years old when he married Cristina. William died in 1349 in the Black Death and his wife Cristina took custody of his son and heir Thomas II.

Roger son of John son of Roger Walloxhall (1328–38d.) a half yardlander died in 1338. He had four daughters of 10, 8, 5 and 2 years old who were taken into the custody of their mother Cristina.[106] In 1349 the eldest daughter Isabella came of age at 21 and entered her father's holding for 2s. and then William de Kemberely paid 2s. for permission to marry her.[107] Alice the second sister entered the other half of the holding in 1350 when she was 19 years old, and married Ralf son of John Walloxhall.[108] The two younger sisters probably died before reaching maturity.

Philip son of Thomas II Lynacre (1297–1335) a half yardlander from Hunnington is noted in the court rolls for the first time as landholder in 1297.[109] In 1316 he was amerced because Juliana his daughter married without permission. Juliana's age was then between 19 and 22.[110]

William atte Lyche (1270–1322d.) a half yardlander from Romsley transferred to his son John half his holding in 1307.[111] Eleven years later John died, and his daughter and heiress Alice was put in the custody of her mother.[112] In 1325 Alice, who was probably

---

[102] BRL 350357 7.7.1311.   [103] BRL 346237 19.7.1318.
[104] BRL 346233 12.1.1312.   [105] BRL 346264 30.6.1333.
[106] BRL 346280 21.1.1338.   [107] BRL 346322 29.7.1349.
[108] BRL 346323 3.2.1350.

[109] He appears in a list of tenants who did not pay a sum of money levied on the community (*Hales Court Rolls*, I, p. 367) (22.7.1297).

[110] BRL 350360 6.10.1316.

[111] The information about this transfer was given in an inquiry held on 11.11.1322 (BRL 346796).   [112] BRL 346794 19.1.1318.

between the ages of 18 and 21, married Richard the son of Thomas Squire.[113]

From a sample of 285 three-generation families who were resident in Halesowen between 1280 and 1349, at least 139 families (49 per cent) had a son or a daughter (80 had a son and 59 a daughter) who probably married between the ages of 18 and 22. This obviously does not constitute an adequate calculation of mean age at first marriage, but it suggests that it is plausible to assume that males and females in Halesowen in the pre-plague period married at an early rather than a late age. Although it seems that men and women married at approximately the same age, there could have been an age gap of three or four years between the spouses at first marriage which our crude method of estimating age at marriage cannot detect.

As mortality in Halesowen in the pre-plague period was heavy, one could expect to find frequent remarriages.[114] Unfortunately, as the names of many wives of local villagers are not given in the court rolls, and as men (unlike women) are never noted in the records as widowers, it is impossible to find out the real number of men who married more than once. Although 725 men are identified as husbands or fathers in Halesowen court rolls between 1270 and 1349, there is evidence that 45 men (6 per cent) married more than once. A more realistic idea about the extent of remarriage in Halesowen can be obtained from the evidence about the marriage of widows. Among the 154 women noted in the court rolls between 1270 and 1349 as widows, at least 97 (63 per cent) married again within a short time of the deaths of their husbands. If such a high proportion of widows in Halesowen remarried it is plausible to assume that at least a similar proportion of widowers, if not a higher one, also managed to do so.

The evidence brought above about the settlement and marriage patterns of Halesowen villagers is compatible with the hypothesis that medieval villagers followed a non-European rather than a European marriage pattern. However, further studies of contemporary villages for which good series of court rolls are available are needed to clarify the issue.

Although it has been argued above that villagers in Halesowen probably married between the ages of 18 and 22, it would be wrong

[113] BRL 346796 13.2.1325.
[114] P. Laslett, *The World We Have Lost* (London, 1971), pp. 103–5.

to assume that all of them succeeded in doing so. Land shortage and low wages forced a certain number of young adults born to middling and especially to poor families to postpone their marriages, and some of them probably never married at all. This is reflected to some extent in the fact that a much lower percentage of middling and poor families than rich ones settled and married their children while the father was alive. But it becomes clearer when we study the incidence of illegitimacy in Halesowen in the pre-plague period.

6. *Illegitimacy*

On many medieval manors single women and widows of unfree status who fornicated had to pay a fine called 'lerwyte' or 'leyrwyte'. On some manors one finds another fine called 'childwyte' which servile women had to pay for bearing children out of wedlock.[115] In the court rolls of the manor of Broughton in Huntingdonshire between 1288 and 1340, 8 leyrwytes and 26 childwytes are recorded.[116] In the court rolls of Halesowen one finds only leyrwytes. Nevertheless, it is clear that these fines were levied on women not only for incontinency but also for conceiving and for giving birth out of wedlock. Usually the clerks recorded in the court rolls the fact that a certain woman fornicated ('deflorata est') and the fine she or her family had to pay, either 12*d*. or 2*s*. But in a few cases more information is available. In the records of the court held in March 1293 it is noted that 'Juliana Thedrich nativa domini deflorata est et impregnata ideo in misericordia.'[117] At the court held in November 1294, the township of Hill was amerced 2*s*. for neglecting to report that Adelina the daughter of William Modi 'suscepit problem extra matrimonium', and Adelina herself was fined 12*d*.[118] In November 1313 the township of Illey was amerced for failure to report that the daughter of William Tiller 'deflorata est et peperit'.[119] If all or the majority of the women who paid leyrwyte in Halesowen conceived

---

[115] See G. G. Coulton, *Medieval Village, Manor and Monastery* (New York, 1960), pp. 91, 477–8; F. M. Maitland, *Select Pleas in Manorial and Other Seignorial Courts*, Selden Society, vol. II (London, 1889), pp. 97–8; P. Vinogradoff, *Villeinage in England* (Oxford, 1892), p. 154; H. S. Bennett, *Life on the English Manor* (Cambridge, 1971), pp. 245–6; Levett, *Studies in Manorial History*, p. 235; Homans, *English Villagers*, p. 169.
[116] Britton, *Community of the Vill*, p. 51.
[117] *Hales Court Rolls*, I, p. 221.
[118] Ibid. I, pp. 310–11.   [119] BRL 346236 18.10.1313.

and gave birth out of wedlock, these fines provide an opportunity to study the incidence of illegitimacy in the parish.

The incidence of illegitimacy in Halesowen in the pre-plague period must have been quite high. In the court rolls from 1270 to 1348, 117 leyrwytes and 220 merchets are recorded. This implies that for each 1.9 women who married, 1 woman gave birth to a child out of wedlock. As the family played a central role in village society, it is hard to believe that peasants favoured extra-marital intercourse. Yet women who conceived and bore children out of wedlock were not stigmatized, as many of them subsequently married – and not below their station. For example, Cristina the daughter of Thomas de Halen shared with her sister Agnes their father's half yardland when he died in 1325.[120] In 1332 Cristina paid 18*d.* as leyrwyte and a year later William atte Mersh a quarter yardlander paid 40*d.* for permission to marry her and to enter her land.[121] In 1325 Alice the co-heiress of Thomas Geoffrey a rich peasant from Oldbury paid a leyrwyte. Yet in 1328 she married a rich peasant Roger Sweyn who paid 10*s.* as a merchet and an entry fine.[122] As far as bastards are concerned, they were not treated as outcasts by their families or by the village community. Although bastards were not allowed to inherit customary land, some of them obviously did.[123]

John Prick a bond tenant from Warley was not only an illegitimate child but was also nicknamed 'the bastard'. Nevertheless, presumably because he was the only heir, he was allowed to take the family holding and only after his death in 1312 did the holding escheat to the lord.[124] However, Geoffrey Bryd from Ridgeacre, another bas-

[120] BRL 346249 15.1.1326.
[121] BRL 346261 20.5.1332; 346264 30.6.1333.
[122] BRL 346249 2.10.1325; 346254 25.10.1328.
[123] The common-law doctrine of bastards being free had to compete with local customs on this point. See J. S. Beckerman, 'Customary law in English manorial courts in the thirteenth and fourteenth centuries', unpublished Ph.D. thesis, University of London, 1972, pp. 118, 156–7. When the custom of the manor came to agree with common law, regarding bastards of unfree parents as free, their former rights of inheritance were extinguished. In Halesowen if the sole heir of a villein was a bastard he was allowed to inherit the customary holding, but only for life. See BRL 346350 23.3.1372. Isolda daughter of Henry de Halen got from the lord a cottage and curtilage: 'Et si dicta Isolda decedat sine herede de corpore suo legitimo ... Thome filio eiusdem Isolde ad terminum vite sue' (ibid.).
[124] 'John Prick dictus bastardus nativeus domini'. His half yardland escheated to the lord and was granted to Richard son of William Linthurst for an entry fine of £2. 6*s.* 8*d.*

tard, did so well that when he died in 1369 his son John was able to secure the inheritance by paying for his father's half-virgate holding the enormous entry fine of £5.[125]

It is possible to identify the socio-economic status of the majority of the women who paid leyrwytes between 1270 and 1348. We can see in tables 12 and 13 that there was a correlation between the incidence of illegitimacy and the socio-economic status of families in the village. The female members of only 5 per cent of the rich families fornicated, but in 11 per cent of the middling and 16 per cent of the poor families they did so. Of the total number of daughters of poor families, at least 26 per cent conceived out of wedlock, but only 16 per cent of the daughters of middling and 5 per cent of the daughters of rich families did so. Moreover, in middling and especially in poor families more than one female member to a family fornicated, while there is no incidence of this at all in rich families. Evidence was found that 26 per cent of the women who gave birth out of wedlock married subsequently. This is clearly an underestimate, since the lists of merchets obtained from the court rolls are incomplete. Yet we can see that rich girls who fornicated had more success in finding husbands than girls from middling and poor families.

During the pre-plague era, as land was in short supply in Halesowen, young villagers who wished to settle in the village and to start a family could not do so unless they inherited land or were provided by their families with land. Therefore women endowed with land or with the means to buy land had little difficulty in finding husbands, whether these women were young girls with dowries or older widows. But cottagers and smallholders often could not endow their daughters with dowries, and the unfortunate girls had to postpone their marriages. Some of them probably never married. Many of them had to leave home and to earn their living as servants and labourers. Some emigrated, and even those who chose to stay on occasionally left Halesowen to seek employment in neighbouring villages. Therefore it is not surprising that girls of status similar to Cristina and Agnes the daughters of Thomas Heath a cobbler from Hawne, who entered with two more sisters their father's tiny holding for 8*d*., were responsible for more than half of the leyrwyte

---

[125] As a son of a bastard was not allowed to inherit his father's customary holding, John Bryd, who was apparently the son of Geoffrey, was declared the son of Felicity Hypkyns, who was Geoffrey's wife. See BRL 346359 2.5.1369.

Table 12. *Women paying leyrwyte in Halesowen 1270–1348*

Status	No. of families	No. of daughters	No. of families whose female members paid leyrwyte	No. of widows	No. of single women	No. of women who subsequently married	Total no. of leyrwytes
Rich	132	137	7 (5%)	2	6 (5%)	5 (62.5%)	8
Middling	294	211	32 (11%)	2	34 (16%)	15 (42%)	36
Poor	322	242	50 (16%)	5	63 (26%)	8 (12%)	68
Unidentified	40	15	5	–	5	–	5
Total	788	605	94 (12%)	9	108 (18%)	28	117

Table 13. *Families who had more than one female member who paid leyrwyte*

Status	Two sisters who paid leyrwyte	Three sisters who paid leyrwyte	Mother and daughter who paid leyrwyte
Rich	–	–	–
Middling	4	–	–
Poor	5	3	2

fines recorded between 1270 and 1348.[126] R. M. Smith has observed that in Redgrave and Rickinghall in the second half of the thirteenth century many of the women who bore children out of wedlock came from poor families.[127]

In contrast, girls who were born to rich villagers were endowed with good dowries. They married young and consequently were at risk as far as pre-marital sex was concerned only for a comparatively short time. Their families, who probably did not want them to marry below their station, took good care that nobody would create a *fait accompli* by seducing them. It appears that the rich girls who fornicated did so not because their families could not provide them with dowries but as a result of unfavourable familial circumstances. For example, Philip Hill, one of the wealthiest peasants in Halesowen, died in 1293 and left a minor son John and three daughters. His widow Juliana took the custody of her son and the holding for £3. 13s. 4d.[128] But she was much more interested in finding a husband for herself than for her daughters. Immediately after the death of Philip she married Thomas Thedrich and in 1301 she married for the third time.[129] Her third husband Roger Cook not only did not take good care of his stepdaughters but even tried to rob one of them of her share in the family holding.[130] So it is not surprising that Alice the daughter of Philip Hill was fined in 1309 for fornication.[131]

[126] On 20.4.1323 Cristina, Matilda, Margaret and Agnes entered their father's holding for 8d. (BRL 346245). In 1327 Matilda married without permission (346252 30.9.1327). In 1334 Agnes had to pay a leyrwyte of 2s. (346269 5.10.1334). In 1336 Cristina paid a 12d. leyrwyte (346275 17.4.1336).

[127] R. M. Smith, 'English peasant life-cycles and socio-economic networks', unpublished Ph.D. thesis, University of Cambridge, 1974, pp. 454–6.

[128] *Hales Court Rolls*, I, p. 226.

[129] Ibid. I, p. 252; II, p. 161.

[130] BRL 346233 24.11.1311; 346234 16.5.1313.

[131] BRL 350353 30.4.1309.

Scolastica the daughter of another rich villager from Hill fornicated in 1327 while her four brothers and her mother were quarrelling violently with each other about the family property.[132]

Many middling families were able to marry their daughters while they were young. But others, especially when they had to provide for several children, could not afford to endow their daughters with dowries. They consequently had to defer marriage and many of them were reported in the court for fornication. For example, Thomas Fisher (1293-1316/18d.) a half yardlander from Cakemoor had three daughters Agatha, Juliana and Edith. In 1312 Agatha the eldest married, but her younger sister Juliana gave birth out of wedlock.[133]

The fact that extra-marital intercourse was so common in Halesowen in the pre-plague period does not necessarily indicate that local women were licentious. Many single women who had intercourse with men might have done so because they were anxious to marry. But as clandestine marriages were very common in contemporary villages, it was quite easy for a man to have sex with a single woman or widow under false pretences and get away with it.[134] We do not have direct evidence to substantiate this hypothesis. But in the second half of the fourteenth century, when it became easier for girls to marry with small or no means, the number of leyrwytes recorded in the court rolls fell considerably, thus suggesting that poverty rather than licentiousness was the reason for the large number of women who bore children out of wedlock.

In the absence of data about birth rates and infant and child mortality it is very difficult to estimate, let alone to compute, percentages of illegitimate births. Smith, however, has used court-roll data to estimate the level of illegitimacy on three Suffolk

---

[132] BRL 356252 13.11.1327. Roger Snode of Hill, Scolastica's father, died in 1323 (346245 6.1.1323). His son John entered the land but his brother Henry claimed that John was a bastard and the holding was seized. As a result John assaulted Henry gravely. John got the land back, probably when an inquiry declared that he was a legitimate child. But the feud between the brothers, in which the other two brothers Robert and Thomas took part, continued for many years. In the court held on 5.1.1323 John was amerced 4d. for calling his mother a 'bytch' and assaulting her with a knife (346243).

[133] BRL 346233 19.4.1312.

[134] See R. H. Helmholz, *Marriage Litigation in Medieval England* (Cambridge, 1974), pp. 22-34; M. M. Sheehan, 'The formation and stability of marriage in fourteenth-century England: evidence of an Ely register', *Medieval Studies*, XXXIII (1972), 234-9; Homans, *English Villagers*, p. 168.

manors in the second half of the thirteenth century. On these manors there were about three to four marriages for every bastard birth, and the percentage of bastard births has been estimated at between 4.9 and 12.3.[135] If our assumption that leyrwytes in Halesowen were paid by women who gave birth out of wedlock is right, the percentage of bastard births in the parish must have been higher than in the three Suffolk villages, since there were 1.9 marriage fines for every leyrwyte.

As many of the illegitimate children were born to poor mothers, it is likely that many of them died in infancy or quite soon afterwards. Yet it would be wrong to underestimate the number of bastards who survived. Some women might have kept their illegitimate children alive because that could have given them a better chance to marry the father. Others might have done so because they had strong motherly feelings, or because they wanted children to comfort and support them in old age. Such women managed to raise their children despite all the economic difficulties which they faced. One of them was Milicentia the daughter of Philip King (1304–49), who supported herself and two illegitimate daughters by brewing ale.[136] Another one-parent family was that of Juliana Balle (1281–1313) the pin-maker who lived with her daughter Edith in Langley.[137]

The evidence obtained from Halesowen court rolls about illegitimacy does not support Homans's claim that primogeniture enabled medieval villagers to restrict and control fertility.[138] It is hard to believe that in a society in which fertility was effectively controlled, the incidence of illegitimacy could be so common as it was in Halesowen in the pre-plague era. The existence of differential illegitimate fertility among strata in the village suggests that the age at first marriage of daughters of well-to-do villagers was lower than that of daughters of less-well-off villagers. But it would be wrong to assume that the mean age at first marriage was high.

[135] See Smith, 'English peasant life-cycles', pp. 454-6.

[136] Milicentia fornicated in 1304 (*Hales Court Rolls*, I, p. 476). In 1317 her father gave her a cottage and a garden in Langley for life (BRL 350360 27.4.1317). From then onwards until her disappearance from the records in 1349 she appears in the records at least ten times every year for brewing ale against the assize. Her daughter Alice is mentioned for the first time in 1336 (346274 17.1.1336) and her second daughter Johanna in 1349 (346323 21.2.1349).

[137] Juliana Balle le Peyneresse fornicated twice, in 1281 (*Hales Court Rolls*, II, p. 84) and in 1293 (ibid. I, p. 230). In 1313 her daughter Edith entered for 2*s*. 6*d*. her messuage and curtilage in Langley (BRL 346234 8.8.1313).

[138] Homans, *English Villagers*, pp. 138, 158-9.

Studies of illegitimacy in pre-industrial societies have shown that often the incidence was more common in communities where the mean age at first marriage was low than in those where it was high.[139]

7. Size of Peasant Families

We have seen that the unequal distribution of wealth in the village created a differential life expectancy at 20, mean age at first marriage and illegitimate fertility among strata of the community. Now we will try to find to what extent the economic status of a villager determined the size of his family.

It was possible to link to families the majority of the individuals identified in Halesowen court rolls between 1270 and 1349. Among the 1,553 males noted in the records 1,377 (89 per cent) were identified either as husbands, fathers, sons or brothers (see table 14). This is to some extent an overestimate, since our sample population does not include males who are noted in the court rolls but whose geographical location or familial relationships could not be found. The names of 225 such males are mentioned in the records between 1270 and 1349. Many of these names are probably aliases of identified villagers, or the names of outsiders, or simply names copied wrongly. But if we assume that each of these names represents a local villager then the percentage of males with familiar relationships is 77. A cautious estimate will put the percentage of recorded males who lived in Halesowen during the period under study and who were linked to families between 77 and 89. Among the 835 women noted in the records between 1270 and 1349, 781 (93 per cent) were identified either as wives, widows, mothers, daughters or sisters. If we add the 103 unidentifiable women mentioned in the court rolls, the percentage of women with familial relationships is 83. Therefore we can assume that between 83 per cent and 93 per cent of the recorded women who lived in Halesowen during the period under study were linked to families.

As women are underrepresented in court rolls, it was assumed that a man and his children constitute a family whether his wife was mentioned or not. In 91 families the fathers died before 1270, but as

---

[139] See Laslett and K. Oosterveen, 'Long-term trends in bastardy in England', *Pop. Studies*, XXVII (1973), 255–85, and Laslett, *The World We Have Lost*, pp. 135–45.

their children are noted in the court rolls between 1270 and 1282, these families were included in the sample of reconstituted families. For example, Thomas and Richard the sons of Henry Schirlet of Hunnington were resident in Halesowen between 1270 and 1307, as their court appearances indicate. Although Henry Schirlet died before 1270, he and his two sons were regarded as a family. In 22 of the reconstituted families only the mothers and their children appear in the records. The children of these families are noted in the court rolls as the sons or daughters of their mothers rather than of their fathers, either because they were bastards or because their fathers died when they were very young. There are 28 additional families consisting only of husband and wife. Their children are not recorded, probably because they died before the age of 12. In all, 788 families were reconstituted from Halesowen court rolls between 1270 and 1349, 738 consisting of father and children above the age of 12, 22 of mother and children and 28 of husband and wife only.

It is very difficult to estimate the proportion of the families living in Halesowen which were reconstituted. In order to obtain a crude estimate we can take the ratio between all the villagers identified as sons and those who were also identified as fathers and as husbands. Among the 105 males who are identified as sons in the records between 1341 and 1349, 26 (25 per cent) probably could not form families because they died in the Black Death before reaching the age of marriage.[140] Of the 79 sons who might have survived, 36 appear in the post-plague court rolls as fathers or husbands. Therefore, of the 1,103 sons over 12 identified in the records between 1270 and 1349, only 1,043 could have formed families before 1349. If all of them stayed in Halesowen and reached the age of marriage and married and their surnames did not change, the percentage of reconstituted families would be 46, since 471 sons were identified as husbands and fathers (see table 14). But a good number of sons were not identified in the court rolls as fathers and husbands because they died below the age of 20, emigrated or remained single all their lives, or because their surnames were changed when they married. If we assume that 6 per cent of all the sons died between the ages of 12 and 19, 15 per cent emigrated, 4 per cent never

---

[140] It is impossible to calculate the age-specific mortality of the age group 12–19. I assumed that their rate of mortality was similar to males in the age group 20–30. But this is only a guess and their true mortality rate might have been much higher.

Table 14. Males noted in the court rolls 1270–1349 and their familial relationships

		Males located geographically or identified as husband, father, brother or son							
	Males for whom neither location nor familial relation is found	Males not identified as father, brother or son		Males identified as father	Males identified as father and as son or brother	Males identified as son or brother but not father		Total identified as sons	Total
Dates		Husband	Not husband			Husband	Not husband		
1270–82	45	2	27	153	174	7	148	329	511
1283–92 (missing)	–	–	–	–	–	–	–	–	–
1293–1300	36	1	24	40	92	2	80	174	239
1301–10	27	1	20	20	58	3	83	144	185
1311–20	39	–	28	14	61	1	77	139	181
1321–30	21	–	29	16	37	1	53	91	136
1331–40	25	1	23	12	24	1	86	111	147
1341–9	32	3	25	11	5	5	105	115	154
Total	225	8	176	266	451	20	632	1,103	1,553

married and 5 per cent changed their surnames with their marriage, the number of identifiable sons who could have formed families would be 760. If these guesses are close to the mark the percentage of reconstituted families is 62. Therefore it is plausible to assume that the proportion of reconstituted families lies between 46 per cent and 62 per cent of all the families living in Halesowen during the period 1270–1349.[141]

From the total number of 788 families obtained from the court rolls between 1270 and 1349, 491 (62 per cent) families were reconstituted on the basis of explicit genealogical data. The linkages for 297 (38 per cent) of the families were indirectly established. Nevertheless, the mean number of offspring per family was computed from all the 788 reconstituted families. This was done because the changes of reconstituting families from explicit data given in the court rolls are not random. Rich families are much better documented than less-well-off families because on average their members attended the manorial court more times – more frequently and over a longer period – than the members of poorer families. Consequently the familial links between villagers who had the same surnames are almost always found in the court records if they were rich but are often missing if they were poor. Therefore, if we calculate the mean number of offspring per family from a sample of families reconstituted only on the basis of explicit genealogical data, the result would be an overestimate, since poorer families are underrepresented in the sample. On the other hand the lumping together of directly and indirectly reconstituted families might introduce uncontrolled errors. We therefore examined the family size estimated for each stratum, comparing the directly established with the indirectly established families. The results, which are very close (see table 15), suggest that the margin of error is small.

In order to find whether there was a correlation between the economic status of a villager and the size of his family, it was necessary to stratify the families reconstituted from the court rolls. The variables used to identify the economic status of the villagers were size of holding, livestock, balance of land transactions, employment of servants and labourers, debts, ale-brewing, participation in village government, pledging and certain offences which were

---

[141] The proportion of families that have been reconstituted from parish registers in France and England is much lower; it rarely reaches 10 per cent. See Hollingsworth, *Historical Demography*, p. 181.

Table 15. *A comparison between the mean number of offspring of directly and indirectly reconstituted families 1270–1349*

	Status	No. of families	No. of sons	No. of daughters	No. of offspring	Mean no. of sons	Mean no. of daughters	Mean no. of offspring
Rich	Directly established families	119	304	123	427	2.55	1.03	3.58
	Indirectly established families	13	32	14	46	2.46	1.08	3.54
Middling	Directly established families	201	302	141	443	1.50	0.70	2.20
	Indirectly established families	93	131	70	201	1.43	0.75	2.16
Poor	Directly established families	131	122	97	219	0.93	0.74	1.67
	Indirectly established families	191	165	145	310	0.86	0.76	1.62
Total	Directly established families	451	728	367	1,089	1.61	0.81	2.41
	Indirectly established families	297	328	229	557	1.10	0.77	1.87

usually committed only by peasants belonging either to the lower or the upper echelons of village society. For example, peasants who were presented in the court for picking firewood from their neighbours' fences and for gleaning sheaves were usually cottagers and smallholders, while those who were often amerced for the damage done by animals to the grass and crops of their neighbours and the lord were usually rich peasants.[142]

Rich peasants in Halesowen had in the pre-plague era about a virgate (25–30 acres) of arable land, held both in the open fields and in severalty in crofts and other small enclosed fields. In addition to their share of pasture on the fallow and on rough grazing, yardlanders had meadowland, which was very scarce, and enclosed plots of rough pasture.[143] They were better endowed with livestock than other villagers. And as they had a surplus of produce to sell in the market, they had the means to buy and to lease more land than their less-well-off neighbours and to farm the best and largest parts of the demesne lands leased by the abbot in the post-plague period. The yardlanders often lent money, grains and livestock to their neighbours and employed them as labourers and living-in servants. Many of them had sub-tenants and some had more than one. In Halesowen rich peasant families brewed ale on a large scale for sale,

[142] Picking firewood from neighbours' fences was done very often by poor villagers who could not afford to buy coal or firewood. It is possible that cottagers were not allowed to collect underwood on the common woodland. In October 1275 the jurymen of Hill presented that 'Henricus Batell, Christina de Werdemor, W. Prutfot, tenent cotagia et ardent heyas vicinorum' (*Hales Court Rolls*, I, p. 69). The right to glean was a recognized form of village welfare; the poor usually were amerced for gleaning a number of sheaves well above the number allowed by custom. For example, in October the jurymen presented that 'uxor Richardi fillie Malle collegit in autumpno de pisis et vessis in campo plus quam collegisse debuerat sed parve quantitatis ideo etc. Matilda Hichecok similar. John le Fox pro una garba similiter' (ibid. II, p. 184). See Page, 'The customary poor law of three Cambridgeshire manors', pp. 125–33.

[143] It is not clear how meadowland in Halesowen was shared by the villagers or whether all the tenants had rights in meadows or had meadowland. But it would seem that yardlanders and many half yardlanders had meadowland which was attached to their holdings. For example, Thomas Clerk of Hasbury a wealthy freeholder died in 1335. In addition to the family holding which was held 'per cartam', his son John inherited customary land bought by his father, viz. some 'lands' *(terra)* which belonged to William Gest and John Squire and two 'platea prati' which belonged to Nicholas atte Broke and Thomas Henry. As freeholders usually paid a lower relief than customary tenants for holdings of the same size, John paid to the lord on entering his father's land only 9s. 1½d. (BRL 346270 3.1.1335). On meadowlands in West Midland villages see R. H. Hilton, *A Medieval Society* (London, 1967), pp. 116–19.

and consequently their members were amerced more often for breaching the assize of ale than were other villagers. The yardlanders dominated the village community, which enabled them to maintain their ascendancy. The representatives of the twelve settlements of the manor who presented the offences committed by the members of their townships[144] – the jurymen, the reeves and the court assessors who evaluated the extent of the damage caused by a villager to his neighbour – were usually elected from the ranks of the rich peasants.[145] They acted as pledges more often than other peasants. They trespassed against the lord and their neighbours with their beasts more often than less-well-off villagers. Like members of other ruling elite groups in other periods, they were grasping and aggressive. The village notables, their wives and sons were presented in the court more often than poorer peasants for causing affray, for assault and for shedding blood.[146]

[144] In the court held on 13.6.1270 we find the following entry: 'Dicunt omnes judicialiter tota communitas ville ubi duo eliguntur de uno hameletto et transgrediuntur quod omnes audientes et circumstantes vicini non contradicentes omnes participent tam de concelamento quam de aquietacione' (*Hales Court Rolls*, I, p. 14).

[145] In Halesowen the villagers elected every year two reeves, a reeve and a sub-reeve or, as they were called in the record, 'major praepositus' and 'minor praepositus' (BRL 346280 31.9.1337). As the reeve had to pay 20s. on taking his office, the sub-reeve 6s. 8d. and the forester or the woodward 3s. 4d., only well-to-do villagers could afford to serve as reeves and foresters. In the records of the court held on 13.10.1339 one finds the text of a concession made by the Abbot of Halesowen to his customary tenants. He conceded that instead of paying 20s. or 6s. 8d. the reeve would pay a fine in accordance with the size of his holding: a yardlander, 7½d., half yardlander, 3½d., quarter yardlander, 2d. and cottager, 1d., and the villagers elected as woodwards would be free of any payment. But for some reason the abbot changed his mind; the text of the concession is crossed out and on the margin the word 'vacat' is written (346291 13.10.1339). However, from the early 1350s reeves and woodwards stopped paying any fine on entering office. The members of the Thedrich family, a wealthy family who had lands both in Oldbury and in Cakemoor, were elected ninety-six times as jurymen and twenty-three times as court assessors between 1270 and 1400. The names of the court assessors appear in the court rolls for the first time in 30.11.1356 (346338). Each year 2 or 4 villagers were elected to fill this key position, and they were always rich peasants. I do not know if the office existed in Halesowen in the pre-plague period.

[146] The Greens from Ridgeacre, like other rich peasants in Halesowen, served many times as 'jurati pacis', but in 1293 'Richard de la Grene venit cum sua potestate et abduxit unam vaccam a custodia Matilda uxoris Rogeri Tixtoris in Wernole ante diem termini cum Johanna matre ipsius Ricard et Henrico clerico fratre suo per quorum auxiliam dictam vaccam abduxit injuste et dicta Matilda levavit huthesium super ipsum juste etc.' Richard was amerced 18d. and his brother Henry was wounded by an arrow shot at him by Nicholas the son of Roger the weaver (*Hales Court Rolls*, I, p. 246). There are other similar examples which show that the rich

Poor families in Halesowen had a quarter of a virgate of land or less. Those among them who had arable land in the open fields and a share in the common pasture often had pigs, sheep and cows but only rarely breeding stock or draught animals. Cottagers and peasants with minute holdings usually had no animals at all except perhaps some poultry, a pig or a sheep. The smallholders were often in debt and had to sell and sub-let their land, while only a few of them could afford to buy and to lease land. They were never elected to fill any public office in the village and only rarely were accepted by the court as pledges. They were often presented for picking firewood from other villagers' fences, for collecting underwood, for gleaning and for stealing corn, foodstuffs, poultry and sometimes even animals from their better-off neighbours and from the demesne.[147] They were frequently maltreated by the more solid members of the community[148] and their offspring were often

used to bully the weaker and poorer members of the community when their interests were at stake. A similar pattern of behaviour has been observed in Broughton during the period 1288–1340. See Britton, *Community of the Vill,* pp. 115–23.

[147] For example, in 1294 it was presented in the court that Alice the wife of William Aluerat stole a quarter of beef and five strikes of oats (*Hales Court Rolls*, I, p. 277). In the court held on 24.2.1276 it was presented that Petronilla the daughter of John Ordrich took 2 cows from the house of Gregory Smethwick to Evesham. Gregory pursued them there and Petronilla took flight (ibid. II, p. 36).

[148] There are many examples which reveal how the humble and poor members of the community were maltreated, exploited and cheated by the solid peasants. In 1306 it was presented in the court that 'canis Thome de Hales [a half yardlander] momordit quendam puerum pauperis et sanguinem detraxit ideo predictus Thomas in misericordia' (*Hales Court Rolls*, I, p. 535). In 1337 the townships of Hill and Lapal presented that John de Knython a rich tenant from Hawne and the lessee of the New Mill and Dalewyk Mill obtained firewood by employing poor villagers to steal it from fences belonging to the abbey and other villages (BRL 346278 8.1.1337). John de Knython was a notorious usurer. For example, in the court held on 3.2.1339 Thomas le Per recognized that he owed him 5s. 7d. (346286). In 1340 Thomas had to lease a plot of meadow to John de Knython. In 1340 John sued William Curtiler for 4 bushels of oats and Ivo Jones for a quarter of oats (346292 29.3.1340). In 1348 John Linacre recognized that he owed John de Knython 6s. 8d. and 3 bushels of wheat; in addition he had to pay 40d. damages for not remitting the debt on time (360320 10.12.1348). Damages which borrowers often had to pay to their lenders were probably disguised interest. If a quarter of wheat in Halesowen in 1348 cost as much as on the Bishop of Winchester's Hampshire manors of Mardon and Ecchinswell, the 40d. damage which John had to pay on the loan of 6s. 8d. plus the 3 bushels of wheat represent interest of 37 per cent. See Titow, *English Rural Society,* p. 99. In 1302 the township of Hawne presented that Lucy the daughter of Petrus Rynger 'depulsat tenentes Petri le Rynger a domo sua injuste' (*Hales Court Rolls,* I, p. 467). In 1294 Richard Cook one of the wealthiest villagers in Ridgeacre was amerced 4d. for trespassing against John de Chisehurst 'garcionis sui' (ibid. I, p. 309). In 1342 it was reported in the court that Richard Notwyk a yardlander from Hunnington shed the

declared 'persona non grata' and were not allowed to stay in the village.[149] Many of the poor families did not maintain a residence in the village for more than one generation, either because their members died from malnutrition or emigrated.

Middling families had usually about half a virgate of land. They were better equipped with livestock than the smallholders, as many of them had draught animals and breeding stock, but the size of their flocks and herds was much smaller than that of the rich peasants. Middling villagers who did not do well appear in the court rolls as borrowers and as vendors and lessors of land. Those who were more fortunate and successful are noted in the records as lenders and as buyers and lessees of land, but not as often as the rich. Although middling peasants played an important role in village government as ale-tasters, foresters and sometimes as jurymen and reeves, it was only a secondary role. They also acted as pledges, but less frequently than their better-off neighbours. Middling families usually succeeded in maintaining residence in the village for a longer period than poor families, but not for as long as the rich.

The Thedriches, rich freeholders from Oldbury, maintained residence in Halesowen from 1270 to 1400. John Thedrich (1294–1336) will serve to illustrate the career of a typical wealthy Halesowen peasant. John appears in the court rolls for the first time as landholder in 1294, five years before the death of his father

blood of his servant Agnes. The township of Hunnington was amerced 12*d*. for not reporting Richard, who was one of the most powerful men in the hamlet. William Ketel of Illey (1356–81) the younger brother of Roger Ketel a well-to-do villager from the same township was a smallholder who was often in debt. His daughters had to earn their living by working as servants in the households of rich peasants. In 1373 he sued Henry Tewenhall a yardlander from Ridgeacre for not providing his daughters who served in his household with enough food and cloth as they had agreed and for beating them *(verberavit se)* (BRL 346352 9.11.1373). On 11.10.1374 it was presented in the court that Juliana wife of William Moor a rich peasant from Lapal and her servant Agnes drew each other's blood. However, it is not surprising that the court presented that Agnes was to blame, and the poor girl had to pay a 10*d*. fine. Agnes was the daughter of William Ketel who on 7.2.1275 sued William Moor for not providing Agnes with two tunics *(tunica)*, as they had agreed (346352).

[149] Richard Bedell a smallholder from Oldbury (1276–93/4*d*.) had two daughters Agnes and Matilda. In May 1293 Agnes had to bring pledges for good behaviour. In October the jury presented that Agnes had received women who burnt the fences of the lord and the villagers and she was amerced 4*d*. In 1294 Matilda and Agnes, who must have starved like other poor villagers as a result of the bad harvest and the very high price of corn, sub-let their holding for eight years to Henry Tinctor. He paid them 8*s*. down and undertook to pay them 1*s*. a year. Seven months later the jury declared that Agnes the daughter of Richard Bedell 'non est competens ad recipiendum infra villam nisi plegios inveniat' *(Hales Court Rolls,* I, pp. 234, 247, 306).

William.[150] He inherited from his father a yardland holding or more, yet in fourteen land transactions he purchased and leased at least another yardland. He leased for life a holding of half a yardland or more, and another smaller holding for a year.[151] He also leased three meadows for his livestock.[152] In 1314 he acquired from the lord a plot of wasteland to enlarge his barn, and in 1320 he bought a parcel of land from his neighbour to extend his courtyard.[153] In 1320 and 1321 he exchanged land with 4 villagers in order to consolidate his lands in one block.[154] He had sub-tenants and at least two living-in servants. During the peak periods he used to employ several extra labourers.[155] He and his wife Agnes were amerced forty-three times for selling ale against the assize. He was a juryman thirty-five times and pledged his neighbours fifty-two times. He sued 7 villagers for various debts. He was amerced twenty times for trespassing against the lord and his neighbours with his animals, which amounted to at least 35.[156] He was amerced eight times for assault and shedding

[150] His father probably gave him the family holding in Oldbury for which John did fealty in 1294 and recognized his obligations, for a rent of 8s. 6d. a year (ibid. I, p. 285). When John's father William died in 1299, the lord took 9s. heriot. The customary tenants of Oldbury were amerced for not reporting that William Thedrich held land from William Fokerham the lord of Warley Wigorn (ibid. I, pp. 329–3). John's mother Agnes brought to her husband as a dowry a holding for which he paid £1. 14s. (ibid. I, p. 261). It is difficult to know exactly the size of the holding which John inherited from his father and mother, but it was probably more than a yardland.

[151] In 1308 Philip son of William Young entered his father's holding for 10s., which indicates that the holding was somewhat larger than half a yardland (BRL 350353 2.10.1308). In 1314 Philip sub-let his holding for life to John Thedrich and Agnes his wife (346235 5.6.1314). In 1325 he leased from the lord William Sclatter's holding for a year (346248 6.2.1325).

[152] In 1227 he leased from Geoffrey Per a meadow in Oldbury called Auedeye for eight crops (Hales Court Rolls, I, p. 379). On 16.4.1309 William Smith of Oldbury sub-let to him for ten years his share in two meadows (BRL 350353) and on 4.12.1321 he leased from William Sclatter his share in Mersh Meadow for ten years (346242).

[153] BRL 346235 28.6.1314; 346238 25.6.1320.

[154] BRL 346238 19.3.1320; 346242 4.2.1321.

[155] In 1305 the jury presented that the holdings of Henry Robines and the 'tenentium' of John Thedrich were damaged by overflow of water (Hales Court Rolls, I, p. 508). In 1299 John was amerced because he kept 2 labourers contrary to the lord's orders (ibid. I, p. 390). Like other villagers, John obtained cheap labour by pledging migrant labourers. In 1322 John stood surety for outsiders who gleaned sheaves wrongly (BRL 346243 6.10.1322). And on 30.10.1299 he was amerced for giving refuge to Margeria Tixtoris (Hales Court Rolls, II, p. 133). And in 1323 he pledged two villagers, a man and a woman who were not allowed to live on the manor (BRL 346245 30.3.1323).

[156] This is the total number of his beasts noted in the entries in which he was amerced for trespassing against his neighbour and the lord.

blood. John Thedrich had between 1294 and 1337 at least 196 court appearances, and the fines and amercements which he paid during this time amounted to £2. 10s. 3d.

William Sclatter (1280–1321/2d.) a bond tenant from Oldbury had about half a virgate of land and a few animals. He was able to afford, like many other middling peasants in the pre-plague era, a living-in servant in his household.[157] He was elected as an ale-taster twice and once as a constable, and acted as a pledge eighteen times. But William, like many other half yardlanders, suffered severe economic hardship as a result of the bad harvests in the early 1290s and in the 1310s. In 1294 William recognized in the court that he owed William Wygge 2s. for a quarter of oats.[158] In the same year he was excused from paying an amercement of a few pence because he was too poor.[159] In 1295 he sub-let 2 selions to Thomas Symond for a term of twelve crops.[160] It seems that in the late 1290s and early 1300s his economic situation improved.[161] But the 'great famine' and the agrarian crisis of 1316–17 hit him very hard. In 1317 he sub-let a plot of land for a term of sixteen years.[162] In 1318 he sold to Richard Geoffrey a yardlander from Oldbury 11 ridges of land.[163] In 1321 he sub-let his meadowland for ten years and sold 3 selions.[164] William had two daughters, but he was unable to provide them with a dowry, and one of them was fined for conceiving out of wedlock.[165] When William died in 1321/2, his daughters paid only 2s. as an entry fine.[166]

Other middling villagers did much better than William Sclatter and were less affected by the recurrent harvest failures between 1293 and 1322. Richard Lynacre a free tenant from Hunnington (1270–1326d.) bought in 1294 a smallholding from Richard Schirlet a neif from the same township. Two months later his nephew

---

[157] On 15.2.1309 he and his servant were amerced for trespassing against the lord (BRL 350353).
[158] *Hales Court Rolls,* I, pp. 313–14 (8.12.1294).
[159] Ibid. I, p. 284 (10.5.1294). [160] Ibid. I, p. 344 (8.7.1295).
[161] From 1298 until the 'great famine' he appears often as a pledge and was elected in 1301 as an ale-taster (ibid. I, p. 430).
[162] BRL 350370 23.3.1317.
[163] BRL 346236 22.3.1318. [164] BRL 346242 4.2.1321.
[165] On 25.4.1313 he was distrained until he paid the leyrwyte for Alice his daughter.
[166] BRL 346252 18.11.1327. His daughters entered their father's land five years after his death because the lord seized the holding and let it to various tenants. The land was seized either because the girls could not pay the entry fine and heriot or because their father was in arrear of rents.

Thomas II Lynacre recognized in the court that he owed him 7s., which he promised to pay in four instalments.[167] William II atte Pyrie a customary tenant from Romsley was able in 1317 to buy the holding of John Couper from Hunnington and to pay an entry fine of £1, although he was only a half yardlander.[168] And Roger Sweyn (1328–43d.) a bond tenant from Oldbury had in addition to a holding of half a virgate a flock of 100 sheep.[169]

William II Lech a bond tenant and smallholder from Oldbury appears in the court rolls from the 1270s as a young boy coming to the court to essoin his father.[170] We do not know when exactly he took his father's holding, as the court rolls for 1283–92 are missing. But when he appears as landholder in the court records of 1293, he was in a very difficult position. In that year he sold a small field, and in 1294 a curtilage and part of a third of a half-virgate holding his mother inherited in Romsley.[171] In 1295 he was sued twice for debt, was amerced for burning fences, and sub-let and sold the rest of his mother's holding.[172] In 1301 he was sued by the lord for 6d. arrears of rent.[173] In 1305 he sold a plot of land, and another in 1313.[174] William was never elected to any public office in the village and never acted as a pledge. When he died in 1315 he left to his son Henry only a cottage and a garden for which the lord demanded a mere 12d. as an entry fine.[175] William Lech was able to save his family from starvation by selling all his land. But other poor villagers had nothing except a miserable cottage, and their life stories, as reflected in the court rolls, are even sadder than that of William. For example, Alice de Schischurst, whose brother William was a servant of John Thedrich and whose nephew John was a servant of Richard Cook, was declared 'persona non grata' in 1275. She was harboured by Wimark and Johanna Green well-to-do widows from Ridgeacre who probably employed her as a servant.[176] In 1276 she found a refuge in the house of Thomas Steinulf from Lapal.[177] But at the end of that year she stole a measure of corn and half a measure of peas

---

[167] *Hales Court Rolls,* I, pp. 301, 314. The size of the holding he bought is not given, but in 1297 he paid 6d. as an entry fine (ibid. I, p. 350).
[168] BRL 350360 26.1.1317.
[169] On 1.9.1339 he was sued by a neighbour for trespass in his field with a flock of 100 sheep (BRL 346289).
[170] *Hales Court Rolls,* II, p. 9 (13.4.1276).
[171] Ibid. I, pp. 253, 264.
[172] Ibid. I, pp. 318, 319, 325, 335.
[173] Ibid. I, p. 433.
[174] Ibid. I, p. 508; BRL 346234 10.1.1313
[175] BRL 350359 30.4.1315.
[176] *Hales Court Rolls,* I, p. 68.
[177] Ibid. I, p. 76.

from her former employer Wimark, then set fire to her house and fled the county.[178]

The variables used to identify the socio-economic status of husbandmen were applied also to artisans. For example, John Walter (1270–1329)[179] a freeholder from Oldbury who was a tanner (barker), was classified as a rich villager because he had several employees in his workshop.[180] He had a large holding which was well stocked.[181] He was amerced thirty-two times for selling ale against the assize and often lent money to his neighbours.[182] He was a representative of Oldbury in the manor court, was elected nineteen times as a juryman and acted as a pledge forty-three times. But Margaret Textor (1298–1321) a weaver from Oldbury was classified as a poor villager, since she was declared 'persona non grata' and often picked firewood from her neighbours' fences and gleaned sheaves.[183]

Halesowen court rolls have sufficient data to undertake a more subtle stratification of village society than the common tripartite one. The biographies of the 1,041 families reconstituted from the court records include more than 40,000 items. However, as the classification of these families was done by hand, it was necessary to adopt the tripartite division of village society. Although this division is not as subtle as one might wish, it enables us to take into account the major socio-economic differences which existed between the peasants when studying the size of their families.

Table 16 sums up the number of children over 12 of all the families reconstituted from Halesowen court rolls between 1270 and 1349, according to their economic status. Fig. 7 and table 17 show the distribution of the rich, middling and poor families according to the number of their offspring. The number of children of local families obtained from the court rolls is only a minimum. Although it was possible to identify in the court records probably the majority of sons of Halesowen families, some of them undoubtedly never

---

[178] Ibid. II, p. 44.   [179] Ibid. I, p. 10; BRL 346254 6.9.1329.
[180] In 1300 he and his son Ralf and his servants assaulted the lord's servant Robert le Norris, who came to John's house, possibly to collect rents (*Hales Court Rolls*, II, pp. 135, 139). In 1304 his servant girl was assaulted by a neighbour (ibid. I, p. 490).
[181] In 1299 he came to the court, did fealty to the abbot, and recognized his services, two suits of court and 8s. 8d. This rent suggests that he had a large holding.
[182] For example, during the agrarian crisis of 1320–3 he sued 3 villagers for debt (BRL 346240/245).
[183] *Hales Court Rolls*, I, p. 382; BRL 346240 13.5.1321.

Table 16. *The number of offspring over the age of 12 in families reconstituted from Halesowen court rolls 1270–1349, by socio-economic status*

Status	No. of families	No. of sons	No. of daughters	No. of offspring	Mean no. of sons	Mean no. of daughters	Mean no. of offspring	Adjusted mean no. of offspring
Rich	132	336	137	473	2.5	1.0	3.6	5.1
Middling	294	433	211	644	1.5	0.7	2.2	2.9
Poor	322	287	242	529	0.9	0.7	1.6	1.8
Unidentified	40	47	15	62	–	–	–	–
Total	788	1,103	605	1,708	1.4	0.8	2.2	2.8

Table 17. *The distribution of rich, middling and poor families reconstituted from the court rolls 1270–1349, by number of offspring*

Status	No. of families	No. of offspring 0	1	2	3	4	5	6	7	8
Rich	132	1 (0.75%)	13 (10%)	17 (13%)	34 (26%)	35 (26%)	17 (13%)	9 (7%)	3 (2%)	3 (2%)
Middling	294	9 (3%)	88 (30%)	91 (31%)	66 (23%)	27 (9%)	10 (3%)	3 (1%)	–	–
Poor	322	18 (6%)	155 (48%)	95 (29%)	38 (12%)	12 (4%)	2 (0.6%)	2 (0.6%)	–	–
Total	748	28 (4%)	256 (34%)	203 (27%)	138 (18%)	74 (10%)	29 (4.0%)	14 (2.0%)	3 (0.4%)	3 (0.4%)

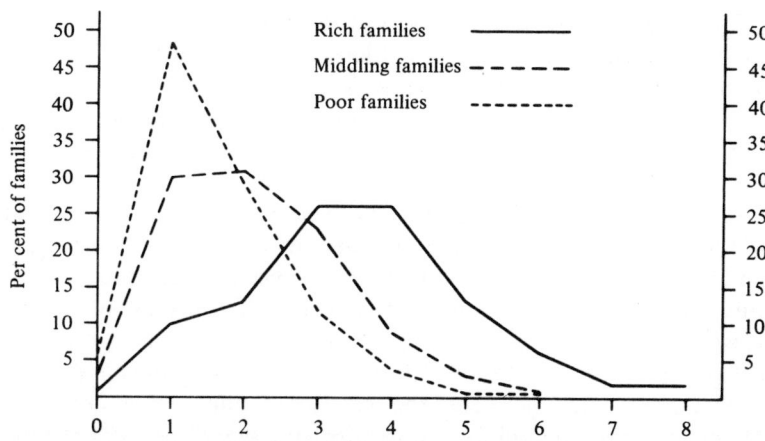

Fig. 7 The distribution of rich, middling and poor families reconstituted from the court rolls in 1270–1349, by number of offspring

entered into observation because they died or emigrated or assumed a new surname in their early teens. Moreover, the number of daughters obtained from the court rolls is too low to be right, as the ratio between sons and daughters is 175 to 100 (women are grossly underrepresented in court rolls). It is interesting to note that there is a correlation between the economic status of a family and the number of its daughters identified in the court records; the ratio of daughters to sons in rich families is 100 to 235, in middling families 100 to 205, and in poor families only 100 to 119. The court rolls represent more faithfully the daughters of the poor than the daughters of well-to-do villagers, because the latter girls had to leave home when they were young. In order to survive they had to glean sheaves, pick firewood from neighbours' fences and steal food from the better-off tenants and from the lord. Moreover, many of them were expelled from the manor and many were pregnant out of wedlock. Therefore the names of the majority of the daughters of cottagers and smallholders appear in the court rolls. But the daughters of the rich and a good number of middling villagers did not have to sustain themselves in this way. And as they also married young many of them never appear in the records with the surnames of their fathers but rather with those of their husbands. Consequently it is possible to identify in the court rolls only a minority of the daughters of rich villagers and half of the daughters of middling tenants.

We do not know the sex ratio in medieval villages in the pre-plague period. There is no evidence to substantiate Russell's assumption that the sex ratio of the adult population in that period was very high.[184] Until further evidence can be found, the assumptions that the sexes were balanced or that the ratio was low are as valid as the assumption that the ratio was high. Therefore we can assume as a hypothesis that there were equal numbers of males and females above the age of 12 in Halesowen in the pre-plague period, and then correct our figures for the imbalance between the sexes. If this hypothesis is true, each family in Halesowen had on average at least 2.8 offspring over 12, but a rich family had on average 5.1 offspring, a middling family 2.9 and a poor family only 1.8.

The correlation between the economic status of a family in Halesowen and the number of its offspring over 12 is very strong. The wealthier a family was, the larger was the number of its children. In a recent study of Redgrave and Rickinghall in Suffolk in the second half of the thirteenth century, it has been shown that a reasonably strong relationship existed between landholding and family size.[185] The analysis of the 1427 tax assessment of the inhabitants of Tuscany has revealed that there was a correlation between the wealth of families and the number of their offspring over the age of 15.[186] The same source has been used to show that in the countryside of Pistoia rich peasant women had more children aged 4 and younger than less-well-off women.[187] A study of twenty villages in southern Poland based on data collected in 1948 has demonstrated that rich peasants had much larger families than those who were poorer.[188]

The unequal distribution of the means of production in medieval villages and the marked differences in living standards it created between sections of the community has been described and stressed

---

[184] *British Medieval Population*, pp. 148–54. For a criticism of Russell's views on the sex ratio in the Middle Ages, see S. L. Thrupp, 'Plague effects in medieval Europe', *Comparative Studies in Society and History*, VIII (1965–6), 475–8.

[185] Smith, 'English peasant life-cycles', p. 119.

[186] Christine Klapisch, 'Household and family in Tuscany in 1427', in *Household and Family in Past Time*, ed. P. Laslett (Cambridge, 1972), p. 274.

[187] Herlihy, *Medieval and Renaissance Pistoia*, pp. 98–100.

[188] Although the inquiry was done in 1948, the data collected concern the size of holding and the number of children in the family, both for the peasants questioned and for their parents. Thus we have data about the fertility of women born between 1855 and 1880: W. Stys, 'The influence of economic conditions on the fertility of peasant women', *Population Studies*, XI (1957), 136–48.

The Population of Halesowen 1270–1348 87

by historians of rural England.[189] The correlation which has been found in Halesowen between wealth and family size confirms their observations. The land shortage, high prices and low wages which existed in Halesowen, as in many other villages in the pre-plague era, had different effects on different sections of the community. The rich became richer and the poor became poorer. Conditions benefited the villagers who were well provided with land and livestock, because they had low labour costs and their surplus produce fetched high prices in the market. Well-to-do peasants suffered losses along with everyone else in the village when the harvests failed, but they were able to sustain these losses better than other villagers. During these crises they not only succeeded in feeding their families, but were even able to lend money and corn to their poorer neighbours and to buy and lease their lands. As the incomes of the yardlanders remained high during the period under study, their children grew up in more spacious and warmer houses than those of their less-well-off neighbours. Richard Ordrich (1301–18d.) a poor villager from Oldbury lived with his family in a humble movable cottage.[190] But Thomas II Brid (1278–94d.) a yardlander from Ridgeacre undertook in 1281 to build for his widowed mother Agnes a two-bay house, 30 feet long and 14 feet wide within the walls, with three doors and two windows, and to provide her each year, in addition to a handsome allowance of wheat, oats and peas, five cartloads of sea coal *(Carbo maris)*.[191] Moreover, the children of well-off peasants were better fed and clothed than the children of poorer villagers. Consequently more children who were born to rich families survived to their twelfth birthday than those born to middling and poor families.

Halesowen villagers who had about 15 acres of arable land suc-

---

[189] Hilton, *Medieval Society*, pp. 114, 121–3; Titow, *English Rural Society*, pp. 73–96; Postan and Titow, 'Heriots and prices on Winchester manors', pp. 172–4; E. A. Kosminsky, *Studies in the Agrarian History of England* (Oxford, 1956), pp. 197–255.

[190] In 1301 Ralf Ordrich a quarter yardlander from Oldbury gave his younger son Richard 'unam placeam terre de capite unius selionis terre in Oldebure ex opposito porte sue ad super edificandum et tenedum ad total vitam ipsius Ricardi. Ita scilicet quod si dictus Ricardus alibi in feodo domini terram vel tenementum adquirere possit ... liceat ei illud edificium ab inde movere et pro sua voluntate in suo proprio tenemento iterum levare sine impedimento' (*Hales Court Rolls*, I, p. 425).

[191] Ibid. I, pp. 166–8. On peasant buildings see Hilton, *Medieval Society*, pp. 94–9; R. K. Field, 'Worcestershire peasant buildings, household goods and farming equipment in the later Middle Ages', *Medieval Archaeology*, IX (1965), 105–45.

ceeded in sustaining their families and in obtaining a surplus to sell on the market in order to pay their rents, amercements, fines, tallages and taxes and to buy things they could not make when the harvests were good or moderate. But when the harvests failed, as they often did in the pre-plague era, many of them – especially those with big families – could not possibly make ends meet. They had to borrow money and corn to render their monetary obligations to the lord and to subsist. These debts burdened their meagre incomes for years and often they had no choice but to sub-let or sell land to remit them. Their living standard was lower than that of their richer neighbours, and fewer of their children – who often must have suffered from malnutrition – survived to the age of 12.

The incomes which cottagers and smallholders obtained from their land or small workshops were too low to satisfy the needs of their families. In order to subsist, poor villagers had to supplement their incomes by working on the demesne or on the farms of better-off villagers. But as real wages were very low their living standard must have been appalling. Many of their children died before they reached the age of 12 as a result of chronic malnutrition, starvation, exposure and diseases. Therefore it is not surprising to find that cottagers and smallholders had on average 67 per cent fewer children over 12 than middling peasants, and 178 per cent fewer than rich ones.

In the absence of birth registration we cannot measure the fertility of women in Halesowen. But it is probable that the marked differences in family size between strata of village society were not only a result of differences in infant and child mortality rates but also of differential fertility. Well-to-do women probably married younger and lived longer than poorer women, and consequently they bore more children.

A. V. Chayanov, in his studies of rural society in pre-revolutionary Russia, developed the theory that the differences between various strata of peasant society are due to demographic differences. The size of peasant holdings and their economic performance increased or decreased in relation to the size of their families.[192] Postan has tried to apply this theory to contradict Kosminsky's Marxist interpretation of the stratification and the inter-

---

[192] *The Theory of Peasant Economy*, ed. D. Thorner, B. Kerblay and R. E. F. Smith (Homewood, Ill., 1966), pp. 53–89.

peasant land market in the second half of the thirteenth century.[193] According to Postan, families well provided with land but deficient in labour found a remedy in the land market by selling or letting what they could not work themselves. On the other hand, men of humble rank, smallholders or wholly landless peasants with large families predominated among the buyers and lessees of land. The only evidence he brings to substantiate this assumption are two examples obtained from court rolls which he claims 'contain a great deal of indirect evidence pointed the same way'.[194] One of the examples is taken from Halesowen court rolls: 'A list of men', he writes, 'who took land from Edith Blanch also appears to be made up of members of "labouring classes" such as Agnes le Seriant or Henry Tinctor.'[195] An erroneous method of establishing the socio-economic status of a villager from his surname or from the fact that he was a sub-tenant seems to have misled Postan here. In a court held in 1281 Edith Blanch and 5 villagers holding land from her were ordered to answer for arrears of rents due from Edith's holding. The names of Edith's sub-tenants were Agnes Seriant, William Wytyng, Henry Tinctor, Thomas Faber and William son of Philip of Wyllinghurst.[196] The villagers called Agnes Seriant and William Wytyng are unidentifiable, since they appear under these surnames only twice. However, the other 3 sub-tenants were neither smallholders nor humble, but members of solid peasant families. Henry Tinctor alias Deystere from Hawne (1274–1307) might have been a dyer. But even if he was, the mere fact that a peasant was a craftsman does not imply *ipso facto* that he was a humble smallholder. In 1278 he obtained from Edith the daughter of William Fremon (alias Edith Blanch) 4 selions and 1 acre in Hunnington, and promised to pay her annual rent of $4\frac{1}{2}d$.[197] In 1280 he acquired from the lord a plot of land for an entry fine of £2 and an annual rent of 15d. The fact that he was not required to bring pledges for the entry fine indicates that he paid in cash.[198] A villager who could pay

[193] Chayanov's influence on Postan's interpretation of the inter-peasant land market has been pointed out recently by Hilton. See his *The English Peasantry in the Later Middle Ages* (Oxford, 1975), pp. 6–7. See Kosminsky, *Agrarian History*, pp. 212–13.
[194] Postan, 'The charters of the villeins', pp. 114–17.
[195] Ibid. p. 117.   [196] *Hales Court Rolls*, II, pp. 96, 107.
[197] At the same time his brother Thomas Tinctor (1272–1307/12d.), who lived in Hasbury and was also a solid tenant, bought from Edith 4 selions for a rent of 2d. (*Hales Court Rolls*, I, p. 105).
[198] Ibid. I, p. 125.

£2 cannot possibly be classified as a humble member of the community. In 1281 he bought from a villager a plot of land.[199] In the 1290s Henry Tinctor was at least in his forties. But the old devil continued to accumulate land. In 1293 Agnes and Matilda the daughters of Richard Bedell a smallholder from Oldbury came to the court and claimed that they had already paid an entry fine for the holding of John Bedell their uncle. It was decided that if they had already paid a fine for the land they should pay 2s. for appealing to the roll, but if they had not they were to pay 6s. 8d.[200] They were pledged by Henry Tinctor, who a year later in 1294 leased their holding for eight years, gave them 8s. in cash and promised to pay an annual rent of 12d.[201] In 1299 Henry's son Richard came of age and acquired land via the market by buying 5 selions from poor Agnes daughter of Richard Bedell.[202] When Henry's son left home and established his own family he did not start to shed his land, although he had no other children. Instead, Henry continued to work his holding with the aid of the cheap hired labour which was so abundant at that time. In 1301 his servant girl Sara is noted in the court rolls.[203]

William the son of Philip Wyllinghurst of Romsley (1280–1301), another sub-tenant of Edith Blanch with Henry Tinctor, was not a humble member of the community but a son of a well-to-do free tenant. Philip Wyllinghurst (1271–99) bought from the lord an acre of land which the lord received from Edith Blanch, probably for an arrear of rent. For this acre of land Philip undertook to pay an annual rent of 11s.[204] Philip was a juryman three times, which is another indication that he belonged to the upper echelons of peasant society. In the 1290s Philip had a granddaughter, but still he continued to accumulate land, since in 1297 he and 2 other tenants were distrained for arrears of rents due from the holding of Thomas Gregories.[205] As land in Halesowen in the last quarter of the thirteenth century was scarce, young villagers could not possibly obtain the capital necessary to buy and even to lease land unless they were

---

[199] Ibid. II, p. 82. [200] Ibid. I, p. 220. [201] Ibid. I, p. 277.
[202] Ibid. I, p. 400. Richard son of Henry Tinctor alias Dyer (1299–1338d.) appears in the records very often, and he was as rich as his father (*Hales Court Rolls*, I, p. 400; BRL 346283 9.9.1338). Both Henry and his son Richard were elected many times as jurymen.
[203] *Hales Court Rolls*, II, p. 161. [204] Ibid. II, p. 43.
[205] His granddaughter is noted in 1300 (ibid. II, p. 119). On the arrear of rents see ibid. I, p. 371.

The Population of Halesowen 1270–1348   91

born to families with means. Their fathers, brothers and other relatives provided them with land,[206] or gave them money or lent them money or acted as their sureties when they borrowed money to acquire land. But landless villagers, cottagers and smallholders had neither the capital nor the credit to purchase or lease land. From hundreds of poor peasants whose careers are documented in the court rolls I found only one case of a villager who was born to a smallholder and succeeded in reaching the top rank of village society.[207] All the peasants who started their life in the village as

[206] In the court rolls between 1270 and 1348, 143 inter-familial land transactions are recorded, 71 of them (50 per cent) between members of rich families, 50 (35 per cent) between members of middling families and 22 (15 per cent) between members of poor families. The rich families constituted only 18 per cent of the families.

[207] William the son of Philip King (1321–69d.) entered his father's quarter virgate for 40d. His father was a neif and his sister Melicentia King had two bastards. Yet despite his humble origins, within ten to twenty years he became the most powerful and one of the richest villagers in Halesowen. He bought his freedom from the lord, since 1340 onwards his name appears frequently among the signatories of deeds (see BRL 351165/176/184/187/191/200/206/212). His frequent appearance as signatory and his presence at almost every court session held during his lifetime suggests that he made his fortune by serving in the manorial administration. Another source of his wealth was usury, since he sued 32 of his neighbours for debt during his lifetime. His land transactions and lands he obtained from the lord are the following:

BRL 350363 9.12.1327: the lord gave him a vacant cottage.
BRL 346253 2.3.1328: sold his land in Cakemoor.
BRL 346260 30.10.1331: bought 2 selions.
BRL 346260 15.4.1332: sold two crofts.
BRL 346270 14.12.1334: exchanged a croft in Lapal.
BRL 346271 8.3.1335: the lord leased to him a vacant holding for sixteen years for an annual rent of 5s. 2d.
BRL 346283 29.10.1337: leased from a villager his part in a field in Illey.
BRL 346284 30.9.1338: leased from Henry Don 5 selions for twenty-nine years.
BRL 346286 3.2.1339: bought the smallholding of Edith Dalby in Lapal; entry fine 6d.
BRL 346314 8.11.1346: bought 4 selions.
BRL 346315 31.1.1347: bought 4 selions.
BRL 346323 Dec. 1349: entered vacant cottage and curtilage; no entry fine.
BRL 346323 13.1.1350: he and his wife Isolda obtained from the lord the half-virgate holding of John Heath of Hill for life; entry fine £1. 6s. 8d.
BRL 346328 15.2.1352: leased from the lord a vacant holding in Lapal for life; entry fine 40d.
BRL 346328 9.5.1352: the lord gave him 2 selions; no entry fine.
BRL 346331 5.10.1353: sold a small plot of land.
BRL 346336 17.2.1355: he appears as 'the Miller', since he leased one of the mills and in 1356 was amerced 2s. for levying excessive toll.
BRL 346356 2.3.1356: leased 2 'dieta' of land from the demesne.
BRL 346343 9.3.1362: at this time William was at least 61 years old and still he and his wife Isolda obtained from the lord 5 selions in Heyefield.
These land transactions do not represent all the freehold which William bought. In

smallholders and succeeded in climbing in order to become solid members of the community were young sons of yardlanders and half yardlanders. They either inherited land when a member of their family died without issue or were helped by their fathers and brothers to acquire additional land. William the son of Philip Wyllinghurst, because his father had the means, was able to buy 3 acres from Edith Blanch in 1280 and to start his own family.[208] In the 1290s he was already a solid member of the community: he was elected like his father as a juryman.[209]

Thomas Faber of Romsley (1270–1302d.), another sub-tenant of Edith Blanch, was a smith and a smallholder.[210] But Thomas was able to acquire land via the land market and to settle in the village although he was a younger son, because he was born to the rich family – the Hills. His eldest brother William, who inherited the family holding, probably helped him in 1270 to lease land and a few years later to buy some land from Edith Blanch.[211] Thomas died without issue in 1302 and the land was probably entered by his grandnephew Richard.[212]

It is clear that in Halesowen the demographic differences between strata of village society were created by economic differences and not vice versa. Land in the pre-plague period was in such short supply that villagers born to poor families who inherited smallholdings or cottages were unable to increase their land resources and incomes. Therefore they had no option but to have small families. Meanwhile, the sons of wealthy villagers could have large families because they inherited sizable holdings or married into land or were helped by their parents and other relatives to acquire land either from the lord or via the land market.

The mean size of peasant families from a few villages in the

1335 he employed William Bond to collect the rents from his tenants. He worked his huge holding with hired labour, since he had only three sons of whom only one Henry (1346–76) survived him. He pledged his neighbours 273 times and acted as juror twenty times. His court appearances amount to 497.

[208] *Hales Court Rolls,* II, p. 71.

[209] Ibid. I, pp. 236, 244, 305, 326.

[210] His name appears in the records (*Hales Court Rolls,* I, pp. 19–461). In 1326 the lord granted him a plot of waste land and permission to build there a smithy and a house (ibid. II, p. 21).

[211] The genealogy of the family is given in *Hales Court Rolls,* I, p. 461. When his nephew Thomas Hill died in 1297 his widow Clementia took the custody of his two sons for £1 (ibid. I, p. 377).

[212] Ibid. I, p. 461.

second half of the thirteenth century has been calculated, and it is interesting to make a comparison with the mean obtained from Halesowen court rolls. But as the size of Halesowen families was measured over the whole period from 1270 to 1349, in which mortality rates were much higher between the years 1293 and 1324 than between the years 1270 and 1292, it was necessary to calculate the mean size of families living in the parish between 1270 and 1282. It was possible to reconstitute from the court rolls between 1270 and 1282 some 174 families who had between them 329 sons and 144 daughters, which gives a mean family size of 4.7. But when we correct these figures for imbalance between the sexes, the mean rises to 5.8. In Redgrave and Rickinghall in Suffolk in the second half of the thirteenth century the mean family size calculated from court rolls data was 4.7 and 4.9 respectively. When corrected for the imbalance between the sexes it rises to a mean of 6.1 and 5.6.[213] On the manors of the Priory of Spalding in Lincolnshire a census from 1268–9 shows that the mean size of serf families was 5.4.[214] The fact that mean family size in Halesowen, where primogeniture was the dominant inheritance custom, was not lower than in villages which practised partible inheritance does not tally with assumptions about the effects which these customs had upon demographic processes in medieval England. According to Homans, primogeniture restricted fertility by pushing up the age of marriage and by preventing more than one son to a family from marrying in his native village, while Joan Thirsk has suggested that the custom of partible inheritance gave easy access to land resources to all sons and increased the likelihood of early marriage and high fertility levels.[215] If the results obtained from Halesowen court rolls can be confirmed by further research on villages which practised unimogeniture, this research will provide us with indisputable proof that different population densities in medieval England were not determined by different inheritance customs, but by other factors.

[213] Smith, 'English peasant life-cycles', p. 104.
[214] H. E. Hallam, 'Some thirteenth-century censuses', *Econ. Hist. Rev.*, 2nd ser., X (1958), 353–4.
[215] Thirsk, 'Industries in the countryside', in *Essays in the Economic and Social History of Tudor and Stuart England*, ed. J. Fisher (Cambridge, 1961), p. 84. See also Thirsk (ed.), *The Agrarian History of England and Wales*, vol. IV, *1500–1640* (Cambridge, 1967), p. 10.

8. *Land Shortage and Population Growth*

When the reserves of reclaimable land in Halesowen were giving out in the second half of the thirteenth century, a rapidly increasing population put a strain upon the available land resources in the parish. The real incomes and consequently the living standard of the peasants fell, and when the parish was hit by a series of harvest failures between 1292 and 1322 mortality rates rose considerably. Yet the crises did not reverse the population trend but only caused a temporary setback. In the late 1320s the population started to increase again, and on the eve of the Black Death it reached almost the peak of the early 1310s. In the long term a slow population growth could have been maintained in Halesowen, although land was in short supply, as a result of a sharp differential fertility and mortality between sections of the population which was caused by an unequal distribution of wealth in the village. The smallholders and cottagers were often reduced to destitution, their expectation of life at 20 fell and the majority of their children died before the age of 12. Consequently poor families in Halesowen failed to keep up their numbers from generation to generation. But other families not only succeeded in reproducing themselves but also in providing a surplus of children which more than counterbalanced the heavy loss of life among the cottagers and smallholders.

The rich, and to a lesser extent the middling villagers, had higher incomes and living standards than their less-well-off neighbours. They married younger, lived longer and had more children. But as many of their children survived to maturity they had to settle and marry more than one son and one daughter. Although they reserved the original family holding for their eldest son and endowed their eldest daughter with a good dowry, the majority of their younger children neither emigrated nor remained single, but settled and married in Halesowen. In the absence of sufficient reserves of reclaimable land, rich and middling peasants settled their younger children on the lands which were previously occupied by their poorer neighbours. Such lands became increasingly available as the economic conditions in the village deteriorated. Many families of small means died out and their holdings were taken up by new tenants. Others had to sell or to sub-let their lands in order to buy food to remit debts and to pay rents, fines and amercements. We have already seen that during and immediately after a subsistence crisis the number of inter-peasant land transactions rose. Fig. 8 shows that this was also true of the number of vacant holdings granted or leased by the lord to the villagers. Table 18 shows that while villagers of small means predominated among the vendors and lessors of land, members of well-to-do families predominated among the buyers and lessees.[216] And table 19 indicates that the rich

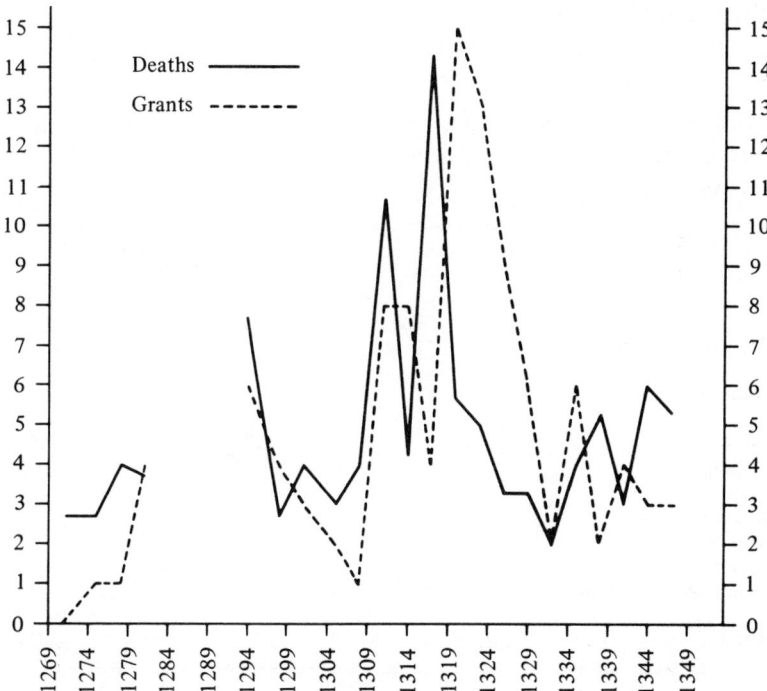

Fig. 8 Number of male deaths (three-year averages) and vacant holdings granted or leased by the Abbot of Halesowen 1270–1348 (per three years)

[216] As the exact size of land sold or leased in the inter-peasant land market is not given, it is impossible to study the volume of the land market. Although table 18 gives only the number of vendors, buyers, lessors and lessees, it does give a fairly faithful picture of the land market, since the great majority of the transactions were of small plots of land of a few selions; only rarely were more than 5 acres leased or sold. In his study of the land market in Redgrave and Rickinghall, Smith has concluded, 'It seems certain that what redistribution was taking place occurred in favour of the upper echelons of the peasant social and economic hierarchy' ('English peasant life-cycles', p. 83).

took the bulk of the holdings which fell vacant after the death of their former holders. In this way the place of families who could not subsist and either died out or emigrated was taken up by the second and third sons and daughters of rich and middling peasants, and the population of the village continued slowly to increase.

The fact that well-off families used any additional land which they acquired to settle and to marry off their younger children prevented them from increasing the size of their holdings for more than one

Table 18. *The socio-economic status of lessors, lessees, vendors and buyers of land in Halesowen 1270–1348 (extra-familial land transactions)*

Status	No. of leases (224)			No. of sales (310)		
	No. of lessors	No. of lessees	Excess of lessees	No. of vendors	No. of buyers	Excess of buyers
Members of rich families	24	58	+34	35	81	+46
Members of middling families	67	60	−7	95	80	−15
Members of poor families	94	23	−71	114	21	−93
Total	185	141	−44	244	182	−62

Table 19. *The status of villagers who took up or leased vacant holdings or parts of vacant holdings from the Abbot of Halesowen 1270–1348*

Status	No. of villagers
Members of rich families	67 (63%)
Members of middling families	34 (32%)
Members of poor families	5 (5%)
Total	106

generation. However, their eldest sons inherited holdings which were sufficiently large to maintain the status of their families in the village and to continue producing more children than they needed for replacement, while their younger sons, who descended in the social scale, had smaller holdings and consequently smaller families than their eldest brothers. For example, John Cook of Ridgeacre (1271–1312d.), who inherited the family yardland holding when his father Richard died in 1301, had four sons and a daughter who reached their twelfth birthday. But his younger brother William (1270–1310d.) had only two sons. Thomas Squire of Romsley (1272–1342d.), who inherited the family yardland holding, had three sons and a daughter. But his brother John (1281–95), who obtained a smaller holding in Hasbury probably through marriage, had only one son. Adam son of Thomas Adam of Hasbury (1302–11d.) a half yardlander had two sons Thomas (1311–34d.) and Philip (1317–34d.). Thomas, the eldest, had two sons and a daughter. His brother Philip, who acquired a smallholding via the land market, had only one son.

Land shortage in Halesowen in the pre-plague period did not stop the population from growing, but only slowed down its growth by widening the economic and consequently also the demographic differences among the strata of village society. These differences created a strong downwards social mobility which a brisk land market reinforced rather than reversed. In other words, when the peasants in the upper stratum of village society could not expand horizontally, since the reserves of reclaimable land were giving out, they had to expand vertically in order to settle their surplus children. This they did by 'colonizing' lands held by the poorer and weaker members of the community whom unfavourable economic conditions pushed either up to heaven or out from their holdings and often from the village altogether.

It is obvious that we cannot draw any general conclusions about the demographic trend in rural England in the pre-plague period from a study of one parish in the West Midlands. And to discover the demographic trend in other rural parishes we have to measure it directly from court rolls or other sources. The indirect economic evidence from which historians have tried to project the movement of the rural population in the pre-plague period is no longer adequate. The same is true of the general conclusions which have been drawn from the fact that mortality rates in villages rose from the last decade of the thirteenth century onwards and reached appalling dimensions during the years 1316–17. Postan writes, 'in medieval England the population could not have continued to increase and must have begun to decline even had the Black Death by-passed the country altogether'.[217] This hypothesis may be right, but without new direct demographic evidence it has exactly the same validity as the opposite hypothesis, namely, that the population of England continued to increase until the Black Death.

[217] *The Medieval Economy and Society* (London, 1972), p. 38.

3. The Black Death

1. Estimates of Black Death Mortality in England

During the years 1347–50 every country of Europe was attacked by the Black Death.[1] In England, the plague raged from about June 1348 to the autumn of 1349.[2] Descriptions by contemporary witnesses leave little doubt that the Black Death was an unparalleled catastrophe.[3] Modern historians, however, differ widely in assessing the overall mortality caused by the plague in England; their estimates vary between 20 and 50 per cent. High estimates of plague mortality are based on ecclesiastical and manorial records. Studies of the records of institutions to benefices in ten dioceses show that the average death rate among the clergy was close to 45 per cent, and a similar rate prevailed among monks in twelve monasteries in various counties.[4] Mortality was even higher among tenants on those manors which have been studied. For example, the death rate on three Cambridgeshire manors of Crowland Abbey was 56 per cent. On the Winchester manors the average rate was 50 per cent; on the Hampshire manor of Bishop's Waltham it was 65 per cent;

---

[1] See E. Carpentier, 'Autour de la peste noire: famines et épidémies dans l'histoire du XIVe siècle', *Annales: E.S.C.*, XVIII (1962), 1062–92. There is a vast literature about the Black Death. I found the following useful: L. F. Hirst, *The Conquest of the Plague* (Oxford, 1953); P. Ziegler, *The Black Death* (London, 1969); T. H. Hollingsworth, *Historical Demography* (London, 1969), pp. 355–74; J. N. Biraben and J. Le Goff, 'La peste dans le haut Moyen Age', *Annales: E.S.C.*, XXIV (1969), 1484–510.

[2] On the plague in England see C. A. Creighton, *A History of Epidemics in Britain from A.D. 664 to the Present Time*, vol. I (Cambridge, 1891); F. A. Gasquet, *The Great Pestilence* (London, 1893); J. Saltmarsh, 'Plague and economic decline in England in the later Middle Ages', *Cambridge Hist. Journ.*, VII (1941), 23–41; Ziegler, *The Black Death*, pp. 120-239.

[3] *Chronicon Galfridi le Baker de Swynebroke*, ed. E. M. Thompson (Oxford, 1889), pp. 98–100. For other references to the Black Death in literary sources, see Creighton, *History of Epidemics*, I.

[4] A. H. Thompson, 'The registers of John Gynewell, Bishop of Lincoln, for the years 1347–50', *Archaeol. Journ.*, LXVIII (1911), 301–60, and 'The pestilences of the fourteenth century in the Diocese of York', ibid. LXXI (1914), 337–47; A. Jessop, 'The Black Death in East Anglia', *The Coming of the Friars and Other Historic Essays* (London, 1906), pp. 168–88. Lunn's results are summed up by J. C. Russell, who also gives data about the mortality in monasteries; see *British Medieval Population* (Albuquerque, N. Mex., 1948), pp. 229–32.

and on twenty-two manors of Glastonbury Abbey the average rate was 54.6 per cent.⁵

Low estimates of the mortality caused by the Black Death are based partly on demographic evidence and partly on economic and other indirect evidence. J. C. Russell has calculated from the Inquisitiones Post Mortem a death rate of between 27.3 per cent and 23.6 per cent and claimed that the level of mortality among the landlords in 1348–9 represents faithfully the level of mortality of the population of England as a whole.⁶ A. E. Levett observed that on the estates of the Bishop of Winchester, despite the fact that many holdings fell vacant during the plague, the majority of them were taken up by new tenants within a short period of time and no immediate profound economic changes were caused.⁷ She therefore assumed that the mortality caused by the Black Death was overestimated both by the chronicles and by historians and argued that 'a loss of one third of the population is an over-pessimistic estimate'.⁸ J. F. D. Shrewsbury recently estimated the national death toll in the Black Death at 5 per cent, on the basis of some dubious assumptions, such as that the plague could not possibly have spread and caused high overall mortality because the major part of England was too thinly populated in 1348.⁹

Some historians have taken the middle road and suggested that the national death toll in 1348–9 was roughly one-third. However, there is no reason to suppose that the average of low and high estimates of mortality provides a more reliable estimate.¹⁰

⁵ F. M. Page, *The Estates of Crowland Abbey* (Cambridge, 1934), pp. 120–5; M. M. Postan and J. Z. Titow, 'Heriots and prices on Winchester manors', in Postan, *Essays on Medieval Agriculture and General Problems of the Medieval Economy* (Cambridge, 1973), p. 171; Titow, *English Rural Society 1200–1350* (London, 1969), pp. 69–72. See also E. Robo, 'The Black Death in the Hundred of Farnham', *Eng. Hist. Rev.*, XLIV (1929), 560; A. Ballard, 'The Black Death', in *Oxford Studies in Social and Legal History*, vol. V, ed. P. Vinogradoff (Oxford, 1916), pp. 181–216; A. E. Levett, *Studies in Manorial History* (Oxford, 1938), pp. 243–85; Russell, *British Medieval Population*, p. 227; D. G. Watts, 'A model for the early fourteenth century', *Econ. Hist. Rev.*, 2nd ser., XX (1967), 547; J. Hatcher, *Plague, Population and the English Economy 1348–1530* (London, 1977), pp. 21–6.

⁶ Russell, *British Medieval Population*, pp. 214–17.

⁷ A. E. Levett, 'The Black Death on the estates of the See of Winchester', in *Oxford Studies in Social and Legal History*, vol. V, ed. P. Vinogradoff (Oxford, 1916), pp. 13-180. ⁸ Ibid. p. 10.

⁹ *A History of the Bubonic Plague in the British Isles* (Cambridge, 1970), pp. 23, 123, and review of it by C. Morris: 'The plague in Britain', *Hist. Journ.*, XIV (1971), 205–15.

¹⁰ J. M. W. Bean, 'Plague, population and economic decline in England in the later

As the great majority of the inhabitants of fourteenth-century England lived in villages, the level of mortality among the peasants in the Black Death is the best guide for an estimate of the national level of mortality. Although the death rates among tenants during the plague have been measured on a good number of manors, many more studies of contemporary villages in various parts of the country are necessary in order to obtain a reliable overall estimate of mortality. The sources which were used to study plague mortality are manorial rentals and accounts, heriots, payments of frankpledge dues and of chevage, and other fiscal records. The figures obtained from these records may either overestimate or underestimate the plague mortality. The method of determining the size of the tenant population of a manor from rentals and accounts, and then computing the death rate from the number of tenants whose deaths are recorded, might overestimate the actual mortality; some deaths could have included those who succeeded plague victims and thus were not in the original population under observation on the eve of the plague.[11] The use of payments of frankpledge dues as a measurement of plague mortality might underestimate the actual mortality if before the plague a number of villagers succeeded in evading these dues. Similarly, the number of vacant holdings in the lord's hands a few months after the plague underrepresents the number of deaths among tenants, since some vacant holdings were taken when the plague was raging. Therefore it is necessary to test the accuracy of the figures obtained from the above-mentioned sources against other records. Good series of court rolls which cover the period between 1330 and 1360 provide an opportunity to measure plague mortality not only among tenants but also among a much wider section of the village population.

2. Mortality in the Parish of Halesowen during the Black Death

Despite the ravages of the plague the manorial administration succeeded in recording the deaths of many tenants. Four court sessions were devoted almost exclusively to registering deaths, and even when the plague exhausted itself in August 1349, the court was still busy for another six months recording conveyances of vacant

Middle Ages', *Econ. Hist. Rev.*, 2nd ser., XV (1963), 426; Ziegler, *The Black Death*, pp. 232–8.
[11] Russell, *British Medieval Population*, pp. 227–8.

holdings and wardships. Consequently it was possible to discover the names of 14 tenants, 13 males and 1 female, whose deaths were not recorded when the plague was raging. The names of 4 other unrecorded victims of the plague are mentioned in the court rolls for 1363, 1370 and 1371.[12]

The plague invaded the parish of Halesowen in May 1349 and subsided in August.[13] The worst month was June, when the deaths of 25 males were recorded in the court rolls (see fig. 9). There is no

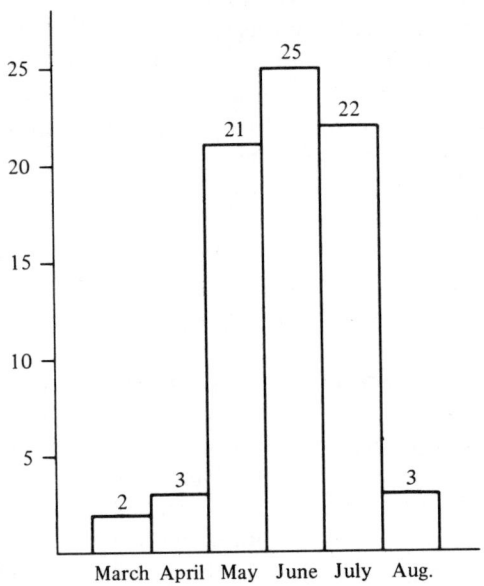

Fig. 9 The course of the plague in the parish of Halesowen 1349 (male deaths recorded in the court rolls)

[12] For example, William Symon of Oldbury appears in the court records for the last time in 1348 for default of court (BRL 346319 8.10.1348). In November 1349 his holding was given to William Jurdan for an entry fine of 40*d*. (346323 11.11.1349). Therefore I assumed that William Symon died in the Black Death. The death of Roger Crone of Hawne was not recorded in 1349. But he left a minor daughter Juliana who came to the court in 1363 and entered her father's holding for 12*d*. In the court it was stated that Roger Crone died in 'prima pestilentia' (346344 8.3.1363). In 1370 Richard son of Henry Robyns from Ridgeacre entered his father's half-virgate holding (346349 20.3.1370). In the same year John son of Roger de Oueley of Lapal entered his father's messuage, toft and a nook (ibid. 16.1.1370). In 1371 John son of Sibille daughter of John Culeth of Warley entered his grandfather John Culeth's holding (346350 10.12.1371). In all three cases it is noted in the records that the villagers died in the first plague.

[13] In August five holdings of deceased tenants were taken up. The deaths of 2 of

doubt that the Black Death was the most devastating disaster that the villagers of Halesowen experienced during the 130 years under study. The plague killed at least 88 peasants, four times the number of deaths recorded during the famine of 1317 and eighteen times higher than the annual average number of deaths recorded between 1340 and 1348. On the eve of the plague 203 male tenants were identified in Halesowen court rolls; 81 of them died in the Black Death.[14] Therefore the death rate of males above the age of 20 was at least 399 per thousand. But as the deaths of some tenants were probably neither recorded nor discovered in later court rolls, the actual death rate must have been higher. If we allow 15 per cent for underenumeration of deaths of male tenants, the rate of mortality rises to 459 per thousand. A cautious estimate will put the death rate of males above 20 in the plague between 399 and 459 per thousand. The fact that the number of resident males above the age of 12 obtained from Halesowen court rolls between 1345 and 1349 is lower by 43 per cent than the number obtained from the court rolls between 1351 and 1355 suggests that the death rate of males above this age was about 430 per thousand. This figure is compatible with available statistical data about the plague mortality in Worcestershire. C. C. Dyer has calculated that on the Bishop of Worcester's manor of Alvechurch, about eight miles south-west of Halesowen, 44 per cent of the tenants died in the Black Death.[15] The death rate among the beneficed clergy in the diocese of Worcester in 1349 was 445 per thousand.[16]

Although the deaths of only 21 women were recorded during the first visitation of the plague, there is little doubt that many more

them, Philip Thomkyns and Richard Williams alias Sclatter, both from Oldbury, had already been recorded in May (BRL 346321 6.5.1349). Therefore it is difficult to know whether the other three tenants mentioned in August, namely John Clerk of Oldbury, Henry Perison of Oldbury and William Hill of Hill, died at that time or in the previous three months (346322 19.8.1349).

[14] In the court rolls between 1347 and the outbreak of the plague in May 1349, 205 tenants were identified as residents in the manor. Three of them, William Walter of Oldbury, John Moulowe of Hasbury and Robert Godyer of Hill, died in April. Only one of them, William Walter, had a son who took the holding. The other two died without issue. Therefore only 203 tenants were exposed to the plague (BRL 346321 15.4.1349).

[15] C. C. Dyer has calculated the death rate of tenants in the Bishop of Worcester's estates from a survey from 1299 and from royal escheators' accounts from 1349: 'The estates of the Bishopric of Worcester, 680–1540', unpublished Ph.D. thesis, University of Birmingham, 1977.

[16] Russell, *British Medieval Population*, p. 222.

died. In the court rolls between 1345 and 1349, 205 women were identified as residents in Halesowen, but in the court rolls between 1351 and 1355 only 119 – a fall of 42 per cent. This suggests that the death rate of women in the plague was as high as that of men. There are no statistical data about mortality of women in the Black Death. Russell has argued that because the Black Death attacked the glands, it might be expected that men were more severely affected, with a higher death rate as a result.[17] Unfortunately, he has not brought forward any evidence to substantiate this assumption.

Indirect evidence obtained from the court rolls suggests that child mortality in the Black Death was very heavy. Seventeen of the villagers who died in the famine of 1316–17 were between the ages of 20 and 39, and 5 of them died childless. But among 26 victims of the plague who belonged to the same age group, 19 (73 per cent) died without issue. As these villagers were landholders, it is reasonable to assume that the great majority of them were married and had at least one child. Therefore, if the Black Death killed more children than the 'great famine', child mortality in the plague must have been catastrophic.[18]

As the plague claimed the lives of so many men, women and children, it is not surprising that whole families were wiped out. Forty of the victims of the plague who were above the age of 20 died without issue, and it is very likely that the wives of most of them died as well. For example, Thomas Hyddeley a yardlander from Lapal was about 30 when the Black Death hit the parish. In July 1349 his death and the death of his wife were recorded in the court rolls, and as his holding was given to his brother John, we can assume that his children died as well.[19] Philip atte Lowe (1304–46d.) a yardlander from Hunnington had two sons Philip II (1334–49d.) and Thomas (1339–49d.) and two daughters Alice (m. 1345) and Juliana (m. 1333).[20] In July 1349 the deaths of Philip II, Thomas and Juliana

---

[17] Ibid. pp. 149, 231–2.
[18] The problem of the susceptibility of children to the plague will be discussed in chapter 4.
[19] Thomas Hyddeley (1339–49d.) entered his father John's (1318–39d.) virgate holding in Lapal in 1339 for an entry fine of 13s. 4d. (BRL 346289 9.6.1339). The death of Thomas and his wife was recorded in July 1349. The holding was given to his younger brother John for a 10s. entry fine (376322 29.7.1349).
[20] Philip atte Lowe is noted in the records between 1304 and 1342 (*Hales Court Rolls*, I, p. 479; BRL 346299). His son Philip II is noted in the records for the first

atte Lowe were recorded in the court rolls and the family holding was given to a new tenant, William of Hill, for an entry fine of £2.[21] Other families were luckier, but they also suffered heavy losses. Thomas Richard a yardlander from Oldbury was probably in his late teens in 1348 when his father Richard died.[22] Philip Thomkyns a wealthy villager from the same township took him and his holding into his custody and married him to his daughter Juliana, who was said to be a minor.[23] Thomas Richard died in the plague leaving a teenage widow and a 1-year-old son Thomas II (1348b.–1393d.).[24] His father-in-law Philip Thomkyns and his brother-in-law John died as well in the Black Death.[25] Philip's minor son Henry and the family holding were given into the custody of Philip's daughter Alice and her husband Thomas Thedrich a yardlander from Oldbury.[26] It is likely that Thomas Thedrich also took custody of his sister-in-law Juliana and her son Thomas II Richard.[27] These examples and others which were found in the record indicate that the plague, unlike the famines, did not spare the rich any more than the poor. Richard atte Hall and William Moulowe lived in the small hamlet of Hill; the former was a poor cottager, the latter a rich yardlander, yet both fell victim to the plague.[28]

---

time on 5.10.1334 and Thomas on 6.10.1339 (346269/291). On 3.6.1333 Philip I paid a merchet for Juliana and on 24.8.1345 his second daughter Alice paid a merchet (346263/312).

[21] Thomas atte Lowe's death was recorded on 6.5.1349 and Philip's on 17.6.1349 (BRL 346321/322). On 29.7.1349 the death of Juliana was recorded (346322). The atte Lowe holding was granted to William Hill in 1350 (346324 30.6.1350).

[22] BRL 346318 16.4.1348.

[23] Ibid. 4.6.1348. Philip Thomkyns took the custody of Thomas Richard and his daughter Juliana for 13s. 4d.

[24] BRL 346321 27.5.1349. Thomas II is mentioned for the first time on 7.3.1352 as a minor under custody. On 5.1.1368 his name appears in the records in a list of villagers amerced for default of court. The fact that he appears as landholder for the first time in 1368 suggests that he was born in 1348 (346328/349).

[25] BRL 346321 27.5.1349.

[26] Thomas Thedrich took the custody for £1 (BRL 346322 19.8.1349).

[27] On 13.1.1350 the lord, who seized Thomas Richard's holding in 1349, leased half of it to Thomas Thedrich. On 7.3.1352 Thomas II Richard's custody was given to Thomas Thedrich for £1. 10s. It seems that at that time Juliana the widow of Thomas Richard died; therefore Thomas Thedrich took the custody of her son formally. But it is possible that he had already taken the young widow and her baby son into his household in 1350 (BRL 346323/328).

[28] Richard atte Halle died in June holding a cottage; the lord seized it and as he had nothing no heriot was taken. William Moulowe died in July holding a yardland which was taken by his son John for a £1 entry fine. The lord took as heriot and mortuary 2 oxen, a horse and a hog (BRL 346322 17.6.1349 and 29.7.1349).

It is often argued that although there is evidence that some localities suffered heavily during the Black Death, the overall mortality was much lower because other villages and hamlets escaped almost unharmed.[29] It is plausible to assume that there were regional differences in the incidence of plague mortality as a result of varying degrees of population density and the nature of the disease, which in its pneumonic and septicaemic form was more lethal than the bubonic. However, there is little statistical evidence, if any, which indicates that there were wide regional differences in England, or that the Black Death caused heavy mortality in one rural settlement while a neighbouring settlement was much less affected.[30] On the manor of Halesowen at least 40 per cent of the tenants died in the Black Death. Table 20 and fig. 10 show, first, that mortality was fairly evenly distributed among the twelve ham-

Table 20. *The geographical distribution of mortality among the male tenants of Halesowen in the Black Death*

Hamlet[a]	No. of observed male tenants who were exposed to the plague	No. of observed male tenants who died in the Black Death	%
Oldbury	30	12	40
Langley	15	5	33
Cakemoor	12	4	33
Warley	11	4	36
Hill	17	6	35
Ridgeacre	15	6	40
Hawne	21	9	43
Hasbury	24	8	33
Lapal	14	7	50
Illey	7	4	57
Hunnington	14	8	57
Romsley	23	8	35
Total	203	81	40

[a] The hamlets are presented from north to south.

[29] Levett, *Studies in Manorial History*, p. 249.
[30] See Saltmarsh, 'Plague and economic decline', p. 36. Hirst wrote of the plague, 'Each pandemic in history has shown a tendency to run its course within a few decades and to show a change of clinical type. The Black Death seems to have been extraordinarily widespread and acute for the first few years and then to settle down to a more typical form with more localized lesions' (*The Conquest of the Plague*, p. 267).

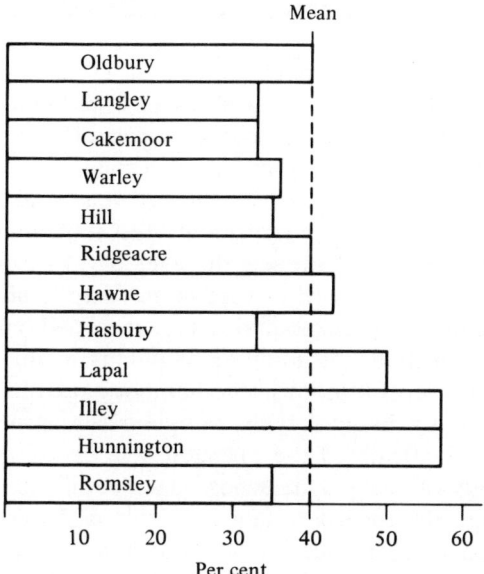

Fig. 10 The geographical distribution of mortality among the male tenants of Halesowen in the Black Death (hamlets presented from north to south)

lets of the parish, given that we do not have a complete record of tenants' deaths and, secondly, that even in those hamlets where the observed mortality was lower than the average it did not fall below 33 per cent.

3. *Estimated Age-Specific Mortality in the Black Death*

Russell has calculated from the records of the Inquisitiones Post Mortem the age-specific mortality of the plague. His figures show that the plague fell more heavily on older men than on the young.[31] P. Goran Ohlin has pointed out that Russell's tables do not give a clear indication that plague mortality rose with age if we separate plague fatality from ordinary mortality. He has argued that it is more plausible to assume that in the devastating outbreaks of the plague age made no difference to this particular risk of death.[32]

[31] Russell, *British Medieval Population,* pp. 216–17.
[32] 'No safety in numbers: some pitfalls of historical statistics', in *Industrialization in Two Systems,* ed. H. Rosovsky (New York, 1966), pp. 78–80.

Data obtained from Halesowen court rolls shed some light on this issue.

It was possible to estimate the age of 71 male victims of the plague. All of them belong to well-documented families who were resident in the parish for at least forty years before 1349. At the time when a victim appeared in the court rolls for the first time as a landholder, it was assumed that he was 20 years old. This is a crude method which tends to underestimate the actual age by between one and three years. However, the ages of 14 of the victims are noted in the records. The results are summed up in table 21.[33] As the deaths of under-20-year-old males were recorded only if they were heirs under custody, the number of deaths in this age group is unrepresentative. But so far as the number of deaths among adults is concerned, it is likely that the sample *is* representative. On this assumption, I calculated the probable age distribution of the 17 adult victims of the plague whose ages could not be estimated directly from the records. Then I estimated the ages of 75 well-documented villagers out of the total number of 122 observed tenants who survived the Black Death. And on the assumption that

Table 21. *The estimated age distribution of males who died in the plague of 1349*

Age group	No. of dead males
20	7
20–9	11
30–9	15
40–9	15
50–9	16
60 and above	7
Total	71

[33] For example, on 12.12.1347 John Miles of Oldbury died and his widow took the custody of his 9-year-old son and heir Philip for 10s. The death of Philip was recorded on 22.5.1349. Therefore he was 11 years old when he died. On 3.2.1350 his sister Juliana took the family holding for an entry fine of 3s. (BRL 346316/321/323). On 6.10.1316 William Langley died and his widow took the custody of his son and heir William II, who was 2 years old. William II Langley died in the plague between 6.5.1349, when he pledged Isabella Hamond, and 19.8.1349 when his widow Amicia married Petrus on the Hill. Therefore William II was 35 years old when he died (350360; 346321/322).

the estimated ages of the 75 survivors of the plague were distributed similarly to the ages of the other 47 survivors which could not be estimated directly from the records, I calculated the probable age distribution of the latter. Eventually I computed the estimated age-specific mortality in the Black Death of male tenants above the age of 20. In order to separate plague fatality from ordinary mortality, I adopted the appropriate table of the United Nations model life-tables.[34] Table 22 shows clearly that plague-fatality rates of males between 20 and 59 rise with age, and fall in the age group above 60. Although the relation between age and plague mortality in Halesowen in 1349 is very similar to that which has been found among the tenants-in-chief, it does not necessarily imply that our observations are valid. The method used to obtain the data is crude and the numbers are too small. Further research on court rolls is needed to verify these figures. But if they should be confirmed it will mean that in the immediate post-plague era villages were populated by a very large group of young people below the age of 40. And this might help us to understand how the rural population succeeded in recovering so rapidly from the ravages of the Black Death.

Table 22. *The estimated age-specific mortality of male tenants in the plague of 1349*

| Age group | No. of tenants | | | | | | Death rate (per thousand) | Plague-fatality rate (per thousand) |
| | Age estimated directly | | Age by projection | | Total | | | |
	Died	Survived	Died	Survived	Died	Exposed to the plague		
20–9	11	29	2.9	18.2	13.9	61.1	227	210
30–9	15	20	4.0	12.5	19.0	51.5	369	346
40–9	15	14	4.0	8.8	19.0	41.8	454	419
50–9	16	6	4.2	3.8	20.2	30.0	673	620
60 and above	7	6	1.9	3.8	8.9	18.7	476	373
Total	64	75	17.0	47.1	81.0	203.1	399	

[34] As it is impossible to calculate the age-specific mortality of Halesowen villagers in the pre-plague period, I adopted the United Nations table used by Ohlin to test Russell's figures (Ohlin, 'No safety in numbers').

4. *The Aftermath of the Black Death*

Life in Halesowen returned more or less to normal without any social or economic upheavals, despite the devastations of the plague. The records of the court held between August 1349 and October 1350 show that the villagers harvested their crops and pastured their animals. They married and bore children in and out of wedlock. They brewed ale against the assize, trespassed against the lord and their neighbours, quarrelled and shed each other's blood, lent money and stood surety for each other, and elected jurymen and other village officials. In Halesowen, as on many other contemporary manors, the holdings of the victims of the plague did not remain vacant. Within a year, the holdings of 76 (82 per cent) deceased villagers were taken up, thirty-two by sons and daughters, twenty by brothers, wives and other relations, sixteen by guardians and eighteen by peasants who had no apparent familial links with the former tenants. Only fifteen holdings of recorded victims of the Black Death are unaccounted for in the records, but there is little doubt that these were taken up as well.[35] Between 1350 and 1360 the abbot granted twenty-five parts of holdings to local villagers, and these must have belonged to the above-mentioned 15 tenants and to others whose deaths in the plague were not recorded.[36]

Although so many vacant holdings were taken up by the survivors of the Black Death, the demand for land in Halesowen did not slacken in the immediate post-plague period. As wages in the parish rose after the plague, the abbey, which worked its demesne only with hired labour, started leasing parts of it in the early 1350s.[37] Twenty-six plots which belonged to the demesne in two big fields, Whitelyfield and Hyefield, were leased between 1351 and 1356.[38]

---

[35] The number of tenants who fell victim to the plague is 93; 88 males (81 adults and 7 minors in custody) and 5 females.

[36] The grants are recorded in BRL 346325–42 and 346814. For example, on 5.10.1353 the lord granted to Henry Don of Hasbury customary land which amounted to 8 selions for an annual rent of 8*d*. and an 18*d*. entry fine (346331). For none of these twenty-five grants of smallholdings, plots of land and parts of holdings are the names of their former holders given in the record.

[37] On 30.9.1354 John atte Broke and Robert atte Broke and on 3.10.1356 David Walsheman, John atte Broke and Thomas le Herdman, Halesowen villagers, were amerced in the court of the Borough of Halesowen for breaking the government statute concerning labour. They were not willing to work for a 'term' but only for a day (BRL 346612/614).

[38] BRL 346326–38.

In addition to a piecemeal lease of the demesne, the Abbot of Halesowen let out all his land in 1355 in the four fields of Cakemoor, and all his land in 1359 in the five common fields of Oldbury. These leases were taken by 4 wealthy villagers for a combined annual rent of £1. 6s. 8d. and an entry fine of £1. 18s. 6d.[39]

The traffic in land between the peasants in the 1350s confirms that the demand for land in the parish was strong. In the period between 1340 and 1349, twenty-seven inter-peasant sales and fifty-two leases of land were recorded in the court rolls. From 1350 to 1359 only twenty-one sales and fourteen leases were recorded. However, in the 1350s, 42 per cent of the buyers and 43 per cent of the lessees acquired whole holdings, while in the 1340s only 20 per cent of the buyers and 13 per cent of the lessees did so. This suggests that the overall volume of land transactions in the 1350s was larger than in the 1340s.[40]

There are not sufficient data to assess land values in Halesowen. But there is indirect evidence which suggests that, on average, land became cheaper. The amount of land available for the survivors of the Black Death was so large that they were more selective than peasants had been in the pre-plague period. The demand for good holdings and good land was very strong, and villagers were prepared to pay very high entry fines in order to acquire them. In 1350 William Hill entered the virgate vacant holding of the atte Lowe family in Hunnington for a £2 entry fine.[41] In 1352 he transferred the holding to Roger Hill, who was prepared to pay an entry fine of £8.[42] A few vacant holdings of half a virgate were taken for entry fines which varied between £1. 6s. 8d. and £1. 13s. 4d. These fines were four or five times higher than the average entry fine for a half

[39] The demesne lands in the four fields of Cakemoor were leased to Richard Perkins and Richard Jurdan for six years; the annual rent was 13s. 4d. and the entry fine 2s. (BRL 346335 20.5.1355). The abbot's land in 'quinque communibus campibus de Oldebury, le Heyefeld, Mutleworth, Radenhullefeld, Rugoweyfeld et le Secherfeld' was leased to Thomas son of William Sweyn and Henry Hill for an annual rent of 12s. 4d. and a £1. 10s. entry fine. It is not specified for how many years this lease was to be (345342 14.8.1359).

[40] The exact size of the land leased or sold in the inter-peasant land market is often not specified in the records. Therefore it is impossible to estimate the amount of land which changed hands in any given period. However, it would appear that, while in the pre-plague period the land market in Halesowen was brisker than in the post-plague era, in the latter period, on average, a larger amount of land was traded in each transaction.

[41] BRL 346324 30.6.1350.   [42] BRL 346328 7.3.1352.

virgate.⁴³ Two crofts which belonged to Richard Gibben of Illey, who died in the plague, were given by the lord in 1350 to 2 tenants for entry fines of 12s. and 16s. respectively.⁴⁴ At the same time the demand for second- or third-rate holdings and marginal lands in Halesowen was weak. In order to induce the villagers to take these lands, the abbot offered them without any entry fines and probably for lower rents. In 1363 he granted to Thomas le Squire from Romsley a croft to be held 'at will' for an annual rent of 9d. and 'nichil dat domino de fine quia ad verum valorem diminuit'.⁴⁵ From the total number of twenty-five vacant holdings and parts of the holdings given by the lord between 1350 and 1360, the entry fines for twelve (48 per cent) were excused.⁴⁶

If land in Halesowen became cheaper in the immediate post-plague period, that explains how the villagers were able to afford to take all the holdings which fell vacant during the Black Death, to lease demesne lands and to buy and lease whole holdings from their neighbours. But it does not explain how the peasants managed to cultivate the same amount of land as they did before the plague, despite the reduction of about 43 per cent in their number. A similar economic situation has been observed on many contemporary manors.⁴⁷ Historians have adopted two hypotheses to explain this surprising phenomenon. The first hypothesis is that a severe shortage of tenants and labour on those manors which suffered heavily during the Black Death did not develop, because there was immigration from manors which had suffered little from the plague.⁴⁸ We have seen that there is no evidence for England that plague mortality was very irregularly distributed within the same area. But even if evidence were found to substantiate this hypothesis, it would

---

⁴³ On 5.10.1356 the lord gave William Osbern's half-virgate holding in Warley to John Perkins of Ridgeacre for life for an entry fine of £1. 13s. 4d. (BRL 346338). The size of William Osbern's holding, which previously belonged to Nicholas de Radewall, is given on 12.4.1391 (346370). On 13.1.1350 William King and Isolda his wife were granted for life the half-virgate holding of John Heath of Hill for an entry fine of £1. 6s. 8d.

⁴⁴ BRL 346323 3.2.1350.   ⁴⁵ BRL 346815 8.9.1363.

⁴⁶ BRL 346323/325/328–9/331–2/337/339.

⁴⁷ See R. H. Hilton, *The Decline of Serfdom in Medieval England* (London, 1969), pp. 32–7; G. A. Holmes, *The Estates of the Higher Nobility in Fourteenth-Century England* (Cambridge, 1957), pp. 114–15. Holmes has observed that incomes of the higher nobility from their manors in the 1370s are generally not 10 per cent lower than they had been in the 1340s (p. 114).

⁴⁸ Levett, *Studies in Manorial History*, pp. 76–86.

not explain the case of Halesowen. The great majority of the vacant holdings in the manor were taken by residents, and in the 1350s there was probably net emigration from the parish. The other hypothesis is that on the eve of the Black Death the imbalance between the rural population and land resources was so serious that many villagers were underprovided with land and the marginal productivity of labour was very low. Therefore, although the population was greatly reduced by the plague, those who survived were capable of taking up the extra land which became available and of working it by using labour more efficiently.[49] It seems that this hypothesis can be applied to Halesowen, especially as the number of villagers in 1347 was almost as high as in 1313 and many of them had been land-deficient. Yet even if there was a large surplus of labour in Halesowen on the eve of the plague, it is hard to see how the peasants could have maintained the pre-plague level of agricultural production when their number was reduced by more than 40 per cent. However, their doing so becomes more plausible if the great majority of the survivors were young people below the age of 40 who could cope with extra hard work, especially during the peak periods, and consequently keep all the land in the village under cultivation.

The Black Death initiated a new phase in the demographic history of Halesowen, not so much for its ferocity as for its further outbreaks in 1361/2, 1369 and 1375, which prevented the population from recovering.

[49] Page, *Estates of Crowland Abbey*, pp. 120–5; Postan, 'Some agrarian evidence of a declining population in the later Middle Ages', *Essays on Medieval Agriculture and General Problems of the Medieval Economy* (Cambridge, 1973), pp. 208–10; A. R. Bridbury, 'The Black Death', *Econ. Hist. Rev.*, 2nd ser., XXVI (1973), 581–9.

4. The Population of Halesowen 1350–1400

1. The Demographic Trend

There are two conflicting views about the demographic trend in the last quarter of the fourteenth and in the fifteenth century. Some historians claim that the demographic recession was confined to 1348–75, while others argue that the population continued to decline well into the fifteenth century.[1] No positive evidence has been brought to show that there was a rapid population recovery after 1375; whereas the facts that in the last quarter of the fourteenth century and in the fifteenth century the prices of corn, land values and rents fell, real wages rose, the area under cultivation shrank and many small rural settlements were abandoned suggest that the population continued to decline after 1375.[2] However, in

---

[1] E. A. Kosminsky, 'The evolution of feudal rent in England from the XIth to the XVth centuries', *Past and Present*, no. 7 (1955), 12–34; J. M. W. Bean, 'Plague, population and economic decline in England in the later Middle Ages', *Econ. Hist. Rev.*, 2nd ser., XV (1963), 423–37; J. Schreiner, 'Wages and prices in England in the later Middle Ages', *Scand. Econ. Hist. Rev.* II (1954), 71–2; A. R. Bridbury, *Economic Growth: England in the Later Middle Ages* (London, 1962), p. 23. The view that the Black Death initiated a long period of demographic decline has been put forward by M. M. Postan, 'Some agrarian evidence of a declining population in the later Middle Ages', *Essays on Medieval Agriculture and General Problems of the Medieval Economy* (Cambridge, 1973), pp. 186–213; J. Saltmarsh, 'Plague and economic decline in England in the later Middle Ages', *Cambridge Hist. Journ.*, VII (1941), 23–41; I. Blanchard, 'Population change, enclosure and the early Tudor economy', *Econ. Hist. Rev.*, 2nd ser., XXIII (1970), 427–45; J. E. Thorold Rogers, *Six Centuries of Work and Wages*, 7th edn (London, 1903), pp. 221–42; J. C. Russell, *British Medieval Population* (Albuquerque, N. Mex., 1948), pp. 260–70. For an excellent summary of the controversy see J. Hatcher, *Plague, Population and the English Economy 1348–1530* (London, 1977), pp. 11–20.

[2] Postan, 'Some agrarian evidence', and his articles 'The fifteenth century' and 'Some social consequences of the Hundred Years Wars', *Essays on Medieval Agriculture and General Problems of the Medieval Economy*, pp. 41–62; Rogers, *Six Centuries of Work and Wages*; R. H. Hilton, 'Enclosure in the fifteenth century', *The English Peasantry in the Later Middle Ages* (Oxford, 1975), pp. 161–73; E. H. Phelps Brown and S. V. Hopkins, 'Seven centuries of building wages', in *Essays in Economic History*, ed. E. M. Carus-Wilson, vol. II (London, 1962); W. Beveridge, 'Wages in the Winchester manors', *Econ. Hist. Rev.*, VII (1936); Hatcher, *Plague, Population and the English Economy*, pp. 36–44; M. W. Beresford, *The Lost Villages of England* (London, 1954); T. H. Lloyd, 'Some documentary sidelights on the deserted village of Brookend', *Oxoniensia*, XXIX/XXX (1964–5), 116–28; C. C. Dyer, 'Population and agriculture on a Warwickshire manor in the later Middle Ages', *Univ. of Birmingham Hist. Journ.*, XI (1967), 113–27.

the absence of data about population movements in rural areas, we know neither the rates of the population decline nor when exactly this trend was reversed. Admittedly, Russell has used a number of manorial extents to measure the post-1377 demographic trend,[3] but we have already seen that there are good reasons to doubt his results.[4] Hollingsworth's estimate of the demographic trend between 1234 and 1489 is based on the generation replacement rates of the tenants-in-chief and therefore does not necessarily represent faithfully the movements of the rural population.[5] Thrupp has attempted to study the demographic trend in a few villages by means of male replacement rates obtained from court rolls.[6] However, as migrations intensified considerably in the post-plague period, such rates are inadequate as a measure of population changes. The underenumeration of sons, as a result of emigration, is so serious that male replacement rates obtained from any post-plague court rolls grossly overestimate the rates of the natural decrease of the village population.[7] The count of the villagers appearing in Halesowen court rolls between 1351–5 and 1391–5 shows that the average annual rate of the decrease of the population of the parish was 0.8 per thousand. But the male replacement rates obtained from the same records imply that the average annual rate of the decline of the population was 11.22 per thousand – an overestimate by a factor of 14.[8]

If the hypothesis that the demographic crisis was primarily confined to the period 1348–75 is rejected, it is necessary to explain why the population continued to decline when there were favourable conditions for its growth: land was cheap, rents were low, real wages were high and seigneurial exactions were greatly reduced.[9] Various hypotheses have been put forward to explain this

[3] Russell, *British Medieval Population*, pp. 266–70.
[4] See p. 2 above.
[5] T. H. Hollingsworth, *Historical Demography* (London, 1969), pp. 375–88.
[6] S. L. Thrupp, 'The problem of replacement-rates in late medieval English population', *Econ. Hist. Rev.*, 2nd ser., XVIII (1965), 101–19.
[7] Hollingsworth, *Historical Demography*, pp. 222–3.
[8] The 122 identified tenants whose deaths are recorded in Halesowen court rolls between 1350 and 1400 had between them 85 sons, which gives an average male replacement rate of 0.697. When we convert this figure to an annual average rate of decrease, the result is 11.22 per thousand.
[9] Hilton, *English Peasantry*, pp. 54–73; id., *Bond Men Made Free* (London, 1973), pp. 230–2; id., *The Decline of Serfdom in Medieval England* (London, 1969), pp. 32–59; C. C. Dyer, 'A redistribution of incomes in fifteenth century England', *Past and Present*, no. 39 (1968), 11–33.

phenomenon. The most common one puts the responsibility for the long demographic recession on the independent action of disease. Russell and Helleiner have argued that the recurrent outbreaks of the plague in the second half of the fourteenth century had short- and long-term negative effects on the population. In the short term they prevented the population from recovering from the devastations of the Black Death. In the long term the further visitations of the plague, which fell more heavily on infants and children than on adults, altered the age structure of the population in the last decade of the fourteenth century in such a way that it had depressing effects on the birth rates in the following decades.[10] Similar negative effects on the population in the fifteenth century were caused, according to Thrupp and Hatcher, by local as well as extra-regional outbreaks of the plague and other infectious diseases.[11] Some historians have suggested that the failure of the population to recover for such a long period might have been caused not only by a rise in mortality but also by a reduction in fertility as a result of delayed marriages and family limitation, or of a widespread reluctance of men to marry.[12]

No sufficient evidence has been brought forward to substantiate any of these hypotheses. In order to test empirically their validity, new demographic data are necessary. In this chapter an attempt will be made to show that such data can be obtained from manorial court rolls. A good series of post-plague court records enables us to measure fairly accurately the changes in the size of a rural population and to study the effects of the recurrent outbreaks of the plague. Moreover, the evidence about marriage, illegitimacy, family size, expectation of life at 20 and the age structure of the adult male population sheds some light on the demographic decline in later medieval England.

Halesowen court rolls from the second half of the fourteenth century survive in abundance: the rolls of only three years are missing, and on average the records of 11.8 court sessions are

---

[10] Russell, *British Medieval Population*, pp. 230–1, 260–70; K. H. Helleiner, 'The population of Europe from the Black Death to the eve of the vital revolution', in *Cambridge Economic History of Europe*, vol. IV (Cambridge, 1967), pp. 10–11.
[11] Thrupp, 'Problem of replacement-rates', pp. 117–18; Hatcher, *Plague, Population and the English Economy*, pp. 57–62.
[12] Helleiner, 'Population of Europe', pp. 69–71; G. Duby, *Rural Economy and Country Life in the Medieval West*, tr. C. Postan (London, 1968), pp. 309–10; Thrupp, 'Problem of replacement-rates', p. 118; E. B. Dewindt, *Land and People in Holywell-cum-Needingworth* (Toronto, 1972), pp. 191–3.

available for each year. The entries in the post-plague court rolls, however, are briefer and less informative than those in earlier rolls. Moreover, as a result of a change in the court's procedure which limited the cases for which pledges were required, the names of local villagers do not appear in the records with the same frequency as in the pre-plague period. But the manorial court continued to deal with the same wide range of cases as it had done before the Black Death, and there is no reason to assume that the population of the manor is less well represented in its records.

The demographic trend obtained from the court rolls between 1351 and 1395 shows that the adult male population, which was reduced considerably by the Black Death, was further diminished in the early sixties by 6 per cent (see table 23). The decline was arrested in the early 1370s when the population suddenly increased by 13 per cent. However, this was only a short-lived recovery. In the 1380s and 90s the population was declining once again. Undoubtedly the fluctuations in the size of the population in Halesowen were caused to some extent by migrations, which were intensified in the post-plague era. Nevertheless, the data provided by the court rolls about mortality and fertility suggest that migrations alone cannot account for the demographic trend in the second half of the fourteenth century.

Table 23. *The population movements 1351–95*

Date	No. of males	Population index
1351–5	270	100
1361–5	255	94
1371–5	289	107
1381–5	275	102
1391–5	252	93

2. Migrations

Studies of English rural society have revealed that the mobility of the peasants was intensified considerably in the post-plague period.[13] This was probably a result of the substantial population

---

[13] Hilton, *Decline of Serfdom*, pp. 32–5; J. A. Raftis, *Tenure and Mobility* (Toronto, 1964), pp. 139–82; F. M. Maitland, 'The history of a Cambridgeshire manor', *Eng. Hist. Rev.*, XXXV (1894), 423–5.

decline after the Black Death and the consequent sharp demand for tenants and labourers which gave the peasants a real opportunity to improve their conditions through migration. Evidence obtained from the court rolls suggests that in Halesowen as in other rural areas the mobility of the population accelerated after the Black Death. The post-plague court rolls, unlike the pre-plague ones, enable us to study migrations in some detail. Admittedly, migration cannot be measured, since the departure of villagers from the manor was only partially recorded in the court rolls. But since peasant surnames stabilized after the Black Death it is possible to measure immigration and to examine how and to what extent newcomers were integrated into the local community.

The number of male immigrants noted in the records between 1351 and 1395 is presented in table 24. The newcomers identified in the court rolls from 1351 to 1355 settled in Halesowen between September 1349 and December 1355. But those noted in the records from 1361–5, 1371–5, 1381–5 and 1391–5 settled in the parish during the years 1356–65, 1366–75, 1376–85 and 1386–95 respectively.

In the forty years from 1353 to 1393 an average of 5.5 immigrants settled in Halesowen each year. The mean number of males identified in the court rolls from 1351 to 1395 is 268.2, so the mean annual male immigration rate was 20.4 per thousand. In the absence of any quantitative data about immigration in other contemporary villages it is difficult to know whether this rate is high or low. In any case, it is clear that the immigration rate in Halesowen rose considerably after the Black Death. In the court rolls for 1331–5 twenty new surnames appear, and twenty-four are similarly recorded for 1345–9. If these are names of newcomers and not

Table 24. *Male immigrants identified in the court rolls 1351–95*

Date	No. of males	No. of immigrants	% of immigrants
1351–5	270	25	9.2
1361–5	255	47	18.4
1371–5	289	55	19.0
1381–5	275	51	18.5
1391–5	252	48	18.8

aliases of old residents, the mean annual male immigration rate from 1333 to 1347 was 6.9 per thousand. This rate is three times lower than the rate which prevailed in the second half of the fourteenth century.

Although we cannot count the number of villagers who left Halesowen every year, there is some evidence which suggests that emigration no less than immigration accelerated after the Black Death. During the period 1300–49 the departure of 38 males from Halesowen is recorded in the court rolls, and 31 from 1350 to 1400. The average number of males noted in the records between 1300 and 1349 is 451.4, so the mean annual rate of recorded male emigration is 1.7 per thousand. But the rate of recorded male emigration from 1350 to 1400 is 2.3 per thousand, a rise of 35 per cent. This figure probably greatly underestimates the actual rise in the emigration rate in the post-plague period. The mean number of sons over 12 per family obtained from Halesowen court rolls between 1350 and 1400 is 1.03, while the mean male replacement rate computed from the same records is 0.697 (see table 25). This means that 48 per cent of the sons identified in the records died or emigrated before the deaths of their fathers. But among the sons noted in the court rolls from 1270 to 1349 only 24 per cent died or emigrated before the deaths of their fathers.[14] The number of recorded sons who replaced their fathers thus declined in the post-plague period by 100 per cent as a result either of a sharp rise in the death rate or the emigration rate of young males. As we will presently see, the expectation of life at 20 of males in Halesowen in the

Table 25. *Male replacement rate 1350–1400*

Date	No. of dead tenants	No. of sons	Replacement rate
1350–9	18	11	0.611
1360–9	35	29	0.828
1370–9	29	18	0.620
1380–9	25	12	0.480
1390–9	22	20	0.909
Total	129	90	Mean 0.697

[14] The mean number of sons per family obtained from the court rolls between 1270 and 1349 is 1.4, but the adjusted mean replacement rate obtained from the same records is 1.128. See tables 4 and 16.

second half of the fourteenth century was higher than in the first half of the century. Therefore the decline in the number of recorded sons replacing their fathers after the Black Death indicates that the emigration rate of young males from Halesowen rose considerably.

Unfortunately, the data about female mobility obtained from the court rolls are scanty. The departure of women from the manor is rarely recorded and many female immigrants are unidentifiable because they often married local villagers and changed their surnames. However, there is no reason to suppose that the pattern of female mobility differed significantly from that of men, and we can assume that the degree of mobility among women in the post-plague period was as high as that among men.

The detailed biographies of immigrants reconstituted from the court rolls between 1350 and 1400 reveal that many of them were related to old Halesowen families by blood or by marriage. As there were constant migrations of men and women to and from Halesowen, many villagers must have had relatives outside the manor. Our sources do not allow us to study the nature of familial relationships which extended beyond the manor. However, it is reasonable to assume that those who left their native villages did not break communication with their families, especially as they often settled in neighbouring parishes. Otherwise it is difficult to explain the many cases found in the post-plague court rolls of non-resident kinsmen of deceased Halesowen tenants who came to the manor and took up their vacant holdings. For example, William de Baresfen from Langley, probably a half yardlander, had three daughters Alice, Sibilia and Margaret.[15] Alice and Sibilia married in Halesowen, but Margaret emigrated to the neighbouring village of Rowley Regis and there married John Turhill. In 1353 William de Baresfen died and his holding was divided equally between his three daughters. Margaret and John Turhill took their share of the family holding and settled in Langley.[16] Thomas Henry a quarter yardlander

---

[15] William de Baresfen (1323–53) (BRL 346244–331). William's father Philip de Baresfen had entered the family holding in 1301 for an entry fine of 13s. 4d., which suggests that the land amounted to a virgate. But in 1333 William sold half of his holding (346264 28.4.1333).

[16] BRL 346331 5.10.1353. John Turhill (1353–1400) was a successful husbandman. He leased a virgate of land and four plots of pasture land from the lord and other villagers for which he paid £3. 11s. 6d. as an entry fine. In 1400, John's brother-in-law transferred to his son Thomas his part of the Baresfen half-yardland holding (346337 27.1.1400).

from Oldbury had three daughters. Of these, Agnes and Juliana married on the manor but Alice emigrated to Derby. Thomas died in the Black Death and Agnes and Juliana shared the holding. But in 1362 Alice's son William de Derby came to Halesowen and claimed his mother's share in the family holding. The manorial court accepted his claim and he took the third part of his grandfather's quarter yardland for a 3s. entry fine.[17] Richard Schirlet a yardlander from Hunnington died in the Black Death. His year-old son Henry was taken into the custody of Roger Hill for nineteen years.[18] But Henry died in 1357 and the holding passed to his next of kin William son of John Schirlet.[19] William died in the mid-1360s without issue and the family holding passed in 1367 to Richard Pachet a kinsman of the Schirlets who lived in Ludlow.[20] Richard Pachet settled in Halesowen, married a local girl and played an important role in village government.[21] Despite the ravages of the Black Death, well-established old Halesowen families were often large enough so that at least a few of their members survived the plague. But in the 1360s and 70s the last representatives of a number of such families were wiped out by the recurrent outbreaks of the plague. Therefore during this period the number of outsiders who came to Halesowen to inherit land increased. Among the 221 immigrants identified in the court rolls from 1350 to 1400 at least 42 (19 per cent) received their holdings by inheritance and, of these, 25 arrived in the parish in the 1360s and 70s.

In addition to newcomers related to old Halesowen families by blood, many immigrants became members of local families through marriage. In August 1349 Alice the daughter of Richard Clerk inherited the yardland holding of her kinsman Thomas Symon, who died in the Black Death.[22] A year later she came to the court with her husband Philip Wilkyns, a newcomer, and surrendered the holding to the lord. Then she and her husband got the holding back

---

[17] BRL 346343 5.2.1362.
[18] BRL 346322 29.7.1349.   [19] BRL 346339 28.6.1357.
[20] William son of John Schirlet is noted for the last time in the records of 1364. Richard Pachet of Ludlow is mentioned in the court rolls for the first time in 1367, as an ale-taster (BRL 336347 6.1.1367). It is very probable that by then he had already obtained the Schirlet holding, since in 1371 he gave the lord 12d. for an inquiry to establish that he was the true heir of Richard Schirlet (346350 29.10.1371).
[21] Richard Pachet (1367–1400) is mentioned in the records (BRL 346347–377). He acted as an ale-taster, juror and assessor. The owner of a large herd, he often lent money to his neighbours.
[22] BRL 346320 19.8.1349.

for life.[23] In 1381 John Colleson from Cradley, who married Lucy the daughter of John Hill of Romsley, came to the court and swore fealty for his wife's holding.[24] Robert Curliter who settled in the township of Hill in the late 1360s obtained a holding on the manor through his marriage to Milicentia the daughter of Philip Hill a yardlander from the township of Hill.[25] At least 75 (34 per cent) of the immigrants mentioned in the court records between 1350 and 1400 obtained their holdings in Halesowen by marrying local women.

Raftis has observed that the proportion of newcomers among the inhabitants of Ramsey village in Huntingdonshire rose considerably after the Black Death. The rise in the immigration rate, according to Raftis, caused social tension and a marked increase in violence in the village. This hypothesis is based on the assumption that the village community was incapable of absorbing and assimilating a large number of immigrants. In order to substantiate this assumption he has claimed that the post-plague court records reveal that newcomers were highly represented among those involved in violence.[26] Raftis may be correct, but the evidence brought by him is inconclusive, as he has failed to show that the proportion of newcomers involved in violence was higher than their proportion in the population. It is clear that newcomers in Halesowen were not involved in violence any more than old residents were. In the courts held between 1371 and 1375, 26 villagers were presented for assault and bloodshed but only 5 of them (19 per cent) were newcomers. In the years 1381–5 and 1391–5 newcomers constituted 16 per cent and 10 per cent respectively of those presented for assault and bloodshed. But we have seen that among the males identified in the court rolls in 1371–5, 1381–5 and 1391–5, the percentage of immigrants amounted to 19, 18.5 and 18.8 respectively. Moreover, there is some evidence which suggests that immigrants who settled in Halesowen in the second half of the fourteenth century were well integrated into the local community.

The major public offices in Halesowen were filled by members of a small group of families which dominated and led the village community for generations. In the pre-plague period it was quite

[23] BRL 346324 30.6.1350.
[24] BRL 346358 1.5.1381. John Colleson (1381–8 /94d.): 346358–822.
[25] BRL 346350 14.1.1372. Robert Curliter (1367–9): 346347–77.
[26] J. A. Raftis, *Warboys* (Toronto, 1974), pp. 219–21, and his article 'Changes in an English village after the Black Death', *Medieval Studies*, XXIX (1967), 163–5.

rare for immigrants to be elected as representatives of townships or as jurors and reeves, but after the Black Death it became fairly common. The lists of reeves, jurors and court assessors obtained from the court records between 1350 and 1400 include the names of 122 villagers who were elected to fill these offices 907 times. Among the 122 notables 28 (23 per cent) were newcomers. For example, Hugo Okene settled in Oldbury in the early 1360s. In 1367 he was elected to act as an ale-taster and in 1368 as a court assessor.[27] Henry de Lodely (Ludlow) settled in Hasbury about 1368. Four years later he was elected to serve as a juror and as an assessor. Between 1372 and 1393 he acted ten times as a juror, six times as an assessor and once as a reeve.[28] Both Bartholomew Cook (1379–1400) and Philip Wilkyns (1350–9) are noted in the court rolls for the first time as jurors. The former acted twenty-one times as a juror and seven times as an assessor, and the latter was elected eleven times as a juror and three times as an assessor.[29] These immigrants, and others who took an active part in village government, were well-off peasants. But this is not the only reason why they were accepted into the ruling elite of the village shortly after their arrival on the manor. All of them without exception were related to old Halesowen families by marriage or by blood. Hugo Okene married Agnes Symon of Oldbury and thus became a member of one of the richest and most influential families in Halesowen.[30] Henry of Ludlow was a kinsman of the Dons, an old well-to-do family from Hasbury.[31] Philip Wilkyns was married to Alice the daughter of John Clerk a yardlander from Oldbury.[32] And Bartholomew Cook acquired his yardland holding through his marriage to Alice of Oldbury.[33]

[27] BRL 346344/348.
[28] BRL 346347/351/354/363/366/367/369/372.
[29] Bartholomew Cook: BRL 346357/358/359/360/363/364/368/369/370/371/372/373/374/375/377/378. Philip Wilkyns: 346325/327/329/331/332/334/335/336/337/338/339/341/342.
[30] In 1372, Hugo and Agnes his wife gave the abbot 40*d*. for recognition of Agnes's right in Thomas Symon's virgate holding (BRL 346350 23.3.1372). In 1375 on the death of Alice Wilkyns, they entered the holding of Thomas Symon (346353 1.8.1375).
[31] His familial relationship with the Dons is mentioned on 28.5.1393 (BRL 346372).
[32] BRL 346324 30.6.1350. He and his wife took the custody and the holding of her minor brother Richard (346342 1.5.1359).
[33] In 1397, Bartholomew Cook's wife Alice died, and the messuage and the virgate holding he was holding in her right were taken by the lord (BRL 346375 27.5.1397).

The election of immigrants related to old Halesowen families to positions of responsibility and authority soon after their arrival on the manor suggests that they were regarded by the villagers as members of local families rather than as aliens, and consequently were integrated fully and smoothly into the local community. And as the majority of the newcomers who settled in Halesowen between 1350 and 1400 were related by blood or marriage to local families, there is no reason to assume that the village community did not absorb and assimilate them.

We saw in table 23 that the inflow of immigrants who settled in Halesowen between 1351 and 1395 was constant. We can therefore assume that the fluctuations in the size of the population of the parish during this period were not caused by immigration. On the other hand, these fluctuations might have been caused by emigration, which cannot be measured. For example, the number of males identified in the court rolls in 1361–5 is lower by 5.9 per cent than the number of males noted in 1351–5. As the mortality of adults in the 1350s was fairly low, the decline of the population of Halesowen in the early 1360s might have been caused by net emigration in the 1350s. Similarly, the rise of the population of the parish in the 1370s and its decline in the 1380s and 1390s might have been a result of changes in the emigration rate. Nevertheless, since it can be shown that there are other demographic factors which provide a plausible explanation for the movements of the population of Halesowen during the period under study, we can assume that emigration was not the determining factor.

3. Mortality

It is well known that the first attack of the plague in 1348–9 was followed by other outbreaks of the disease which affected England as a whole. However, it is not clear how many such outbreaks occurred. According to Russell there were only three general outbreaks of the plague: in 1361, 1369 and 1375.[34] But on evidence drawn from literary sources, J. M. W. Bean and others have claimed that the plague attacked the country again in 1390, 1400 and

---

But it is probable that Bartholomew paid the customary fines and regained the land, since he was elected again as juror in 1398 (346376 2.10.1398). It is not clear to which family his wife belonged.

[34] *British Medieval Population*, pp. 276–8.

several other times during the fifteenth century.[35] The data obtained from Halesowen court rolls between 1350 and 1400 enable us to find how many times the population of the parish was hit by the plague and to estimate its losses. In addition it is possible to determine whether the mean annual adult death rate in the second half of the fourteenth century was higher or lower than in the pre-plague period.

The number of males whose deaths are observed directly or indirectly in the court rolls from 1350 to 1400 is presented in table 26 and fig. 11. We can see in fig. 11 that there were three periods of high mortality in Halesowen during the period under study: 1361–3, 1367–9 and 1373–5. Undoubtedly the heavy mortality in these years was caused by the plagues of 1361–2, 1369 and 1375. However, it is difficult to trace the course of these plagues and to estimate accurately the death toll which they took, since not all the deaths were recorded in the month in which they occurred. For

Table 26. *Male deaths obtained from Halesowen court rolls 1350–1400*

Date	No. of courts	No. of deaths
1350–2	39	3
1353–5	46	6
1356–8	48	4
(1359)	11	5
1361–3	30	15
(1364)	10	1
1367–9	37	19
1370–2	29	5
1373–5	38	13
1376–5	34	8
1379–81	45	6
1382–4	38	8
1385–7	41	9
1388–90	31	7
1391–3	35	7
1394–6	27	8
1397–9	18	5
(1400)	9	5
Total	566	134

[35] Bean, 'Plague, population and economic decline', pp. 427–30. See also Hollingsworth, *Historical Demography*, p. 385.

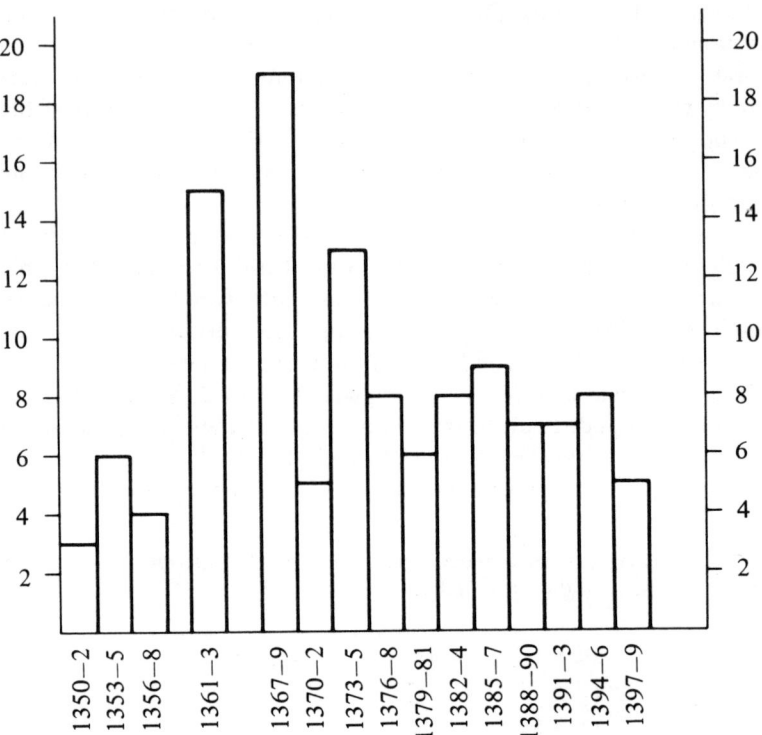

Fig. 11 Male deaths obtained from the court rolls 1350–1400 (three-year periods)

example, we know that William Holy died in the plague which erupted in the summer of 1369, yet his death was not recorded until May 1370.[36] The observations following should therefore be regarded as numerical hypotheses which need verification against comparable data from other villages in the West Midlands.

It seems that the plague invaded the parish of Halesowen for the second time in the winter of 1361–2. The deaths of 9 male tenants are recorded in the court rolls from September 1361 to October 1362. But there is good evidence that at least 4 other tenants lost

---

[36] The death is recorded on 15.5.1370 (BRL 346349). In the court held on 8.4.1394 it is stated that William died in the 'Second Pestilence' (346374).

their lives in the plague, although their deaths are not recorded.[37] In the court records of 1361–4, 140 males were identified as resident tenants. Therefore the death rate of males over 20 in the plague was at least 93 per thousand. But since underenumeration of deaths in our records is probably 51 per cent, the death rate was about 140 per thousand.[38] This estimate is comparable with other estimates of the losses suffered among clergymen and peasants in 1361–2. The death rate among the clergy of the diocese of York in the second plague was estimated at between 94 and 133 per thousand, and on the Hampshire manor of Bishop's Waltham at 130 per thousand.[39] On the other hand, the tenants-in-chief, who did not suffer as many losses as the clergy and the peasantry in the first visitation of the plague paid a higher death toll in 1361 – as high as 227 per thousand.[40]

The third plague probably hit the parish in the summer of 1369. In the court rolls from January to June 1369 no deaths are recorded, but in July the deaths of 8 males and 7 females are recorded. The deaths of another 8 men and 2 women are registered in later courts, and they probably also fell victims to the plague. The number of male tenants identified in the court rolls from 1361 to 1364 is 140, and 151 in the court rolls from 1371 to 1375. Therefore we can assume that 145 tenants were exposed to the plague of 1369. If this assumption is right, the rate of mortality among the males over 20 was at least 110 per thousand. But as there was a 51 per cent underregistration of deaths, the actual rate was about 167 per thousand. Unfortunately, data about the mortality in 1369 in other

---

[37] The 4 tenants are mentioned in the court rolls regularly until 1361–2 and then their widows are noted. For example, Philip Coldwell from Ridgeacre is noted for the first time in 1336 (BRL 346278 16.10.1336) and for the last time on 6.10.1361. On 27.4.1362 his widow Juliana was amerced for default of court (ibid.). This implies that Philip died between October 1361 and April 1362 when the plague was probably raging in the parish.

[38] In the court rolls of 1361–4, 140 male tenants are noted; in 1371–5, 151, and in 1391–2, 121. We can therefore assume that the mean number of tenants resident in the parish from 1350 to 1400 was about 137. The mean annual number of recorded deaths of tenants in the court rolls from 1350 to 1400 is 2.8, which gives a minimum mean annual death rate of males over 20 of 20.4 per thousand. But the expectation of life at 20 of tenants who died between 1380 and 1400 was 32.5 years, which in a stable population corresponds to an annual death rate of 30.7 per thousand. Consequently, a 51 per cent underregistration of deaths can be assumed.

[39] Russell, *British Medieval Population*, p. 222; J. Z. Titow, *English Rural Society 1200–1350* (London, 1969), p. 70.

[40] Russell, *British Medieval Population*, p. 217.

rural areas are not available. But the death rate among the tenants-in-chief in 1369 has been estimated at 131 per thousand and among the clergy in the diocese of York at between 104 and 156 per thousand.[41]

In 1375 the villagers experienced the century's fourth and last outbreak of the plague. Although it is not clear when exactly the disease erupted, there is little doubt that mortality in 1375 was high. In the court rolls of 1374 no male deaths are recorded, but there are 6 in 1375 and 6 in 1376. This is the highest number of deaths recorded in the court rolls for any two consecutive years between 1370 and 1400. As 151 male tenants are identified in the court rolls in 1371–5, the death rate of males over 20 in the fourth plague was at least 79 per thousand. But if we allow for underregistration of deaths the rate rises to 120 per thousand. Russell has estimated the death rate of the tenants-in-chief in 1375 at 125 per thousand.[42]

To sum up, in the plague of 1361–2 the death rate of males over 20 in Halesowen was about 135 per thousand; in 1369, 161 per thousand; in 1375, 117 per thousand. Although these observations are crude and the margin of error is fairly wide they suggest that the mortality of adults in the second, third and fourth outbreaks of the plague was much lower than in the first outbreak.

It was possible to estimate the ages of 38 tenants who died in the plagues of 1361–2, 1369 and 1375. The results are presented in table 27. If the age structure of the population did not change significantly between 1349 and 1375, our figures suggest that (as in the first outbreak of the plague) the risk of death rose with age.

Table 27. *The estimated ages of males who died in the plagues of 1361–2, 1369 and 1375*

Age	Number of dead
20–9	3
30–9	5
40–9	9
50–9	12
60 and over	9
Total	38

[41] Ibid. pp. 222, 217. [42] Ibid.

The Population of Halesowen 1350–1400   129

Russell calculated the age-specific mortality in the four plagues and stated that 'as men grew older the plague was more fatal to them'.[43] But as the samples obtained from Halesowen court rolls and from the records of the Inquisitiones Post Mortem are too small, more data are needed to verify this hypothesis.

Although deaths of women are underregistered in our records, there is some evidence which suggests that the second, third and fourth plagues did not spare the women of Halesowen. The mean annual number of recorded deaths of women between 1350 and 1400 is 2.2. In the court rolls of 1361–2 the deaths of only 3 women are recorded. However, our sources reveal that the mortality of women rose significantly in the third and fourth plagues: in 1369–70 the deaths of 9 women are recorded and in 1375–6 there are 6. Therefore it is reasonable to assume that the low number of the deaths of women recorded in 1361–2 was the result of omission, and that the second plague like the later ones took a heavy toll of life among the women of the parish.

Data about infant and child mortality in the plagues which followed the Black Death are not available in Halesowen court rolls. However, it would seem that infants and children were as susceptible to these plagues as they were to the pestilence of 1349. Contemporary chroniclers reported that the plagues of 1361–2 and 1369 fell very heavily on infants and young children[44] and the disease of 1361 was even called 'la mortalité des enfauntz'.[45] It is hard to believe that a disease which took a heavy toll of life among young children in England and on the Continent spared the children of Halesowen. Moreover, the hypothesis that the rate of child mortality in the plagues of 1361–2, 1369 and 1375 was very high explains the marriage and population trends obtained from the court rolls between 1375 and 1395 and the unusual age structure of the adult male population in 1393.[46]

Despite the exposure of the population of Halesowen to three outbreaks of the plague in the second half of the fourteenth century, the mean annual death rate of adults was lower than in the pre-plague period. The mean number of male tenants identified in the

[43] Ibid. pp. 219–20.
[44] The descriptions of the chronicles are summed up in C. A. Creighton, *A History of Epidemics in Britain from A.D. 664 to the Present Time*, vol. I (Cambridge, 1891), pp. 114–24, 302.
[45] *The Anonimalle Chronicle*, ed. V. H. Galbraith (Manchester, 1927), p. 50.
[46] See sect. 8 below.

court rolls from 1300 to 1348 is 210, and the deaths of an average 5.2 tenants are recorded each year. From 1350 to 1395 the mean number of male tenants is 137, and the deaths of an average 2.8 tenants are recorded each year. The mean annual rate of male deaths obtained from the court rolls from 1300 to 1348 is therefore 24.8 per thousand, and from 1350 to 1400 only 20.4 per thousand, a decrease of 16 per cent. In order to find whether this decrease reflects a fall in the actual death rate of adults in the second half of the fourteenth century and is not merely a change in the registration of deaths, we can compare the life expectancy at 20 of the villagers who died between 1300 and 1348 and of those who died between 1350 and 1400.

We have seen that the life expectancy at 20 of tenants whose deaths are recorded in the court rolls 1300–48 was 30.2 years. But as the deaths of smallholders and cottagers were underrecorded in the court rolls, we estimated the life expectancy of males at 20 at between 25 and 28 years. But the life expectancy at 20 of 105 tenants from a sample of 134 males whose deaths are recorded in the court rolls between 1350 and 1400 was 32.5 years. Further, while in the pre-plague period there was a marked difference between the life expectancy at 20 of poor tenants and that of middling and rich ones, this difference was greatly reduced in the second half of the fourteenth century. Thomas Fisher a smallholder from Oldbury died in 1363 when he was about 62 years old.[47] When Thomas's son John died in 1393, his heir was excused from paying a mortuary, since John was too poor. Yet when John Fisher died he was at least 50 years old.[48] Thomas atte Mersh from Hawne, a tenant of small means, died in 1399 at 66.[49] In our sample of 105 tenants, 20 (19 per cent) were smallholders and cottagers, and their expectation of life at 20 was 30.6 years. Therefore we can assume that the actual life expectancy at 20 of males in Halesowen in the period 1350–1400 was about 32.5 years. This means that after the Black Death there was an increase of between 4.5 and 7.5 years in the life expectancy of 20-year-old males in Halesowen.

[47] BRL 346240 13.5.1321 – 346344 8.3.1363.
[48] John Fisher entered his father's messuage and 4 'dieta' of land on 8.3.1363 for an entry fine of 2s. He died on 19.11.1393 holding a cottage and a few parcels of land. As 'he had nothing', his son Richard was excused from paying death duties (BRL 346344–73).
[49] BRL 346331 5.10.1353 – 346377 22.10.1399. His native holding amounted to three cottages. He was often heavily in debt and in arrears of rents and fines.

This rise in the life expectancy of adults in Halesowen in the second half of the fourteenth century was probably a result of an improvement in the living standard in the village. As land was relatively abundant, the proportion of families with a quarter virgate of land or less decreased; whereas before the Black Death such families constituted 43 per cent of the total number of families in the village, after the Black Death they were only 35 per cent.[50] Furthermore, the income and consequently the living standard of smallholders and cottagers must have risen with the rise in wages after the plague. But references to peasants who were too poor to pay fines and a large number of pleas of debt found in the court rolls from 1350 to 1400 show clearly that poverty did not disappear from Halesowen in the post-plague period.[51] There is no doubt that when harvests failed in the second half of the fourteenth century many families experienced grave hardships. But as cottagers and smallholders did not suffer from chronic malnutrition as they probably did in the first half of the fourteenth century, crop failures did not cause such high mortality as in that period. For example, Phelps Brown's index shows that prices, which were at a low level between 1376 and 1390, rose considerably in 1391.[52] Evidence obtained from the court rolls shows that there was a grave harvest failure in Halesowen in 1390. In the records of the years 1389–90, nine pleas of debt and three land transactions are registered; but in 1391–2 the number of pleas of debt rises to thirty-seven and that of land transactions to eight. Yet the number of deaths recorded in 1391–2 does not rise: in 1391 the deaths of 2 males and 3 females are recorded, and in 1392 those of 3 males and 3 females.[53]

4. *The Marriage Trend*

The marriage fines recorded in the court rolls from the second half of the fourteenth century can be used to trace the marriage trend in

---

[50] See sect. 6 below.

[51] The references to the poverty of tenants are usually found in the cases in which payment of heriot or mortuary was excused by the lord. For example, on 27.4.1369 William Hill a quarter yardlander from Romsley died, and since 'nichil habuit pro herieto' the heriot was not levied on his heir (BRL 346816).

[52] E. H. Phelps Brown and Sheila V. Hopkins, 'Seven centuries of the prices of consumables, compared with builders' wage-rates', in *Essays in Economic History*, ed. E. M. Carus-Wilson, vol. II (London, 1962), p. 184.

[53] BRL 346368–72.

the parish, on the assumption that the changes in the number of merchets reflect similar changes in the number of marriages contracted by the villagers. This assumption might be true for 1349–85, since in this period the abbey regularly levied merchets on its customary tenants. The rate of the fine, which was 2s. before the Black Death, was raised to 6s. 8d.[54] In the last fifteen years of the century – probably as a result of the tenants' resistance, which assumed a violent form in 1386 when the bondmen of Romsley rebelled – the abbot had to stop exacting merchets.[55] In the court rolls from 1349 to 1385, some 57 marriage fines are recorded, but from 1386 to 1400 only 1. We can therefore use the marriage fines to trace the marriage trend in Halesowen during the period 1349–85, but can only guess the direction of the trend in the last fifteen years of the century.

The number of observed and estimated merchets obtained from the court rolls between 1349 and 1399 is presented in table 28. In fig. 12 the merchets estimated from the court rolls between 1300 and 1400 are presented as a percentage of the males identified in the same records.

We can see in fig. 12 that in the period which immediately followed the Black Death, proportionally more marriages were contracted in Halesowen than in any other three-year period in the fourteenth century. A similar upsurge of marriages after the Black Death occurred in the parish of Givry in Burgundy. The plague which devastated the parish between August and November 1348 caused the deaths of more than 60 per cent of the population. In 1349, 86 marriages were recorded in the parish register, whereas before the plague the annual average of marriages was only 26.[56]

The number of marriages in Halesowen rose sharply again in the

[54] Occasionally, poor tenants and villagers who enjoyed the special favour of the lord paid between 12d. and 40d. as merchet. For example, the daughter of Roger Crone a quarter yardlander payed a merchet of 12d. in 1363 (BRL 346344 8.3.1363). In 1362 the abbot allowed Juliana the daughter of Thomas Squire a yardlander from Romsley to pay only 2s. as merchet, since her father 'est amicus domini' (346814 28.4.1362). On the other hand, rich girls like Agnes the daughter of Thomas Hikemon of Romsley paid as much as 9s. for the lord's permission to marry (346359 5.2.1382).
[55] Our knowledge of the revolt comes from a record of proceedings before the justices of oyer and terminer, of which the abbot kept a copy. See BRL 347156 and Hilton, *English Peasantry*, p. 63.
[56] P. Gras, 'Le registre paroissial de Givry (1334–1357) et la peste noire en Bourgogne', *Bibliothèque de l'Ecole des Chartes*, C (1939), 295–308.

Table 28. *Observed and estimated merchets obtained from the court rolls 1349–1400*

Year	No. of available court sessions	No. of estimated court sessions	No. of observed merchets	No. of estimated merchets
1349 (from May)	11	11	5	5.0
1350	16	19	2	3.6
1351	8	18	3	6.7
1352	15	17	5	5.7
1353	7	18	0	0.0
1354	14	17	2	2.4
1355	17	17	2	2.0
1356	18	18	1	1.0
1357	16	17	0	0.0
1358	13	18	0	0.0
1359	11	18	2	3.3
1360	–	–	–	–
1361	4	18	1	4.5
1362	9	18	1	2.0
1363	16	17	6	6.4
1364	10	18	1	1.8
1365	–	–	–	–
1366	–	–	–	–
1367	7	18	1	2.6
1368	14	17	4	4.9
1369	15	18	2	3.6
1370	12	18	0	0.0
1371	4	18	0	0.0
1372	13	17	2	2.6
1373	15	18	0	0.0
1374	12	18	3	4.5
1375	9	18	0	0.0
1376	4	18	0	0.0
1377	14	18	1	1.3
1378	16	18	0	0.0
1379	14	16	1	1.1
1380	15	15	1	1.0
1381	16	16	1	1.0
1382	15	15	4	4.0
1383	13	16	2	2.5
1384	10	15	3	4.5
1385	15	15	1	1.0
1386	12	16	0	0.0
1387	14	16	0	0.0
1388	10	15	0	0.0
1389	7	15	0	0.0
1390	11	15	0	0.0
1391	11	15	0	0.0
1392	13	15	1	1.1
1393	11	15	0	0.0
1394	10	16	0	0.0
1395	4	16	0	0.0
1396	13	16	0	0.0
1397	8	15	0	0.0
1398	2	15	0	0.0
1399	8	15	0	0.0
1400	9	15	0	0.0
Total	561	931	58	80.1

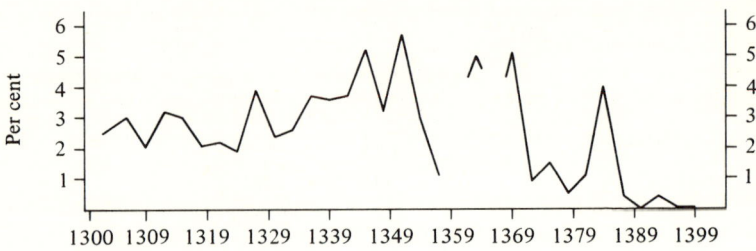

Fig. 12 The marriage trend in Halesowen 1300–99, based on estimated marriage fines presented as a percentage of the males identified in the court rolls (three-year periods)

years 1361–3 as a reaction to the second visitation of the plague in 1361–2. It would seem that during the first two decades following the Black Death the marriage rate in the parish was high. In the court rolls from the period 1325–48, in which the population of the parish was rapidly recovering from the losses it suffered in the 1310s, the mean annual number of estimated merchets constitutes 1.25 per cent of the males identified in these records. In the court rolls from 1349 to 1369 the mean annual number of estimated merchets constitutes 1.2 per cent of the males noted in the same records.

As many marriages were contracted in Halesowen between 1349 and 1369, the birth rate must have been at a high level and the number of marriages should have increased from the late 1360s onwards. And indeed we can see in fig. 12 that during the years 1367–9 the marriage rate was as high as in 1361–3. But in the 1370s and the 1380s the trend reversed and the number of marriages declined. Whereas the mean annual number of estimated merchets obtained from the court rolls between 1349 and 1369 is 3.1, between 1370 and 1385 it is only 1.5. The marriage rate in Halesowen declined during this period as a result of the recurrent outbreaks of the plague which followed the Black Death. As these plagues took a much higher toll of life among children than among adults, the proportion of young adults in the village in the period 1370–85 was lower than in the period 1349–69. Therefore the number of marriages decreased during the years 1370–85 and the same trend probably continued in the late 1380s and in the 1390s.

The hypotheses adopted to explain the marriage trend in

Halesowen are compatible with the demographic trend obtained from the court rolls in 1351–95. The fact that more villagers are identified in the court rolls from 1371–5 than in the records from 1351–5 and 1361–5 (see table 23) suggests that the Black Death was followed by a boom in the birth rate. And the fall in the number of villagers noted in the court rolls from 1381–5 and 1391–5, although the population of the parish was free from further attacks of the plague, indicates that many of those born in the 1350s and 60s lost their lives in the second, third and fourth plagues.

5. *The Age at Marriage*

We have found evidence which suggests that although land was in very short supply in Halesowen in the pre-plague period, the villagers married in their late teens or early twenties. It is reasonable to assume that in the post-plague period, as land became relatively abundant and wages rose, the peasants married as early in life as in the previous period, or even earlier. In the court rolls from the second half of the fourteenth century there is evidence which supports this hypothesis.

In the pre-plague period many sons of Halesowen villagers did not wait for their father's death or retirement in order to acquire a holding. However, since there was a shortage of land, sons of smallholders and of middling peasants sometimes had to wait until the death of their father before they were able to obtain land. In the post-plague period the number of sons who acquired a holding during the father's lifetime increased. In the court rolls between 1270 and 1349 evidence was found that among the 740 sons who settled in Halesowen, 283 (38 per cent) did so while their fathers were alive. There is evidence that of the 261 sons noted in the court rolls from 1350 to 1400, 141 settled in Halesowen. Of the latter, 76 sons (54 per cent) did so while their fathers were still alive. The number of sons who settled in the village while their fathers were living rose after the Black Death, probably as a result of the increase in the supply of land, which enabled young villagers not only from well-to-do families but also from families of small means to acquire land. The fact that 54 per cent of the sons who settled in the parish after the Black Death did so while their fathers were living, despite the high rate of infant and child mortality during the period 1349–75, suggests that practically every young villager who reached the age of 20 and wished to settle in Halesowen acquired a holding without any difficulty. If on obtaining a house and some land each young man in the parish immediately married, his age at first marriage in the post-plague period was about 20.

This hypothesis can be tested by using genealogies of local families reconstituted from the court rolls between 1350 and 1400. Robert Hill a quarter yardlander from Romsley is noted for the first time in the court records as landholder in 1367, two years before the death of his father William.[57] In 1384 Robert died and his son John, who was probably between the ages of 17 and 19, took up the family holding.[58] It seems that at that time John married and had a son, since twelve years later in 1396 his son was amerced for trespassing against the lord.[59] This indicates that he was at least 12 years old; otherwise the court would have amerced his father. Richard Pitway a half yardlander from Romsley appears in the court rolls for the first time as tenant in 1344.[60] In 1363 his son Thomas, who was between the ages of 19 and 21, married Agnes the daughter of John Yeldentre.[61] John Hiddeley (1349–94d.) from Lapal inherited his brother's yardland holding when he died in the Black Death.[62] In 1369 John was amerced 12d. for marrying off his 20-year-old son Henry without permission.[63] I found by applying this method that among the 261 sons noted in the court rolls between 1350 and 1400 at least 32 (12 per cent) married at about the age of 20. As the genealogical method is effective only in cases where the first-born sons survived to maturity, the percentage of men married at about 20 obtained from the records probably represents a general trend.

Genealogies of local families reveal a significant number of cases in which women married even earlier than men. William Gregory (1349–86d.) a smallholder from the township of Hunnington is noted for the first time in the records as landholder in 1349.[64] In 1368 his daughter Felicity paid 40d. as a marriage fine, which shows that she married between the ages of 19 and 21.[65] Similarly, Juliana

---

[57] He was amerced for default of court (BRL 346347 6.10.1367).
[58] BRL 346821 1.7.1384.   [59] BRL 346823 18.4.1396.
[60] He was amerced for default of court (BRL 346812 2.7.1344). Richard died in 1375 leaving a holding of half a virgate which was taken by his son Thomas for a 6s. 8d. entry fine (346817 3.8.1375).
[61] BRL 346815 8.9.1363.
[62] BRL 346322 29.7.1349.   [63] BRL 346348 28.4.1369.
[64] Noted in the court rolls as tenant from 1349 to 1368 (BRL 346322–65).
[65] BRL 346348 28.4.1369.

the daughter of William Adam (1351–1400d.) was between 12 and 15 when she married in 1363.[66] Agnes the daughter of Adam Hurne (1338–68/70d.) was between 13 and 16 when she married in 1351.[67] And Johanna the daughter of John Hychcok (1363–87d.) was between 14 and 17 when she married in 1377.[68] Of the 119 daughters noted in the court rolls from 1350 to 1400, at least 15 (13 per cent) married between the ages of 12 and 19. It is likely that the mean age at first marriage fell after the Black Death, since girls of small means were able to marry as early as their better-off neighbours.

If the age at first marriage of women fell significantly in the post-plague period, as our data seem to suggest, there must have been an age gap of a few years between the spouses. A quite similar marriage pattern prevailed in the villages around Prato in Tuscany in 1372; the mean age at first marriage of males was 22.3 and of females 15.3.[69]

Thrupp has gained the impression from a study of the manorial court rolls of Wilburton on the edge of the Isle of Ely that there was some lassitude on the part of village men in the late fourteenth and early fifteenth century about remarrying after a first spouse had died.[70] However, in the Halesowen post-plague court rolls there is evidence which reveals a strong desire on the part of the peasants who lost their wives to remarry. Juliana the wife of Philip Boury of Ridgeacre (1359–1400) died in 1378.[71] In 1382 Philip's second wife died, but in the same year he married his third wife Margaret (1382–96).[72] The first wife of Henry de Lodeley (1358–93/7d.) from Hasbury died in 1370.[73] Alice his second wife is mentioned in the court rolls between 1373 and 1379.[74] We do not know when Alice died, but in the court records of 1393 a third wife Agnes is

[66] William Adam is noted in the records from 1351 to 1400 (BRL 346328–77). Juliana his daughter paid a marriage fine on 2.8.1363 (346344).

[67] Adam Hurne is noted in the records from 1338 to 1368 (BRL 346285–347). In the court held on 27.4.1370 his widow Agnes bought half a yardland holding (346349). We can therefore assume that Adam died between 1368 and 1370. His daughter Agnes paid a marriage fine on 5.10.1351 (346327).

[68] John Hychcok is noted in the court rolls from 1363 to 1387 (BRL 346343–365). His daughter paid 8s. as a marriage fine on 29.7.1377 (346354).

[69] D. Herlihy and C. Klapisch-Zuber, *Les toscans et leurs familles* (Paris, 1978), p. 207.

[70] 'Problem of replacement-rates', p. 112.

[71] BRL 346355 28.4.1378.

[72] BRL 346539 26.2.1382. Margaret was amerced many times between 1382 and 1396 for brewing ale against the assize (346359–74).

[73] BRL 346349 15.5.1370.   [74] BRL 346531 15.6.1373 and 28.4.1379.

noted.[75] Among the 253 heads of families identified in the court rolls from 1350 to 1400, at least 25 (10 per cent) married more than once. The majority of these peasants belonged to the top rank of village society. Evidence about second and third marriages of less-well-off villagers is not available in the court rolls, not because they did not remarry, but probably because the names of their wives simply do not appear in the records as frequently as the names of the wives of their richer neighbours.[76]

In the pre-plague period, as land was in short supply, widows with land usually found no difficulty in remarrying. But after the Black Death, as more land became available, they seemed less attractive as spouses. A number of Halesowen widows probably succeeded in remarrying because they were very well endowed with land and were still reasonably young. For example, Alice the daughter of John atte Lyche a wealthy villager from Romsley was married to Roger Spring (1357–80d.); after his death she married Roger atte Lowe (1334–96d.) a widower from Hunnington.[77] She could have been in her thirties at the time of her second marriage. Among the 39 widows noted in the court rolls for 1349–1400, at least 10 (26 per cent) remarried. But of 154 widows identified in the records from 1270 to 1348, at least 97 (63 per cent) succeeded in remarrying. The decline of the marriage rate of widows in the post-plague period must have raised the marriage rate of young women, and therefore the plague was probably one of the factors which caused the mean age of women at first marriage to fall.

6. *Illegitimacy*

Thrupp has suggested that illegitimacy rates may have risen in medieval villages in the immediate post-plague era, although this suggestion is not supported by any concrete evidence.[78] However, there *is* some evidence which suggests that the illegitimacy rate in Halesowen not only failed to rise after the Black Death but in fact fell sharply.

In the court rolls from 1349 to 1386, 56 merchets and only 9

[75] BRL 346372 28.5.1393.
[76] Women are very badly represented in the post-plague court rolls, but as the ale industry in Halesowen was concentrated in the hands of the rich villagers, their wives, who were very often amerced for brewing ale against the assize, are better represented in the court records than the wives of less-well-off peasants.
[77] BRL 346822 3.5.1392.   [78] 'Problem of replacement-rates', p. 113.

leyrwytes are recorded, although 220 merchets and 117 leyrwytes are registered for 1270–1348. It is unlikely that the number of leyrwytes fell during the period 1349–86 because the manorial administration did not collect these fines as extensively as in the previous period. If the Abbey of Halesowen intensified seigneurial exactions after the Black Death by raising the rate of marriage fines by about 300 per cent, it is hard to believe that such a profitable source of revenue as leyrwytes was given up. Moreover, if the abbey exacted very high merchets from bondwomen, it does not make sense that at the same time it provided them with an opportunity of evading these fines by neglecting to levy leyrwytes. Therefore it would seem that the number of leyrwytes fell sharply after the Black Death because a much smaller number of women than in the pre-plague period conceived and gave birth out of wedlock. In the pre-plague period the majority of leyrwytes were paid by dowerless women from poor families who, unlike their richer neighbours, had to postpone their marriages or to remain single all their lives. Young peasants of small means who could have married them were unable to do so because they could not acquire land and support a family. But after the Black Death, when more land was available and wages rose, it was much easier for such young peasants to start a family. Consequently, dowerless girls could marry at the same low age as dowered ones, and the number of pre-marital conceptions dropped sharply. With the rise in the marriage rate of young dowerless girls, the marriage rate of widows fell. This is reflected in the fact that 4 of the 9 leyrwytes recorded in the court rolls between 1349 and 1396 were paid by widows, while only 8 per cent of the leyrwytes recorded in the pre-plague court rolls were paid by widows.

7. *Size of Peasant Families and Social Stratification*

We have seen that the expectation of life at 20 in Halesowen in the post-plague period rose, and that the mean age at first marriage of women probably fell. Therefore one would expect that the size of peasant families increased during this period. Yet the data obtained from the court rolls suggest that the size of Halesowen families contracted in the second half of the fourteenth century.

The quality of the genealogical data obtained from the post-plague court rolls is better than of those obtained from the pre-plague records, since peasants' surnames stabilized after the Black

Death. Of the 253 families identified in the court rolls from 1350 to 1400, 189 were reconstituted on the basis of explicit genealogical data. But such families constitute only 62 per cent of the total number reconstituted from the court rolls between 1270 and 1349. On the other hand, the number of males whose familial relationships can be traced declines in the post-plague court rolls. It was possible to link to families 89 per cent of the males identified as resident in the court rolls from 1270 to 1349. But among the 550 males identified in the court rolls from 1350 to 1400 it was possible to link only 422 males (77 per cent) to families (see table 29). The percentage of single men is higher in the post-plague court rolls than in those of the pre-plague period as a result of the different rate of infant and child mortality in the two periods. As women are under-represented in our records, we often discover that a villager was married only from the appearance of his children's names in the court rolls. But since more villagers lost their children before they could have appeared in the manorial court (i.e. before the age of 12) after the plague period than before it, the number of males identified as single rose in the court rolls from 1350 to 1400.

We have seen that families reconstituted from the court rolls between 1270 and 1349 may number between 46 per cent and 62 per cent of all the families living in the parish during this period. It is likely that the percentage of families reconstituted from the court rolls between 1350 and 1400 is lower. If all the 261 sons above 12 identified in the court rolls reached the age of marriage, married and settled in Halesowen, the percentage of reconstituted families would be 36, since 93 sons are noted also as fathers or husbands. But if 40 per cent of all the sons noted in the records did not establish families because they died young, emigrated or remained single all their lives, the number of sons who could have formed families would be 156.6. If this guess is close to the mark, the percentage of reconstituted families is 59. We can therefore assume that the proportion of reconstituted families lies between 36 per cent and 59 per cent of all the families living in Halesowen during the period 1350–1400.

Table 30 sums up the number of children above 12 in all the families reconstituted from the court rolls between 1350 and 1400 according to their economic status. Table 31 and fig. 13 show the distribution of rich, middling and poor families according to the number of their offspring.

Table 29. *Males noted in the court rolls 1350–1400 and their familial relationships*[a]

Date	Males for whom neither location nor familial relationship is found	Males located geographically or identified as husband, father or son							
		Identified as father or son		Identified as father	Identified as father and son	Identified as son but not father		Total identified as son	Total
		Husband	Not husband			Husband	Not husband		
1350–9	22	–	30	53	31	3	27	61	144
1360–9	31	3	14	28	22	4	34	60	105
1370–9	39	2	35	23	21	4	42	67	127
1380–9	20	1	23	26	3	3	34	40	90
1390–1400	35	1	26	24	–	2	31	33	84
Total	147	7	128	154	77	16	168	261	550

[a] Males noted in the court rolls from 1350 onwards whose first appearance in the records was before 1350 are not included. However, I include in the table 46 males identified in the court rolls from 1350 to 1359 as fathers although they had been noted in earlier records (36 as sons and 10 as single men).

Table 30. *The number of offspring over the age of 12 in families reconstituted from Halesowen court rolls 1350–1400, by economic status*

Status	No. of families	No. of sons	No. of daughters	No. of offspring	Mean no. of sons	Mean no. of daughters	Mean no. of offspring	Adjusted mean no. of offspring
Rich	60	89	35	124	1.5	0.6	2.1	3.0
Middling	89	88	43	131	1.0	0.5	1.5	2.0
Poor	81	56	36	92	0.7	0.4	1.1	1.4
Unidentified	23	28	7	35	–	–	–	–
Total	253	261	121	382	1.0	0.5	1.5	2.1

Table 31. *The distribution of rich, middling and poor families reconstituted from the court rolls 1350–1400, by number of offspring*

| Status | No. of families | No. of offspring | | | | | | | | |
		0	1	2	3	4	5	6	7	8
Rich	60	2 (3%)	21 (35%)	16 (27%)	15 (25%)	4 (7%)	2 (3%)	–	–	–
Middling	89	7 (8%)	45 (51%)	28 (31%)	6 (7%)	3 (3%)	–	–	–	–
Poor	81	14 (17%)	51 (64%)	9 (11%)	5 (6%)	2 (2%)	–	–	–	–
Total	230	23 (10%)	117 (51%)	53 (23%)	26 (11%)	9 (4%)	2 (1%)	–	–	–

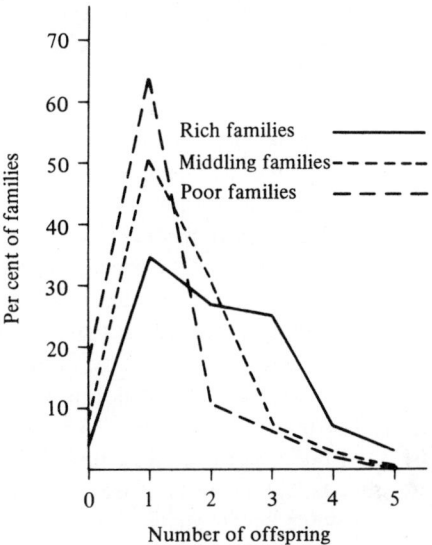

Fig. 13 The distribution of rich, middling and poor families reconstituted from the court rolls 1350–1400, by number of offspring

The mean number of offspring above the age of 12 per family obtained from the court rolls between 1350 and 1400 is 1.5. But this mean has to be corrected because of the underrepresentation of women. If the sexes were balanced, the mean number of offspring in the period under study would be 2.1. The unadjusted mean number of children to a family estimated from the court rolls between 1270 and 1349 is 2.2 and the adjusted mean is 2.8. Although our figures are crude, they suggest that the size of Halesowen families declined by about 25 per cent after the Black Death. This decline was probably a result of the heavy infant and child mortality in the four outbreaks of the plague between 1349 and 1375. If Halesowen families had on average only one son and one daughter over 12, it is not surprising that they failed in the second half of the fourteenth century to keep up their numbers from generation to generation.

We can see in table 30 and fig. 13 that a correlation between the economic status of peasant families and the number of their offspring still existed in the second half of the fourteenth century. The rich peasants, who had in this period large holdings of a virgate or more, had 33 per cent more children per family than half yardlanders and 53 per cent more children than smallholders and cottagers; and half yardlanders had 30 per cent more children than smallholders. However, the difference in the mean number of offspring between rich, middling and poor families is smaller than in the previous period. In the pre-plague period rich peasants in Halesowen had 38 per cent more children than middling and 65 per cent more children than poor peasants. And middling peasants had 39 per cent more children than smallholders. The narrowing of differences between the number of offspring of rich and middling and middling and poor families but the failure of those differences to disappear in the post-plague period indicates that the villagers' standard of living did not rise as high as one might have expected. The rise in the income of cottagers, smallholders and half yardlanders after the Black Death enabled them to sustain times of dearth better than in the pre-plague period, and consequently their expectation of life increased. But the rate of mortality of their infants and young children, who were more susceptible than adults to food shortage and to the cold, must have risen considerably in lean years, while the children of their better-off neighbours, who suffered a good deal less from hunger and cold, were able to survive.

Although the supply of land in the second half of the fourteenth century was much greater than in the previous period, there is no evidence in our records to support Chayanov's theory that the size of the family determined the size of its holding. One finds neither smallholders enlarging their holdings when the size of families increased, nor tenants of large holdings curtailing their tenements when the size of their families decreased. For example, William Derby inherited in 1362 a third of a quarter virgate from his grandfather.[79] William had three sons, yet when he died in 1370 he left to his son William junior the same minute holding; and William was excused from paying a heriot because his father was too poor.[80] John Fisher (1363–93d.) inherited from his father a messuage and 4 'dietas' of land in Oldbury and Langley.[81] Although John had at least two sons, he was forced to decrease his holding instead of

[79] BRL 346343 5.2.1362.
[80] His sons John, Thomas and William junior are mentioned in the court records of 1370 and 1379 for the first time (BRL 346349/356). The death of William Derby is recorded in the court held on 16.1.1370 (346349). The land was taken by his eldest son William junior.
[81] BRL 346344 8.3.1363.

increasing it, as he sold part of it in 1368.[82] John died in 1393 holding a cottage and a few parcels of land, and as he was poor his son Richard was excused from paying death duties.[83] John de Moulowe (1348–73d.) from the township of Hill married Matilda the co-heiress of Thomas Hill, who brought him half a virgate of land as a dowry.[84] In 1379 he inherited from his father William a whole yardland, and in 1355 he purchased the other half of his wife's family's yardland holding.[85] Like John Fisher, he had two sons who survived to maturity, but when he died in 1373 his son John II inherited a holding of two yardlands.[86] Richard de Moulowe (1348–1401d.) the brother of John I de Moulowe was the richest peasant in Halesowen.[87] He obtained a yardland holding through his marriage to the widow of Philip Hill.[88] He bought two tofts, two curtilages, a messuage, two crofts and three-quarters of a virgate from his neighbours.[89] It is difficult to estimate the real size of his holding, as only transactions in customary land are recorded in the court rolls, and it is likely that he bought freehold land as well. In any case, Richard had land in the townships of Hill, Cakemoor, Lapal and Warley. In addition, he must have had a large herd, as he was sued fifty-four times for the damage his beasts caused the lord and his neighbours. Despite the fact that Richard's economic activities exceeded those of any other villager, he did not restrict them when he grew old or when his two sons left the manor in

[82] His two sons Richard and Robert are noted in the court rolls for the first time in 1393 and 1399 respectively (BRL 346373/377). In 1368 he sold to Ralf son of John Walloxhall a toft, a cottage and a curtilage in Oldbury (346347 19.7.1368).
[83] BRL 346373 19.11.1393.   [84] BRL 346323 11.11.1349.
[85] His father died in the Black Death and he entered the family holding of a yardland for a 20s. entry fine (BRL 346322 29.7.1349). He purchased from his brother-in-law Philip de Coldwell the other half of Thomas Hill's yardland holding, and paid an entry fine of 13s. 4d. (346335 15.4.1355).
[86] John de Moulowe had two sons Simon and John II. In 1370 he obtained for Simon a half yardland in Hill for an entry fine of 46s. 8d. (BRL 346349 6.2.1370). But Simon did not remain in the village: it was declared in the court that he was living abroad (346358 17.10.1380). John II therefore entered his father's holding of two yardlands in 1373 for an entry fine of £2 (346351 4.5.1373).
[87] Richard de Moulowe is noted 342 times in the court rolls between 1348 and 1401 (BRL 346317–78).
[88] Philip Hill left two minor daughters when he died in 1349, Agnes and Milicentia. In 1353 Agnes surrendered her share in the family holding to Richard, who promised to pay her 2s. a year for the rest of her life. We know about this agreement because Agnes sued Richard in 1380 for not keeping to his annual payment (BRL 346357 4.4.1380). Milicentia, Agnes's sister, married Robert Curliter. In 1372 Richard and Robert divided between them Philip Hill's yardland holding (346350 14.1.1372).
[89] Richard's land transactions are recorded in BRL 346349/353/364/369/371.

1390.[90] In 1391 he even bought more land.[91] Both Richard and John de Moulowe, like other rich peasants in Halesowen, employed living-in servants and labourers.[92] These peasants of substance were less dependent than their less-well-off neighbours on the labour of their children. They sold a large part of their produce on the market and consequently were able to pay the high wages demanded by agricultural labourers. Therefore, despite the fact that rich peasants in Halesowen had in the post-plague period an average of 42 per cent fewer children to a family than in the previous period, they managed to farm probably twice as much land.

We have seen that in the pre-plague period a combination of land shortage and a higher survival rate among the children of well-to-do villagers than among the children of their less-well-off neighbours created a strong downward social mobility. In the second half of the fourteenth century this movement was arrested as a result of a greater supply of land and a lower survival rate among the children of peasants who belonged to the upper echelons of village society. After the Black Death the number of rich and middling families with more than one son and one daughter who survived to maturity declined. In these families younger children who wished to settle in the village did not have to descend in the social scale. As the supply of land greatly increased, younger sons were usually able to obtain the same amount of land as their senior brothers and to maintain their social position in the village. For example, Thomas the son of Richard Hill of Romsley (1362–1400) inherited a yardland holding from his father in 1362.[93] His brother John (1357–93d.) also acquired a yardland holding, probably through a good marriage.[94] The two brothers, who often quarrelled, were successful farmers and both played an important role in village government.[95] The brothers Thomas (1364–75d.) and Richard (1363–1409d.) Squire from

[90] In the court held on 20.4.1390 it was declared that Richard de Moulowe's two sons were living outside the manor.

[91] On 11.10.1391 he bought a messuage and a curtilage in Hill from John Smith.

[92] John de Moulowe's servants are noted on 26.4.1357 (BRL 346339) and on 28.4.1369 (346348). Richard de Moulowe's servants are mentioned in 1380 and 1388 (346359/367). In addition, Richard was sued twenty-eight times by various villagers for the money he promised to pay them for certain jobs, such as ploughing.

[93] BRL 346814 28.7.1362.

[94] When John Hill died, his son John II inherited a yardland holding (BRL 346822 7.3.1393).

[95] The two brothers acted many times as jurors, pledges and court assessors.

Romsley were also both substantial tenants.[96] In 1371 Thomas and Richard with their uncle John Squire and their nephew John atte Lych leased the demesne lands in Romsley for the abbot for a term of sixteen years at an annual rent of £2.[97]

The substantial population decline in Halesowen in the post-plague period not only stopped the downward movement in the social scale but even reversed it to some extent. During this period the number of cottagers and smallholders in Halesowen declined, as it did in many other villages. In the pre-plague period they constituted 43 per cent of the population of the manor, but only 35 per cent in the second half of the fourteenth century. At the same time the proportion of wealthy peasants in the population rose from 18 per cent to 26 per cent. Nevertheless, the evidence obtained from Halesowen court rolls does not support Postan's hypothesis that a strong upward social mobility in the post-plague period prevented a polarization of village society.[98]

The stratum in Halesowen to profit most from the demographic crisis and the new opportunities which were opened up to the peasants after the Black Death was that of the rich villagers rather than, as Postan has argued, that of smallholders and cottagers. Almost all the wealthy peasants in Halesowen inherited a great deal of land from close and distant relatives. Richard Gilbert (1326–49d.) a well-to-do peasant from Illey died without issue in the Black Death. His relative Roger Ketel (1347–97), another wealthy villager, entered the land for an entry fine of 16s.[99] Simon Perkins (1381–1400) from Ridgeacre inherited from his mother Alice half a virgate (1384), from his uncle Thomas half a virgate (1385) and from his father John (1391) a whole virgate or more.[100] Inheritance was not the only way in which the wealthy villagers increased the size of their holdings. They took the best and largest holdings which fell vacant after the Black Death and throughout the fourteenth century, because they were able, unlike their less-well-off neighbours, to pay the high entry fines demanded by the lord for such holdings. For example, in 1349 Thomas and Philip atte Lowe

---

[96] Thomas Squire is noted in the court rolls between 1364 and 1375 (BRL 346344–817). His brother Richard is noted in the records for 1363–1409 (346344–824).
[97] BRL 346816 27.6.1371.
[98] 'Medieval agrarian society in its prime: England', *Cambridge Economic History of Europe*, vol. I, 2nd edn (Cambridge, 1966), pp. 630–2.
[99] BRL 346343 3.2.1350.   [100] BRL 346359/364/370.

from Hunnington died childless and the family yardland holding was escheated to the lord. In 1350 he gave it to William Hill for an entry fine of £2.[101] In 1359 William transferred the holding to his brother Roger, who had to pay a fine of £8 for the lord's permission.[102] Another member of the Hill family, William (1377–97), acquired in 1397 the vacant holding of Thomas Don of Hasbury (1344–82), which amounted to half a virgate, for an entry fine of £3. 6s. 8d.[103] Of the thirty-six vacant holdings of a quarter virgate or more which were taken intact by new tenants in the period 1350–1400, twenty (55 per cent) were taken up by rich peasants, although they constituted only 26 per cent of the population of the manor. The rich villagers also accumulated land through the inter-peasant land market, as table 32 indicates. And the most successful among them were able to farm the largest and the best parts of the demesne lands leased by the abbey *en bloc*.[104]

Table 32. *The socio-economic status of lessors, lessees, vendors and buyers of land in Halesowen 1350–1400*

	No. of leases (32)			No. of sales (81)		
	No. of lessors	No. of lessees	Excess of lessees	No. of vendors	No. of buyers	Excess of buyers
Members of rich families	12	16	+4	17	25	+8
Members of middling families	11	8	−3	25	21	−4
Members of poor families	9	4	−5	30	9	−21
Total	32	28	−4	72	55	−17

[101] BRL 346324 30.2.1350.
[102] BRL 346327 7.3.1352.   [103] BRL 346375 27.5.1397.
[104] For example, the demesne lands in Cakemoor were leased by Richard Jurdan and Richard Poskyns for an annual rent of 13s. 8d. Radwall Grange was leased in 1369 to Henry Green for an annual rent of £2. 16s. 8d. The abbey demanded the same rent for Romsley Grange from Thomas Pitway in 1366 and from the Squires in 1371. All these farmers were very wealthy peasants who bought land from their neighbours, obtained vacant holdings, employed hired labour, lent money on a large scale to their less-well-off neighbours and belonged to the ruling elite of the village. The demesne leases are recorded in BRL 346335/346/349/816.

In the pre-plague period, wealthy villagers had to provide for many children and therefore the size of their holdings did not increase from generation to generation although they purchased land from their neighbours and obtained vacant holdings from the lord. But in the post-plague period, as the survival rate of their children fell, they were able to transfer intact to their heirs all the land which they had accumulated during their lifetimes. Admittedly the number of wealthy peasants who died without issue increased in the second half of the century. But in such cases there were always collaterals either in Halesowen or elsewhere who came and took up the vacant holdings and continued to accumulate more land.[105] Thus the landed resources of the rich peasants grew from generation to generation and the gap widened between them and the rest of the villagers. In this period a number of wealthy Halesowen families laid the foundations on which their descendants climbed into the ranks of the yeomanry in the fifteenth and sixteenth centuries. For example, Adam de Melley (1352–91) of the township of Illey inherited from his father John half a yardland and half a yardland from his mother Alice Yeldentre, and obtained a third half yardland by marrying Lucy the daughter and heiress of John Pyrie. Towards the middle of the sixteenth century one of his descendants Henry Melley farmed 690 acres, of which 580 were pasture, for an annual rent of £9. 3s. 7d. He also held with Richard Harries, a descendant of another old Halesowen family, 440 acres of pasture and wood for a rent of £5.[106]

There is no doubt that in the second half of the fourteenth century a number of middling peasants like Adam de Melley succeeded in climbing to the top rank of village society, and their place was taken by smallholders like the Hurnes from Hasbury.[107] However, the vast

---

[105] For example, Robert Atte Lyche died in 1392 without issue. His three-quarter-yardland holding was taken by his nephew Thomas atte Lyche for an entry fine of 40s. (BRL 346822 23.2.1392). In 1396 Thomas transferred all his lands in Romsley to his relatives Thomas and Richard Squire (346823 20.4.1396). In the same year Thomas and Richard Squire leased from the abbot the demesne lands in the three common fields of Romsley for twelve years, with a right to half of the harvest services of the customary tenants of Romsley, for an annual rent of 13s. 8d. (ibid. 14.4.1396).

[106] BRL 347162. See also R. K. Field, 'The Worcestershire peasantry in the later Middle Ages', unpublished M.A. thesis, Birmingham University, 1962, pp. 207–9.

[107] John Hurne from Hasbury died in 1339 leaving to his son Adam a quarter virgate of land (BRL 346287 24.2.1339). It is likely that Adam obtained more land immediately after the Black Death, since in 1352 he was elected as an ale-taster and

majority of the half yardlanders, smallholders and cottagers could not take advantage of the economic opportunities which existed after the Black Death to the same extent as their richer neighbours. They lacked the money and the credit necessary to acquire, to stock and to farm large holdings. Therefore, although their income and living standard probably rose in the post-plague period, the gap between them and the rich peasants widened rather than narrowed.[108]

8. The Age Structure of the Adult Population in the Early 1390s

Russell and Helleiner have argued that the recurrent outbreaks of the plague in the 1360s and 1370s altered the age structure of the population at the end of the fourteenth century in such a way that it had a depressing effect on the birth rates in the following decades.[109] This hypothesis is compatible with the age structure of the adult population obtained from Halesowen court rolls from the early 1390s.

It is difficult to estimate the age distribution of Halesowen villagers in the 1390s, since migrations to and from the parish intensified considerably in the post-plague period. Although we do not know at what age peasants usually migrated, it is reasonable to assume that they did so in their twenties and thirties rather than in their forties and fifties. Therefore, if we measure only the ages of native-born villagers and not of immigrants, we will underestimate the size of the age groups 20–9 and 30–9. In order to overcome this bias it is necessary to measure the ages of native-born villagers as well as of immigrants. In the court rolls from 1391 to 1395, 255 villagers are identified as residents, and there is good evidence that 121 of them were tenants. We assumed that when each one of these tenants appeared for the first time in the court rolls as a landholder he was at

in 1355 as a reeve (346329/336). Adam died between 1367 and 1370, as his name is noted in the records for the last time in 1367 and that of his widow appears in 1370 (346347/349). In 1370 his widow Agnes acquired a half-yardland holding. We do not know the sizes of the holdings of his two sons Thomas (1359–83) and John (1372–93d.). But the fact that both of them acted as court assessors and jurors suggests that they were well-off peasants (346327–72).

[108] A similar development in Leicestershire has been observed by Hilton; see *The Economic Development of Some Leicestershire Estates in the Fourteenth and Fifteenth Centuries* (Oxford, 1947), pp. 94–5, 129–30.

[109] Russell, *British Medieval Population*, pp. 230–1, 260–70; Helleiner, 'The population of Europe from the Black Death to the eve of the vital revolution', pp. 10–11.

least 20 years old. Then we assumed that the age distribution of these tenants represents the age distribution of all the villagers over 20, males as well as females. It is likely that we underestimated the real age of a number of immigrants, yet we obtained some crude idea of the age structure of the adult population in the early 1390s. Fig. 14 represents the estimated age composition of the adult population of Halesowen in 1350 and 1393.

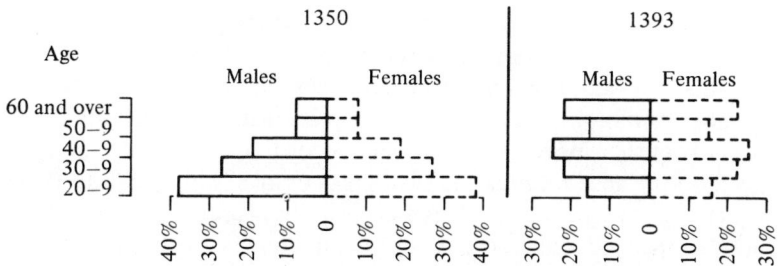

Fig. 14 The estimated age structure of the adult population of Halesowen in 1350 and 1393

We can see clearly in the figure that the adult population in Halesowen in 1393 was much older than in 1350. In 1350 tenants in their twenties and thirties constituted 65 per cent of the tenant population of the manor, but in 1393 only 38 per cent. The change was probably a result of a sharp difference in the life expectancy of children and of adults. In the decades which followed the Black Death the life expectancy of adults over 20 rose, while that of infants and children fell considerably as a result of the recurrent outbreaks of the plague. Therefore the population of the parish was overwhelmed at the end of the fourteenth century by the middle-aged and elderly and was doomed to a long period of stagnation and decline.

Appendix: The Distribution of Marriage Fines over the Year

When we estimated the actual number of merchets collected by the Abbot of Halesowen, we assumed that the fines were equally distributed over the year. In order to check this assumption, we examined the monthly distribution of merchets in the nine years for which all records survived. Fig. 15 shows that except in May and October the number of merchets recorded each month is more or less the same. It is likely that more merchets were recorded in May and October because in these months the two 'great courts' were held. In these courts the townships and jurymen usually presented marriages of bondwomen contracted without permission, i.e. without the payment of a marriage fine. But it is also possible that in these months

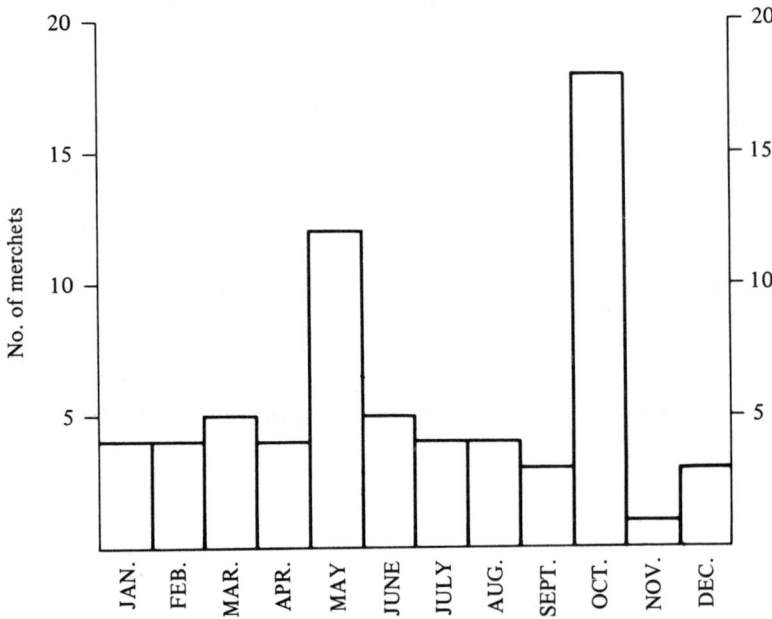

Fig. 15 The distribution of marriage fines over the year (obtained from the records of 1301, 1312, 1313, 1328, 1335–8, 1348)

the number of marriages, and not only of marriage fines, rose. More marriages were contracted in October because the peasants, who had just finished the harvest, were better off then than at any other time during the year. The rise in marriages in May may be connected with the religious and popular festivals celebrated during this month.

As more merchets were recorded in October and May than in other months, we grossly underestimated the number of actual merchets in the years for which the 'great courts' are missing. Nevertheless, it appears that this does not invalidate conclusions based on the merchet statistics obtained from the court rolls 1295–1385. We argued that there was a significant rise in marriages during the period 1336–48, because the number of merchets estimated from the court rolls between 1336 and 1348 exceeds the number of merchets estimated from the same source between 1316 and 1335. In the court rolls from 1336 to 1348 the records of six 'great courts' are missing, two from October and four from May. But in the court rolls from 1316 to 1335 the records of only four 'great courts' are missing, two from October and two from May. Therefore it is likely that the real rise in the number of marriages in the thirteen years which preceded the Black Death was even sharper than the one which emerges from the statistics of estimated merchets presented in table 8. The same is true of the marriage trend obtained from the post-plague court rolls. We claimed that the number of marriages, which was at a high level in the period 1349–69, fell in the period 1370–85. In the court rolls from 1349 to 1369 the records of seven 'great courts' are missing, two from October and five from May. But in the court rolls from 1370 to 1385 the records of only four 'great courts' are missing, two from October and two from May. It is therefore possible that the decline in the number of marriages in the period 1370–85 was even steeper than the one revealed by the estimated merchets presented in table 28.

Bibliography

PRIMARY SOURCES

Manuscript Sources

Birmingham Reference Library. [Cited as BRL]
    The Court Rolls of the Manor of Halesowen 1269–1400: nos. 346201 et seq.
    The Court Rolls of the Borough of Halesowen 1272–1400: nos. 346512 et seq.
    The Court Rolls of Romsley 1293–1400: nos. 346790 et seq.
    Account Rolls, 1361–2, 1362–4 and 1368–9: nos. 347130 et seq.
    Report of Commission of Oyer and Terminer 1386: no. 347156.

Printed Sources

Anonimalle Chronicle, The, ed. V. H. Galbraith. Manchester, 1927.
Chronicon Galfridi le Baker de Swynebroke, ed. E. M. Thompson. Oxford, 1889.
Court Rolls of the Manor of Hales 1272–1307, ed. J. Amphlett, S. G. Hamilton and R. A. Wilson. 2 vols. Worcestershire Historical Society, 1910–33. [Cited as *Hales Court Rolls*]
Domesday Book, vol. I. Record Commission, 1783.

SECONDARY SOURCES

Unpublished Theses

Beckerman, J. S. 'Customary law in English manorial courts in the thirteenth and fourteenth centuries'. Ph.D. thesis, University of London, 1972.
Dyer, C. C. 'The estates of the Bishopric of Worcester, 680–1540'. Ph.D. thesis, University of Birmingham, 1977.
Field, R. K. 'The Worcestershire peasantry in the later Middle Ages'. M.A. thesis, University of Birmingham, 1962.
Smith, R. M. 'English peasant life-cycles and socio-economic networks'. Ph.D. thesis, University of Cambridge, 1974.

Monographs and Articles

Baker, A. R. H. 'Evidence in the "Nonarum Inquisitiones" of contracting arable lands in England during the early fourteenth century', *Economic History Review*, 2nd ser., XIX (1966).

'Some evidence of a reduction in the acreage of cultivated lands in Sussex during the early fourteenth century', *Sussex Archaeological Collections*, CIV (1966).

'Contracting arable lands in 1341', *Bedfordshire Historical Record Society*, X/XI (1970).

Ballard, A. 'The Black Death', in *Oxford Studies in Social and Legal History*, vol. V, ed. P. Vinogradoff. Oxford, 1916.

Bean, J. M. W. 'Plague, population and economic decline in England in the later Middle Ages', *Economic History Review*, 2nd ser., XV (1963).

Bennett, H. S. *Life on the English Manor*. Cambridge, 1971.

Beresford, M. W. *The Lost Villages of England*. London, 1954.

Beveridge, W. H. 'Wages in the Winchester manors', *Economic History Review*, VII (1936).

'Westminster wages in the manorial era', *Economic History Review*, 2nd ser., VII (1955–6).

Biraben, J. N. and J. Le Goff. 'La peste dans le haut Moyen Age', *Annales: Economies, Sociétés, Civilisations*, XXIV (1969).

Birrell, J. R. 'The forest economy of the Honour of Tutbury in the 14th and 15th centuries', *University of Birmingham Historical Journal*, VIII (1962).

'Peasant craftsmen in the medieval forest', *Agricultural History Review*, XVII (1969).

Blanchard, I. 'Population change, enclosure and the early Tudor economy', *Economic History Review*, 2nd ser., XXIII (1970).

Bridbury, A. R. *Economic Growth: England in the Later Middle Ages*. London, 1962.

'The Black Death', *Economic History Review*, 2nd ser., XXVI (1973).

Britton, E. *The Community of the Vill*. Toronto, 1977.

Cambridge Economic History of Europe, vol. I: The Agrarian Life of the Middle Ages, 2nd edn, ed. M. M. Postan. Cambridge, 1966.

Carpentier, E. 'Autour de la peste noire: famines et épidémies dans l'histoire du XIVe siècle', *Annales: Economies, Sociétés, Civilisations*, XVII (1962).

Carus-Wilson, E. M. 'An industrial revolution of the thirteenth century', in *Essays in Economic History*, ed. Carus-Wilson, vol. I. London, 1954.

'Evidences of industrial growth on some fifteenth century manors', in ibid. vol. II. London, 1962.

Chambers, J. D. *Population, Economy and Society in Pre-Industrial England*. London, 1972.

Chayanov, A. V. *The Theory of Peasant Economy*, ed. D. Thorner, B. Kerblay and R. E. F. Smith. Homewood, Ill., 1966.

Coulton, G. G. *Medieval Village, Manor and Monastery*. New York, 1960.

Creighton, C. A. *A History of Epidemics in Britain from A.D. 664 to the Present Time*, vol. I. Cambridge, 1891.

Darby, H. C. and I. B. Terret (eds.). *The Domesday Geography of Midland England*. Cambridge, 1954; 2nd edn, 1971.

Dewindt, E. B. *Land and People in Holywell-cum-Needingworth*. Toronto, 1972.

DuBoulay, F. R. H. *The Lordship of Canterbury*. London, 1966.
Duby, G. *Rural Economy and Country Life in the Medieval West*, tr. C. Postan. London, 1968.
Dyer, C. C. 'Population and agriculture on a Warwickshire manor in the later Middle Ages', *University of Birmingham Historical Journal*, XI (1967).
  'A redistribution of incomes in fifteenth century England', *Past and Present*, no. 39 (1968).
Faith, R. J. 'Peasant families and inheritance customs in medieval England', *Agricultural History Review*, XIV (1966).
Farmer, D. L. 'Some grain price movements in thirteenth-century England', *Economic History Review*, 2nd ser., X (1957–8).
Field, R. K. 'Worcestershire peasant buildings, household goods and farming equipment in the later Middle Ages', *Medieval Archaeology*, IX (1965).
Fourquin, G. *Les campagnes de la région parisienne à la fin du Moyen Age*. Paris, 1964.
Gasquet, F. A. *The Great Pestilence*. London, 1893.
Glass, D. V. and D. E. C. Eversley (eds.). *Population in History*. London, 1965.
Goubert, P. 'En Beauvaisis: problèmes démographiques du XVIIe siècle', *Annales: Economies, Sociétés, Civilisations*, VII (1952).
Gras, P. 'Le registre paroissial de Givry (1334–1357) et la peste noire en Bourgogne', *Bibliothèque de l'Ecole des Chartes*, C (1939).
Hajnal, J. 'European marriage patterns in perspective', in Glass and Eversley (eds.).
Hallam, H. E. 'Some thirteenth-century censuses', *Economic History Review*, 2nd ser., X (1958).
  'Population density in the medieval fenland', *Economic History Review*, 2nd ser., XIV (1961).
Harvey, B. F. 'The population trend in England between 1300 and 1348', *Transactions of the Royal Historical Society*, 5th ser., XVI (1965).
Harvey, P. D. A. *A Medieval Oxfordshire Village: Cuxham, 1290 to 1400*. Oxford, 1965.
Hatcher, J. *Rural Economy and Society in the Duchy of Cornwall, 1300–1500*. London, 1967.
  Plague, Population and the English Economy 1348–1530. London, 1977.
Helleiner, K. H. 'Population movement and agrarian depression in the later Middle Ages', *Canadian Journal of Economics and Political Science* XV (1950).
  'The population of Europe from the Black Death to the eve of the vital revolution', in *Cambridge Economic History of Europe*, vol. IV, ed. E. E. Rich and C. H. Wilson. Cambridge, 1967.
Helmholz, R. H. *Marriage Litigation in Medieval England*. Cambridge, 1974.
Herlihy, D. 'Population, plague and social change in rural Pistoia 1201–1430', *Economic History Review*, 2nd ser., XVIII (1965).
  Medieval and Renaissance Pistoia. London, 1967.

Herlihy, D. and C. Klapisch-Zuber. *Les toscans et leurs familles.* Paris, 1978.
Hilton, R. H. *The Economic Development of Some Leicestershire Estates in the Fourteenth and Fifteenth Centuries.* Oxford, 1947.
  'The content and sources of English agrarian history before 1500', *Agricultural History Review,* III (1955).
  'Peasant movements before 1381', in *Essays in Economic History,* ed. E. M. Carus-Wilson, vol. II. London, 1962.
  A Medieval Society. London, 1967.
  The Decline of Serfdom in Medieval England. London, 1969.
  Bond Men Made Free. London, 1973.
  The English Peasantry in the Later Middle Ages. Oxford, 1975.
  'Gloucester Abbey leases of the late thirteenth century', ibid. (repr.).
  'Lord and peasant in Staffordshire in the Middle Ages', ibid. (repr.).
  'Rent and capital formation in feudal society', ibid. (repr.).
  'Social structure of rural Warwickshire in the Middle Ages', ibid. (repr.).
Hirst, L. F. *The Conquest of the Plague.* Oxford. 1953.
Hollingworth, T. H. 'A demographic study of British ducal families', in Glass and Eversley (eds.).
  Historical Demography. London, 1969.
Holmes, G. A. *The Estates of the Higher Nobility in Fourteenth-Century England.* Cambridge, 1957.
Homans, G. C. 'The rural sociology of medieval England', *Past and Present,* no. 4 (1953).
  English Villagers of the Thirteenth Century. New York, 1970.
Hyams, P. R. 'The origins of the peasant land market in England', *Economic History Review,* 2nd ser., XXIII (1970).
Jessop, A. 'The Black Death in East Anglia', *The Coming of the Friars and Other Historic Essays.* London, 1906.
Kershaw, I. *Bolton Priory: The Economy of a Northern Monastery.* Oxford, 1973.
  'The great famine and agrarian crisis in England 1315–22', *Past and Present,* no. 59 (1973).
King, E. *Peterborough Abbey 1086–1310: A Study of the Land Market.* Cambridge, 1973.
Klapisch, C. 'Household and family in Tuscany in 1427', in *Household and Family in Past Time,* ed. P. Laslett. Cambridge, 1972.
Kosminsky, E. A. 'The evolution of feudal rent in England from the XIth to the XVth centuries', *Past and Present,* no. 7 (1955).
  Studies in the Agrarian History of England. Oxford, 1956.
Krause, J. 'The medieval household: large or small?', *Economic History Review,* 2nd ser., IX (1956–7).
Laslett, P. *The World We Have Lost.* London, 1965; 2nd edn, 1971.
Laslett, P. (ed.). *Household and Family in Past Time.* Cambridge, 1972.
Laslett, P. and K. Oosterveen. 'Long-term trends in bastardy in England', *Population Studies,* XXVII (1973).
Le Roy Ladurie, E. *The Peasants of Languedoc.* Chicago, 1974.

Levett, A. E. 'The Black Death on the estates of the See of Winchester', in *Oxford Studies in Social and Legal History,* vol. V, ed. P. Vinogradoff. Oxford, 1916.
  Studies in Manorial History. Oxford, 1938.
Lloyd, T. H. 'Some documentary sidelights on the deserted village of Brookend', *Oxoniensia,* XXIX/XXX (1964–5).
Lucas, H. S. 'The great European famine of 1315, 1316, and 1317', in *Essays in Economic History,* ed. E. M. Carus-Wilson, vol. II. London, 1962.
Maddicot, J. J. 'The peasantry and the demands of the Crown 1294–1341', *Past and Present Supplement,* I (1975).
Maitland, F. M. *Select Pleas in Manorial and Other Seignorial Courts.* Selden Society, vol. II. London, 1889.
  'The history of a Cambridgeshire manor', *English Historical Review,* XXXV (1894).
Miller, E. *The Abbey and Bishopric of Ely.* Cambridge, 1951.
Morris, C. 'The plague in Britain' (review of Shrewsbury, *A History of the Bubonic Plague in the British Isles*), *Historical Journal,* XIV (1971).
Nash, T. R. *Collection for the History of Worcestershire.* 2nd edn. 2 vols. London, 1799.
Ohlin, P. G. 'Mortality, marriage and growth in pre-industrial populations', *Population Studies,* XIV (1960).
  'No safety in numbers: some pitfalls of historical statistics', in *Industrialization in Two Systems,* ed. H. Rosovsky. New York, 1966.
Page, F. M. 'The customary poor law of three Cambridgeshire manors', *Cambridge Historical Journal,* III (1930).
  The Estates of Crowland Abbey. Cambridge, 1934.
Phelps Brown, E. H. and S. V. Hopkins. 'Seven centuries of building wages', in *Essays in Economic History,* ed. E. M. Carus-Wilson, vol. II. London, 1962.
  'Seven centuries of the prices of consumables, compared with builders' wage-rates', in ibid.
Postan, M. M. 'Histoire économique: moyen âge', *Rapports du IXe Congrès International des Sciences Historiques.* Paris, 1950.
  'Medieval agrarian society in its prime: England', in *Cambridge Economic History of Europe,* vol. I, 2nd edn, ed. Postan. Cambridge, 1966.
  The Medieval Economy and Society. London, 1972.
  'Some agrarian evidence of a declining population in the later Middle Ages', *Essays on Medieval Agriculture and General Problems of the Medieval Economy.* Cambridge, 1973.
  'Some social consequences of the Hundred Years Wars', ibid.
  'The charters of the villeins', ibid.
  'The chronology of labour services', ibid.
  'The fifteenth century', ibid.
  'Village livestock in the thirteenth century', ibid.
Postan, M. M. and J. Z. Titow. 'Heriots and prices on Winchester manors', in Postan, *Essays on Medieval Agriculture and General Problems of the Medieval Economy.* Cambridge, 1973.

Raftis, J. A. *The Estates of Ramsey Abbey: A Study in Economic Growth and Organisation.* Toronto, 1957.
Tenure and Mobility. Toronto, 1964.
Warboys. Toronto, 1964.
'Social structures in five East Midland villages', *Economic History Review,* 2nd ser., XVIII (1965).
'The concentration of responsibility in five villages', *Medieval Studies,* XXVIII (1966).
'Changes in an English village after the Black Death', *Medieval Studies,* XXIX (1967).
Robinson, W. C. 'Money, population and economic change in late medieval Europe', *Economic History Review,* 2nd ser., XII (1959–60).
Robo, E. 'The Black Death in the Hundred of Farnham', *English Historical Review,* XLIV (1929).
Rogers, J. E. T. *A History of Agriculture and Prices in England 1259–1793,* vols. I–IV. Oxford, 1866–82.
Six Centuries of Work and Wages. 7th edn, London, 1903; 9th edn, 1908.
Russell, J. C. *British Medieval Population.* Albuquerque, N. Mex., 1948.
'The pre-plague population of England', *Journal of British Studies,* V (1966).
Saltmarsh, J. 'Plague and economic decline in England in the later Middle Ages', *Cambridge Historical Journal,* VII (1941).
Schofield, R. S. 'Historical demography: some possibilities and some limitations', *Transactions of the Royal Historical Society,* 1971.
Schreiner, J. 'Wages and prices in England in the later Middle Ages', *Scandinavian Economic History Review,* II (1954).
Sheehan, M. M. 'The formation and stability of marriage in fourteenth-century England: evidence of an Ely register', *Medieval Studies,* XXXIII (1971).
Shrewsbury, J. F. D. *A History of the Bubonic Plague in the British Isles.* Cambridge, 1970.
Slicher van Bath, B. H. *The Agrarian History of Western Europe, A.D. 500–1800.* New York, 1963.
Stys, W. 'The influence of economic conditions on the fertility of peasant women', *Population Studies,* XI (1957).
Thirsk, J. 'Industries in the countryside', in *Essays in the Economic and Social History of Tudor and Stuart England,* ed. J. Fisher. Cambridge, 1961.
'The family', *Past and Present,* no. 27 (1964).
Thirsk, J. (ed.). *The Agrarian History of England and Wales,* vol. IV: *1500–1640.* Cambridge, 1967.
Thompson, A. H. 'The registers of John Gynewell, Bishop of Lincoln, for the years 1347–50', *Archaeological Journal,* LXVIII (1911).
'The pestilences of the fourteenth century in the Diocese of York', ibid. LXXI (1914).
Thrupp, S. L. 'The problem of replacement-rates in late medieval English population', *Economic History Review,* 2nd ser., XVIII (1965).

'Plague effects in medieval Europe', *Comparative Studies in Society and History,* VIII (1965-6).
Titow, J. Z. 'Evidence of weather in the account rolls of the Bishopric of Winchester 1209-1350', *Economic History Review,* 2nd ser., XII (1959-60).
'Some evidence of the thirteenth century population increase', *Economic History Review,* 2nd ser., XIV (1961).
'Some differences between manors and their effects on the condition of the peasant in the thirteenth century', *Agricultural History Review,* X (1962).
English Rural Society 1200-1350. London, 1969.
Victoria County History of Worcestershire. 4 vols. London, 1901-24.
Vinogradoff, P. *Villeinage in England.* Oxford, 1892.
Waites, B. 'Medieval assessments and agricultural prosperity in northeast Yorkshire, 1292-1342', *Yorkshire Archaeological Journal,* XLIV (1972).
Watts, D. G. 'A model for the early fourteenth century', *Economic History Review,* 2nd ser., XX (1967).
Worcestershire County Council Handbook. Worcester, 1910.
Wrigley, E. A. 'Family limitation in pre-industrial England', *Economic History Review,* 2nd ser., XIX (1966).
'Mortality in pre-industrial England: the example of Colyton, Devon, over three centuries', *Daedalus,* XCVII (1968).
Population and History. London, 1969.
Wrigley, E. A. (ed.). *An Introduction to English Historical Demography.* London, 1969.
Ziegler, P. *The Black Death.* London, 1969.

Index

ale-brewing, 12, 70, 76–7, 80, 138n
Alvechurch, 103
Aston, 30

Birmingham, 4, 30
Black Death: aftermath, 110–13; age-specific mortality, 107–10; geographical distribution of mortality, 106–7; mortality, 99–105
Broughton, 64

Chayanov, A. V., 88, 144
children, survival of, 87–8, 144, 149; see also daughters; family; sons
coal, 8
court rolls: and demographic analysis, 11–24; Halesowen, 4n, 10, 116–17; as historical source, 2–4
Coventry, 30
Cradley, 122
craftsmen, 83, 89–90, 92
Crowland Abbey, 99

daughters: settlement and marriage patterns, 50–60, 85, 94–7, 136–7; see also family; illegitimacy; marriage
debts, 37, 76, 78n, 81–2
demesne leases, 4, 110–11, 147–8
Derby, 121
Domesday Book, 4
Dudley, 30
Dyer, C. C., 103

economy: condition of the local village, 30, 37–41, 86–8, 90–2, 131, 144; nature of the local peasant, 6–8; see also family; land; land market
emigration, 119–20; see also mobility
enclosures, 29
entry fines, 29–30, 112–13
Evesham, 30
expectation of life, 43–5, 58, 60, 130–1

family: and economic status, 74–83, 142–4; and immigration, 120–4; and land, 50–1, 94–7, 131, 144–6; one-parent, 70, 72; reconstitution, 17–21, 71–4, 140–1; size, 83–8, 92–3, 142–3; see also land market; marriage; peasants
famine, see subsistence crises
fertility, 88
fields, 6–7

Glastonbury Abbey, 100
gleaning, 37, 38, 78, 83

Hajnal, J., 50
Halesowen: abbey of, 5, 35n; borough of, 5–6; history of the manor, 4–5; parish of, 5; townships of the manor of, 6
Harborne, 23, 31
Hatcher, J., 116
Helleiner, R. H., 116
Hereford, 31
Hinderclay, 34
Homans, G. C., 50, 55, 57

identification of persons, 11–12, 21–3
illegitimacy, 64–71, 138–9
immigration rate, 118–20; see also mobility
inheritance, 50, 56–7, 70; and family size, 93, 147

Kidderminster, 23
Kings Norton, 4n, 30

labourers, see servants
land: accumulation of, 96–7, 145–6, 149; legal age for holding, 43; reclamation, 6–7, 28–9; shortage and population growth, 94–8; supply of, 29–30, 131, 144; values, 29–30, 111–12
land market, 2n, 37, 76, 78–9, 80–2, 85–92, 95–7, 111, 145–6, 148
Levett, A. E., 100
leyrwyte, 64–5, 139
life expectancy, see expectation of life
livestock, 7, 76, 78–9, 80–2
Ludlow, 121

maintenance agreements, 22n, 23n, 87
manorial court, 2
marriage: age at, 60–4, 136–7; and economic status, 58–60, 64; and land, 66–7, 135–6; patterns, 50–9, 135–6; trend, 47–50, 131–5; *see also* daughters; illegitimacy; sons
meadowland, 76, 80n
merchet, 45–7, 131–4, 152–3
mobility: geographical, 30–1, 117–24; social, 90–2, 97, 146–50
mortality: child, 104, 129, 134–5, 143–4; crises, 38–41; measurement of, 33n, 34–5, 46n; post-Black Death age-specific, 128–9; rates, 44–5, 126–30; trends of, 36–7, 124–6; women, 35, 42–3, 103–4, 129; *see also* Black Death
mortuary, 35n

Newport, 31
Northfield, 30

offices in the village, 74, 77, 79–80, 122–4
Ohlin, P. G., 107

peasants: poor, 30, 33, 38–40, 43, 51–2, 58–60, 64, 66–8, 76n, 77n, 78–9, 82–3, 87–8, 91–2, 94, 130–1, 141–3, 144–5, 149–50; middling, 52–3, 58–60, 64, 66–9, 79, 81–2, 87–8, 94–7, 130–1, 141–4, 149; rich, 40–1, 52, 54, 58–60, 64, 68–9, 76–7, 79–81, 87, 89–90, 94–7, 130, 141–3, 145–50; *see also* family; marriage; stratification
pledging, 20, 36n, 77
population: age structure of, 150–1; growth and land shortage, 94–8; rate of decline of, 115; rate of growth of, 30; trends, 24–8, 31–2, 114–17
Postan, M. M., 27–8, 88–9

Raftis, J. A., 11, 12, 133
Redgrave, 34, 68, 86, 93, 95n
rents, 8–9, 114
replacement-rates, 32–4, 115, 119
Rickinghall, 68, 86, 93, 95n
Rowley Regis, 120
Russell, J. C., 2, 100, 104, 107, 115–16, 128

servants, 76, 78n, 79n, 80, 82–3, 90, 146
services, 8–9
sex ratio, 85–6
Shrewsbury, J. F. D., 100
smallholders, *see* peasants
Smethwick, 30
Smith, R. M., 69
sons: emigration of, 119–20; marriage and settlement patterns of, 50–60, 94–7, 135–6, 143–4, 147, 149; *see also* family; inheritance
Spalding, priory of, 93
standard of living, 43–5, 94, 130–1, 144
stratification, 74–83; and family size, 88–92, 144–9; *see also* peasants
subsistence crises, 38–41, 45
surnames, 3–4, 11–12, 15–16, 22, 139

tenants: court-roll appearances of, 35n, 36n; number of, 10, 28, 35, 127–8; obligations of free and customary, 9; proportion of free and bond, 10
Thirsk, J., 93
Thrupp, S., 32, 34, 116, 137–8
Titow, J. Z., 29, 43

villeins, 4; *see also* tenants
violence, 23n, 77, 78n, 83n, 122
virgate, size of, 8

Walsall, 31
Warley Wigorn, 30
Warwick, 30
Wick, 31
widowers, 137–8
widows, 63, 67–8, 138
women, 25–6, 41–2, 64–71, 103–4, 120; *see also* family; illegitimacy; marriage

DATE DUE			
GAYLORD			PRINTED IN U.S.A.